Smithsonian

Q&A

THE ULTIMATE QUESTION
AND ANSWER BOOK

CATS

HarperCollins books may be purchased for educational, business, or sales
promotional use. For information, please write: Special Markets Department,
HarperCollins Publishers, 10 East 53rd Street, New York, NY 10022.

Produced for HarperCollins by:

HYDRA PUBLISHING
129 MAIN STREET
IRVINGTON, NY 10533
WWW.HYLASPUBLISHING.COM

FIRST EDITION

Library of Congress Cataloging-in-Publication Data has been applied for.

ISBN-10: 0-06-089112-2
ISBN-13: 978-0-06-089112-1

06 07 08 09 10   QW   10 9 8 7 6 5 4 3 2 1

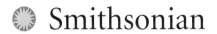

Smithsonian

Q&A

THE ULTIMATE QUESTION
AND ANSWER BOOK

CATS

John Seidensticker and Susan Lumpkin

Collins
An Imprint of HarperCollinsPublishers

CATS

Contents

1   **The Nature and Wonder of Cats**

5   **CHAPTER 1:** What is a Domestic Cat?

21   **CHAPTER 2:** Domestic Cat Details

37   **CHAPTER 3:** The Cat's Body

55   **CHAPTER 4:** How Cats Sense the World

69   **CHAPTER 5:** Domestic Cats as Predators

87   **CHAPTER 6:** Social Life

READY REFERENCE

102 Describing the Breeds

106 The Breeds

Cultures throughout the world depict cats in their art, such as this stylized Chinese lion figurine.

The round-eyed, stocky British shorthair is but one of the many domestic cat breeds.

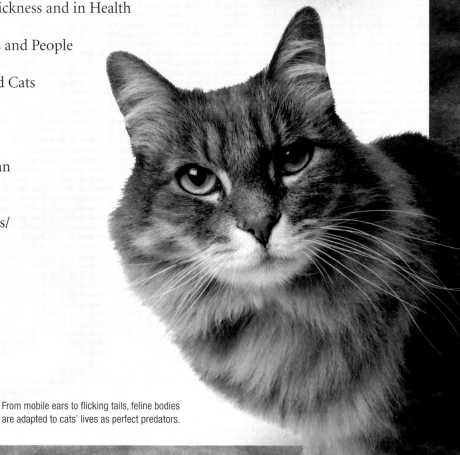

There are an estimated 800 million domestic cats in the world today.

119 CHAPTER 7: Males and Females

137 CHAPTER 8: Bringing Up Babies

151 CHAPTER 9: A Day in the Life

167 CHAPTER 10: In Sickness and in Health

179 CHAPTER 11: Cats and People

193 CHAPTER 12: Wild Cats

204 Glossary

208 Further Reading

210 At the Smithsonian

212 Index

218 Acknowledgments/
Picture Credits

From mobile ears to flicking tails, feline bodies are adapted to cats' lives as perfect predators.

THE NATURE AND WONDER OF CATS

From tabbies to tigers, members of the cat family are easy to recognize. Even small children know a "kitty" when they see one—even if it is a full-grown tiger. The feline family resemblance is so strong because all cats are first and foremost polished hunters. Moving sinuously with grace and power, cats seem always ready to begin a slow stalk or explode into a deadly pounce. Large, close-set eyes and twitching ears hint at keen senses superior to ours. Powerful legs with

Above: Even the most docile of house cats retain their wild, predatory sides.

Left: As are all cats, the tiger is a powerful hunter.

lethal claws and short, canine-tipped jaws reveal cats to be hunting machines. From time immemorial, they have excited our imaginations, arousing terror, loathing, respect, or love, depending on the cat and the circumstance. Only in the last few thousand years have domestic cats shared our homes, not so much as renters but as co-owners. Yet, they have never joined with us completely. Our cats live double lives, enjoying domesticity but slipping back into their wild sides, seemingly at will.

One of the most popular of the pedigreed breeds, the Abyssinian cat is valued for its wild-looking coloration.

Domestic cats link our human-dominated world with the splendor and mystery of the natural world. Domestic cats and wild cats have the same armaments, camouflaged coats, behaviors, and ancestors. In the 33 million years that wild cats have been on the scene, their basic structure has not changed. Neither has that of domestic cats in the few thousand years that they have graced our presence, in contrast to the extreme structural changes that have resulted from the selective breeding of domestic dogs. Settling into a particular form early in its evolution and sticking with it to the present, as the cat family Felidae has done, is rare among the families of mammals. Nonetheless, 39 species of wild cats are recognized today, and all of them display variations on the common cat theme as adaptations to different climates, habitats, and prey. Our domestic cat, now recognized as a species in its own right, closely resembles the 30 species of small wild cats in both form and function.

Wild cats and domestic cats differ greatly in abundance. There are an estimated 400 million domestic cats and at least that many feral cats (domestic cats living wild) in the world today. Yet, although nearly a billion domestic and feral cats share our world, perhaps fewer than one million total individuals of the 39 species of wild cats are alive today. Entire species or populations of wild cats, from the largest tigers to the smallest black-

footed cats, are in danger of extinction or are species of conservation concern. The critically endangered Iberian lynx of Spain and Portugal, for example, is now down to fewer than 200 individuals. No wild cat species has become extinct in the historic past, but the geographic ranges of all of them have continued to shrink in the face of human activities. Tigers, for example, today occupy only seven percent of their historic range. In contrast, domestic cats have tagged along as people moved to new areas and now live nearly everywhere in the world except in the frigid polar regions. Australia and New Zealand, for example, did not have native wild cats; domestic cats

Although populations of wild cats have steadily decreased in the last 100 years, domestic cats, especially the feral ones, are flourishing.

arrived with the first European settlers. Today, these domestic cats turned feral endanger native mammals and birds, and have even caused some to go extinct.

The cult of the cat spans human history, mixing ancient fears and profound respect. Just knowing a big cat is around sharpens perceptions, for in such a matchup, humans are not the dominant species, but merely prey. The natural historian David Quammen wrote, "Great cats remind us that we are just another flavor of meat." Nonetheless, humans seem to have always wanted to associate with these perfect hunting machines through art, adornment, trophies, magic, and religion—and living with their smaller, safer relatives. In some animistic religions, shamans are believed to be transformed into cats during certain rites. Black cats and witches were linked so completely that both were persecuted until not so long ago. The ancient Egyptians called a cat a *miu,* which means "one who mews," and they honored their domestic cats, associating them with the cat goddess Bastet. They also mummified cats as offerings and buried hundreds of thousands in tombs. Today we too honor our pet cats. The death of a beloved cat is a painful experience for a cat owner, and we frequently pay our respects by interring our pet's remains in our backyard or a nearby pet cemetery.

To watch a favorite pet cat lounge languidly in a ray of sunlight and then see it, in a flash, grow completely tense and focused on a bird that has alighted on a feeder outside the window is to marvel at the work of nature and to delight in living with a perfect predator. To walk into a living room and find the shredded

The number of Iberian lynx in Spain and Portugal *(Lynx pardina)* has dwindled to a mere 200 individuals, mostly living in protected areas.

ruin of an expensive chair, and know that there is little to be done about it except reupholster, reveals how complex the human-cat relationship is.

Cats help people to learn about and appreciate nature, provide them with companionship, and even help them to bear life and death more easily. And they are just fun to be around.

The cat has long been thought a mysterious animal, both repelling and fascinating humans. At various times in history and in various places in the world it has been revered as a goddess or associated with witches.

CHAPTER 1

WHAT IS A DOMESTIC CAT?

Domestic cats can range from working animals to much-loved pets. We value them as rodent catchers, and treasure them as companions. By studying domestic cats, scientists learn critical new facts about basic biology and diseases, which benefits humans. Cats entertain us.

Yet, as every cat owner knows, each cat has its own personality, its own routine, its own likes and dislikes. This makes sweeping generalizations difficult. Even scientists who study cats caution that

there is still much to learn about these familiar animals. This makes domestic cats mysterious and attractive to some people and repulsive to others. During the last decades, scientists have been watching cats carefully and gradually discovering their secrets, as well as probing our own complicated relationships with cats. Although much remains to be learned, we know more about domestic cats than about any other species of cat—more, for that matter, than about most mammals.

Above: Domestic cats, which are sometimes referred to as "mousers," have long been valued for their hunting skills.

Left: Like this contented house cat, many domestic cats are fortunate enough to be welcomed into human homes.

Cats are Mammals

Q: What is a cat?

A: A cat belongs to the family Felidae, order Carnivora, class Mammalia, subphylum Vertebrata. In other words, like us, cats are mammals, and as members of the class Mammalia they are vertebrates, or animals with backbones. The first animals with backbones appeared more that 500 million years ago. Backbones link mammals with fish, birds, reptiles, and amphibians. Mammals differ from the other vertebrates in having hair and feeding young milk produced by mammary glands (hence the word "mammal").

Cats and all mammals and birds are warm-blooded, or more technically, homeothermic, which means that they regulate body temperature through energy metabolism rather than depending solely on behavior and the local ambient temperature. Mammals trace their pedigree

Right: The marsupial mammals, such as the kangaroo, complete much of their early development inside a pouch on the mother's body.

Below: All cats, both wild and domestic, are placental mammals, which means that they give birth to live young that have been nourished through a placenta inside the mother's uterus.

through the reptiles, as do birds, but evolved from different reptilian ancestors than birds did. The mammal-like reptiles were well developed by 250 million years ago. The ancestors of today's true mammals diversified 180 million years ago when their ancestors split from the ancestors of today's egg-laying mammals—the duck-billed platypus and the echidna, or spiny anteater. By 135 million years ago, an ancestor that give birth to relatively well-developed young nourished through the placenta in the mother's uterus differentiated from the pouched marsupial mammals, represented by today's opossums and kangaroos.

These groups—egg-laying mammals (monotremes), pouched mammals (marsupials), and the placental mammals (including cats and humans)—represent the evolution of three diverse mammalian reproductive mechanisms. Today there are more than 5,400 species of mammals. Only about 300 species are marsupial mammals, and there are only 5 species of monotremes; all other mammals are placentals. Cats, and humans, are in the majority group of placental mammals, but we should not think of the placental reproductive system as advanced and the other two as primitive. If the ancestral characteristics are advantageous under present conditions for a mammal species' way of life, there is no pressure to evolve.

There are 29 orders of mammals, including the order Carnivora to which cats belong. Scientists disagree, however, about which orders are most closely related to the Carnivora. Those who compare the bones of various species to determine relationships suggest that the Carnivora is most closely related to the ant- and termite-eating pangolin order; then to the hoofed, grass- and leaf-eating mammals; then to the bats; and then, most distantly, to the primates (including humans). Those who study genetics to determine relationships present evidence that groups the Carnivora with the whales, bats,

and hoofed mammals. Primates, rodents, and tree shrews form another group more distantly related to the Carnivora.

Whatever its nearest mammalian relatives, the Carnivora arose from a miacoid, one of a small group of arboreal, domestic cat–sized carnivorans that first appeared in the forests of the Northern Hemisphere 60 to 80 million years ago. After the extinction of the dinosaurs about 65 million years ago, the Age of Mammals began in earnest, with mammalian species experiencing rapid diversification. By about 40 million years ago, the Carnivora had divided into two groups. One, the catlike Feliformia, eventually came to include today's cats, hyenas, civets, mongooses, and the now-extinct catlike nimravids. The second group, the Caniformia, eventually came to include today's dogs, foxes, wolves, bears, raccoons, weasels, skunks, badgers, otters, and a now-extinct group called bear-dogs.

The Carnivora order of mammals is divided into two groups, the catlike Feliformia group, which is made up of today's cats and catlike animals such as the mongoose and hyena, and the dog-like Caniformia group, which includes dogs, wolves, foxes, and animals such as this fisher.

The cats are a variation on a common theme.
—JOHN EISENBERG

Cats and Other Carnivores

Q: How do cats differ from other carnivorous animals?

A: All cats, big and small, belong to the order Carnivora, one of 29 mammalian orders. There are about 15 families in the order (although the number keeps changing). The Carnivora is divided into catlike and doglike forms. A key anatomical difference between the catlike and doglike carnivores lies in the tympanic bulla, which is part of the skull between the eardrum and the base of the outer ear. Occurring on each side of the skull and housing the ossicle of the middle ear, this bony chamber is filled with air and serves as a resonating chamber. In some species of both groups of carnivores, the tympanic bulla may be inflated, which increases hearing sensitivity. The catlike carnivorans, however, possess a unique arrangement in the tympanic bulla. Each bulla is divided by a septum that varies in depth in different species and enables them to hear with greater acuity the sound frequencies that match the calls of their primary prey. This septum is absent from the doglike carnivorans. It also explains why a domestic cat can hear sounds that you or even your dog may not hear, especially in the higher frequencies.

The word Carnivora means "meat-eater," but many of the members of the Carnivora supplement their meat diet with plant material, and some, such as the giant panda, eat mostly plant material. Cats are the rarest of exceptions—they eat meat only. For this reason, scientists have coined the term hypercarnivore to describe them. Despite the range in size—from 2 pounds to 660 pounds (about 1–300 kg)—found in the family Felidae, all cats are adapted to hunt for live, mostly vertebrate prey. As a result, cats form a remarkably homogeneous group.

The approximately 250 species in the order Carnivora are not the only meat-eating mammals. There are frog-catching bats, mouse- and rabbit-eating Virginia opossums, squid-eating sperm whales, and many other different mammals that rely on flesh for their sustenance. What then unites cats and dogs and separates them from bats and whales? The flat, shearing blades on the fourth premolars of the upper jaw and the first molar of the lower jaws—a paired set of teeth called the carnassials—define the Carnivora. Some members of the order, bears for example, have lost these shearing blades, in what scientists call secondary adaptations, to increase their efficiency for including plants in their diets. In the cats, however, the carnassials have retained the ideal shape for slicing meat. A relatively short digestive system, resulting from the easy digestion of meat, is characteristic of

Among the distinguishing features of a cat is the unique structure of its tympanic bulla, the round bone behind the ear, and the flat, shearing blades of its carnassials.

A Cat's Skull

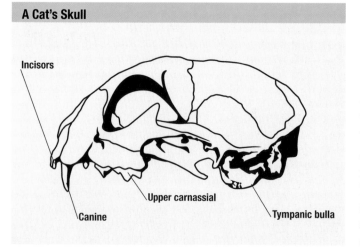

Incisors

Upper carnassial

Canine

Tympanic bulla

carnivores. Hypercarnivores have shorter digestive systems than do carnivores that include other foods in their diet. A cat has a digestive system where length is about four times its head and body length, while a red fox, which includes fruits, nuts, and insects in its diet, has a gut length of about five times its head and body length.

Among the carnivores, the cats are the most dramatically adapted for a predatory lifestyle. They are sleek runners and stealthy ambush hunters possessing a unique combination of stabbing and slicing teeth, powerful jaws, flesh-ripping razor claws, strong and agile bodies with flexible limbs, and excellent binocular vision.

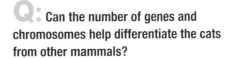

Q: Can the number of genes and chromosomes help differentiate the cats from other mammals?

A: No. Wild and domestic cats have roughly 50,000 genes, about the same number as humans. Most wild cats and the domestic cat possess 19 chromosome pairs, 15 of which are invariant among all the species. The small spotted wild cats of South and Central America differ from the domestic cat and the other wild cats in having only 18 chromosome pairs.

Most cats possess 19 pairs of chromosomes, except for the small spotted cats of South and Central America, such as the margay. Margays have "eye-spots," or black-ringed spots located behind each ear, which give onlookers the impression that they are being watched from behind.

Scientists have dubbed cats "hypercarnivores" because they eat a strictly meat-only diet. Their teeth and digestive tract are well adapted for this diet.

Cat Origins

Q: Where and when did cats evolve?

A: The ancestors of today's cats first appeared in the fossil record about 33 million years ago. Fossils of the first cat, the dawn cat, *Proailurus*, were found in Europe where it lived in the Oligocene epoch (about 33 to 24 million years ago). Members of this species, or a group of closely related species, were the size of today's largest domestic cats, and their morphology, or shape and structure, suggests that they were arboreal. Cat fossils are very rare or absent from the early to mid-Miocene epoch (about 23 to 17 million years ago), so biologists call this the "cat gap." Fossils of *Pseudoaluria*, related to but distinct from the dawn cat,

first appear in China, Europe, and North Africa during the early Miocene, and by the mid-Miocene abruptly appear in the fossil beds of the Middle East, Mongolia, and India. By 17 million year ago, *Pseudoaluria* entered North America. For the remainder of the Miocene, there was an increase in the diversity of cat fossil species. Using molecular genetic phylogenetic reconstruction—that is, analyzing genes to determine evolutional history—scientists have traced the various modern groups of wild cats, called lineages, back more than 10 million years to the late Miocene.

Above right: *Smilodon fatalis*. There were several independent families of saber-toothed cats coexisting during the Cenozoic, Miocene, and Pliocene eras.

Below: A skull of a saber-toothed cat. The saber teeth were likely not used to grab prey, but to fatally wound it. Too much pressure on the teeth might have broken them.

Q: What are some extinct cats?

A: The most spectacular species of extinct cats is the magnificent saber-toothed tiger, *Smilodon fatalis*, the fossils of which have been found in the La Brea tar pits in downtown Los Angeles and date back about 10,000 years. These saber-toothed cats are called tigers because this species was approximately tiger-sized. This name is misleading, however, because there were many saber-toothed cat species, most of them smaller than tigers, and none of them directly related to the tiger we know today. Modern tigers, as are all modern cat species, are conical-toothed.

The term saber-toothed refers to the size and shape of the upper canines, which resemble long, curved sabers. There are no cats with specialized saber-teeth living today, although the saber-toothed trait was an adaptation that at least some cat species had for most of the cats' fossil history and even appears earlier in noncat groups. At present, we are going through a "saber-tooth gap." After *Pseudoaluria* appeared on the

scene about 17 million years ago, the Nimravidae, or paleofelids (old cats), immediately began to decrease, and then became extinct. At the same time, there was an increase in the neofelids (new, or true, cats). These are the cats of the family Felidae to which the modern domestic cat belongs. These new cats, presumably because they were better at being catlike, outcompeted the old cats.

A second spectacular fossil cat is the American lion *(Panthera atrox)*. Fossils of these have also been found in the La Brea tar pits. These are directly related to today's lions, although the American lion was huge. Some were estimated to weigh 760 to 1,150 pounds (345–522 kg). Modern male African lions average about 330 to 550 pounds (150–250 kg).

The American lion was the largest cat found in the La Brea tar pits of Los Angeles, California. Its enormous size even extended to the length of its tail, which was nearly four feet long, almost matching the length of its torso.

The Wild Cats

Q: How many species of cats are there today?

A: The most recent authority, *Mammal Species of the World*, third edition, lists 40 species in the family Felidae. Two decades ago, the answer to this question would have been 36, and one decade ago, 37. The diversity of forms in the family Felidae is a subject of ongoing study and debate among specialists. Taxonomy, the science of classification, is never static; it always questions old assumptions and seeks clarification. For example, a population of small wild cats is found on Iriomote Island, just east of Taiwan in the Pacific Ocean. When scientists first described these cats, they classified them as a separate species; later, they included them as a subspecies of the leopard cat, which lives in mainland Asia. Most recently, they have returned them to full species rank. In order to explain speciation, the origin of isolation between populations must be resolved. This information is simply not known about many wild cat populations.

Recently, biochemical methods have been used as a basis for further clarifying relationships. As techniques have improved, our understanding of the relationships among the species in the family Felidae has improved. Relationships are determined by looking at molecular similarities among the genes and chromosomes of the various species. Biologists have been able to resolve the cat lineages back to about 10 million years ago. Ancestors of some species diverged before

this time, and it is not certain how some fit into the currently recognized lineages. Many budding species did not survive. There are many fossils of long-extinct cats, but most speciation events will never be known. All the cats we know today are the result of one long evolutionary process that led to several cat lineages.

The *panthera lineage* includes the clouded leopard, lion, tiger, jaguar, and snow leopard, all Old World in distribution with the exception of the New World jaguar. The *lynx lineage* includes the bobcat, Iberian lynx, Canada lynx, and Eurasian lynx, a mix of Old and New World species. The *leopard cat lineage* is entirely Asian in distribution and includes the leopard cat, the Iriomote cat, the fishing cat, the flat-headed cat, the rusty-spotted cat, and the Pallas's cat. The *bay cat lineage* includes the bay cat, the marbled cat, and the Asian golden cat, and is restricted to Southeast Asia. The *caracal lineage* includes the African golden cat, the serval, and the caracal. The African golden cat is restricted to Africa's tropical rain forests, but the caracal's range

Right: There are four species of Lynx. These stocky, mostly cold-adapted cats are found in northern Asia, Europe, and North America.

Below: The snow leopard is a member of the panthera lineage. Panthera also includes the lion, tiger, jaguar, and clouded leopard. Snow leopards live in extremely cold climates, and are insulated by their thick fur coats.

extends through Africa and into India. The *puma lineage* includes the puma and the small jaguarundi of the New World and the cheetah of Africa and Asia. The *leopardus lineage* includes the small cats of South and Central America: the ocelot, the margay, the oncilla, the Chilean pampas cat, the Pantanal cat, the Argentinean pampas cat, the kodkod, the Geoffroy's cat, and the Andean mountain cat.

The final lineage is the *Felis lineage,* which includes the domestic cat and the wildcat, along with the sand cat, the Chinese mountain cat, the jungle cat, and the black-footed cat.

In the formal classification of the living cats, all members of the panthera lineage are included in the subfamily Pantherinae. All the others lineages fall into the subfamily Felinae.

Some specialists think, however, that these distinctions will be revised.

Above left: With its short legs and long, thick, pale-gray fur, the Pallas's cat, a member of the leopard cat lineage, is adapted to live in harsh-climate areas of central Asia in semi-deserts, hilly areas, and in steppes with rocky out-crops. Locally it is known as the rock wildcat.

Above right: The puma, also called the mountain lion, is the second-largest New World cat. It is related to cheetahs, which once lived in North America, too.

Left: Servals, proficient at hunting rodents, also hunt birds, fish, frogs, lizards, and insects. They have been recently classified in the caracal lineage.

The Origins of the Domestic Cat

Below left: The European wildcat *(Felis silvestris silvestris)* is shy and untamable, so its ancestors were probably not the source of domestic cats.

Below right: Bronze figure of a cat with kitten, made in Egypt about 664 to 332 bce. Domestic cats were first depicted in Egyptian art about 2,000 to 4,000 years ago.

Q: What species of cat was first domesticated?

A: The source species of the domestic cat is the Old World wildcat. Genetic analyses indicate that the domestic cat is more closely related to the African wildcat subspecies, *Felis silvestris lybica*, than to the European wildcat subspecies, *Felis silvestris silvestris*. Some authorities consider the domestic cat to be its own species, *Felis catus*. Other authorities designate them as *Felis silvestris catus*, a subspecies of its wild source species. A cat's jawbone excavated from one of the earliest human settlements on Cyprus, dated to about 8,000 years ago, is the earliest clear sign of a familiar relationship between humans and cats. No wild cats occurred naturally on Cyprus; the colonists who first arrived by sea must have brought cats with them. Because wildcats and domestics are so similar, it is not easy for scientists to tell if the skeletal material they find at sites with human remains is from the wild or domestic forms. This is true of the remains found in Jericho (modern Israel) dating 7000 to 6000 bce and in an Indus Valley site dating 2000 bce. The finding in Cyprus of a cat carefully buried alongside a person, however, suggests that it was, if not domesticated, a treasured pet.

Specialists generally agree that African wildcats were domesticated in Egypt between 4,000 and 5,000 years ago. Cats began to figure in Egyptian art about 2000 bce, or 4,000 years ago. There is one exceptional picture of a cat wearing a collar dating to about 2600 bce. By about 1600 bce domestic cats clearly and frequently

appear in art, shown sitting under chairs, eating fish, playing, and helping people hunt birds in the Nile Delta's papyrus swamps. From Egypt, domestic cats very slowly dispersed throughout Europe and Asia, tagging along with traders and with the great movements of people.

Q: Have people domesticated any other cat species?

A: Although cats of a few species have been tamed, wild cats possess many of the traits that have made other species impossible to domesticate: They are solitary and territorial, have nasty dispositions, and often do not breed well in captivity. As carnivores, they do not efficiently convert food biomass into meat for humans to eat. One prominent authority defined domestication as a wild animals' transformation into something more useful to humans through selective breeding. If the first domestic cats' use to us was their superb rodent-catching skills, there would be little reason to attempt to change them.

Attempts to tame European wildcats have been largely unsuccessful, even hand-reared kittens. As adults they are exceptionally shy and intractable. In contrast, Dr. James Serpell reports that "the African subspecies, however, appears to possess a far more docile temperament, and they often live and forage in the vicinity of human villages and settlements." Some authorities have argued that as domestic cats spread from Egypt through Europe and Asia, a certain amount of hybridization occurred between them and European wildcats, jungle cats (*Felis chaus*),

and even Pallas's cats. There are domestic cats in Indian villages that look almost exactly like the wild jungle cats.

In historical times, cheetahs and, to a lesser extent, caracals have been tamed, if not domesticated. In the Middle East and in India, cheetahs were captured and trained to hunt gazelles beginning about 1,000 years ago, and this practice continued into the twentieth century. Caracals were trained to hunt birds and hares. Cheetahs are an especially difficult species to breed in captivity and thus all but impossible to domesticate.

Today, thousand of large cats—lions, tigers, and pumas—are maintained and bred as pets in backyards and small compounds in North America and Europe. In China, Thailand, and several other Asian countries, tigers are maintained in what are known as tiger "farms" and are managed to produce large numbers of cubs. These tiger farms are tourist destinations and have been reported to supply tiger organs (illegally) for locally produced traditional medicine.

Although captured individuals were trained to hunt in times past, cheetahs did not breed in captivity, and were therefore never domesticated.

Close Relatives

Q: What species are the closest relatives to the domestic cat?

A: The domestic cat and the wildcat, the source species for the domestic cat, are in the Felis, or domestic cat, lineage, along with the elusive Chinese mountain cat, the sand cat, the jungle cat, and the black-footed cat. The cats in this lineage are small cats of Asia and Africa. All of them can climb but are primarily terrestrial hunters. All of the wild species are solitary-living; feral domestic cats, in contrast, will live in groups where there is a concentrated rich food supply, such as on farms and around dumps and harbors.

Right: The black-footed cat shares its lineage with the domestic cat. It is one of the smallest wild cats.

Below: The feet of sand cats are padded heavily with hair to protect them from the hot desert sand.

One of the greatest challenges all small cats face is to avoid becoming prey to larger avian and terrestrial predators.

The black-footed cat is an extremely small cat, weighing less than about four pounds (2 kg), and lives in dry habitats in southern Africa. It rivals the rusty-spotted cat from India and Sri Lanka and the kodkod from South America for the title of smallest wild cat. Its tawny to cinnamon-buff fur is marked with black or brown spots that form bands on the head, neck, and tail. It has conspicuous black "boots," rounded ears, large eyes, and a black-tipped tail less than half the length of its head and body. Its skin is pink, unlike the pigmented skin of the other spotted cats. This little cat feeds on rodents, shrews, and small birds, and also larger birds such a bustards that are twice its size or larger.

The sand cat and black-footed cat do not overlap in their distribution in Africa. The sand cat lives in true sand deserts in North Africa, on the Arabian Peninsula, in Pakistan, and east of the Caspian Sea. It is tan in color, with a stocky build, and the ears set wide on the sides of its head. In the harsh landscapes where this little cat lives, it finds sustenance in small mammals, reptiles, and birds.

One of the rarest of small cats, the Chinese mountain cat is a small, stocky cat with relatively short legs. Its thick, fur coat is pale yellow and gray, ticked with longer dark-brown or black guard hairs. It lives in the dry mountain and shrub steppe of western China. Rodents and pikas (small relatives of rabbits), birds, and pheasants are its primary prey.

The jungle cat is slightly heavier and taller than a domestic cat. It has plain, unspotted fur that varies from tawny brown to reddish. The black tips on its guard hairs give it a speckled look. It is an elegant cat with tufted ears, a short tail, and long limbs. The jungle cat is found throughout south Asia, Asia Minor, and into Egypt. This is not a cat of the deep jungle as its name suggests, but instead lives in tall grass, thick brush, riverside swamps, and reed beds. It feeds on rodents, small birds, and occasionally frogs.

Widely distributed and adaptable, jungle cats live in a variety of habitats.

Domestic Cat Ancestors Today

Q: Where does the wild ancestor of the domestic cat live today?

A: Wild ancestors of the domestic cat live in Asia, Africa, and Europe. Scientists have divided these wildcat species into three groups: the thickset, heavily furred, forest-living wildcat subspecies from Europe, *Felis silvestris silvestris*; the lighter-bodied steppe wildcat subspecies of Asia, *Felis silvestris ornate*; and the longer-legged African subspecies, *Felis silvestris lybica*. There is, however, considerable variation within regions, and currently there is no uncontroversial genetic or morphological definition of a wildcat.

The modern wildcat itself is thought to have descended from the now-extinct Martelli's cat, *Felis lunensis*, known from fossil remains in Europe dating back two million years. The transition from Martelli's cat to the modern wildcat is thought to have occurred in Europe less than 450,000 years ago. But fossils from Africa and the Middle East date back to less than 130,000 years ago, suggesting that the wildcat rapidly expanded its range at that time because of habitat shifts caused by climate change.

The current accepted scientific thinking is that about 50,000 years ago the long-established European wildcat moved out of Europe, and this coincided with the evolution of the steppe wildcat form in the Middle East, from which it quickly spread eastward into Asia and southward into Africa. If this is the case, then we have essentially two lines or types rather than three: the forest-living cat of Europe and the steppe-living cat of Africa and Asia.

Q: Can a domestic cat breed with a wildcat?

A: Yes, domestic cats do breed with wildcats, and this has greatly confounded our understanding of relationships between wildcats and wild-living domestic cats. It is difficult for scientists to distinguish between domestics and wildcats without sophisticated statistical and genetic techniques. After the domestic cat was derived from the Middle East–North African steppe wildcat group at least 4,000 years ago, it has proceeded to colonize nearly the entire world with human assistance. Until recently, domestic cats were left to wander at will—and into the habitats of their wild relatives, which made it easy for them to breed with their wild counterparts.

As might be expected, the morphology of the wild-living domestic cats is more similar to that of African wildcats than

The African wildcats *(Felis silvestris lybica)* can be found in every African habitat except the arid deserts and the pure rain forests. These cats are thought to be the ancestors of Egypt's domesticated cats.

it is to that of European wildcats. The farther from the center of domestic cat origin, the more noticeable the effects of hybridization become. For instance, conservationists are especially worried about free-living domestic cats hybridizing with the forest-living wildcats of Scotland and Europe. Hybridization between wildcats and domestic cats is also a serious threat to the ability of wildcats to continue to exist unaffected by human-caused disturbances, including those created by pet animals.

Q: **What is the difference between a wildcat and a domestic cat?**

A: Domestic cats have diverse coat color patterns and may breed year-round; wildcats show far less coat variability and are seasonal breeders. Domestic cats also tend to have proportionately smaller brains, jaws, and teeth, shorter legs, and

longer digestive tracks than wildcats. We do not know exactly how the domestication of the cat occurred, but studies have revealed that selection for tameness and affection for people can turn a line of wild red foxes into doglike pets in a mere 20 years. Domestication appears to elevate levels of the neurotransmitter serotonin, which has a calming effect. Certain coat colors in domestic cats are also associated with temperament. The most common coat colors in domestic cats today are blotched tabby, black, and orange, all colors correlated with calmer cats than the agouti, or striped tabby, which is the ancestral coat color.

Left: Scottish wildcats live in the forests of Scotland. Conservationists worry about their mating with free-living domestic cats.

Below: Orange domestic cats are known for their calm temperaments.

The domestic cat is a contradiction. No animal had developed such an intimate relationship with mankind, while at the same time demanding and getting such independence of movement and action.

—*DESMOND MORRIS*

CHAPTER 2

DOMESTIC CAT DETAILS

All domestic cats are the same species, with very few genetic differences among the assorted breeds and populations in various parts of the world. Those few differences, mostly in fur color, pattern, and length, account for the diversity of free-ranging and feral cats you may see in your neighborhood or as you travel from place to place. You may see standard tabby cats, orange cats, and shorthaired and longhaired black cats. You may also see stocky, robust cats and slen-

der, delicate cats, whose genetic ancestors originated in Europe and Asia, respectively. Some variations in fur color pattern are more common in one place than another. Orange cats, for example, are most common in Asia Minor. Variations in fur and build also account for most of the differences among the standard pedigree breeds, Siamese and Maine coon, for example. Most pedigree breeds have been created recently, with breeders intensively selecting for traits that vary naturally within the species or that appear as a result of chance mutations.

Above: Domestic cat color patterns vary between breeds as well as within a litter.

Left: Although some people believe that black cats are unlucky, others prefer cats with rich, all-black fur.

Breeds New and Old

Q: How many breeds of domestic cats are there?

A: It depends on whom you ask. Even among cat fanciers—people who breed pedigreed cats and register them with the various governing bodies that set breed standards—the number of recognized breeds depends on the governing body in question. For example, the Cat Fanciers Association, one of the largest registries of pedigreed cats, recognizes 41 breeds. The American Cat Fanciers Association lists 48 breeds. The Canadian Cat Association counts 44. The International Progressive Cat Breeders' Alliance recognizes 73.

Noted cat biologist Desmond Morris described 80 breeds, some of which no longer exist, in a 1996 book. And new breeds are being created all the time.

The breeds listed by these various organizations refer to pedigreed cats—those whose ancestry can be traced back over several generations. Serious competitive cat breeders try to perfect the cats they breed to conform to the standards set by the organizations. According to the Cat Fanciers Association, "The ideal [pedigreed] cat is a perfectly proportioned animal, of pleasing appearance and superb refinement, a sophisticated version of a domesticated feline."

All cat fanciers recognize certain long-established breeds, and these are also familiar to the general public. Persian cats, with their very long fur and pug noses, aristocratic Siamese cats, and American shorthairs, which most closely resemble the run-of-the-mill house cat, are examples. Other recognized breeds, such as curly-furred LaPerms and chocolate-colored Havana browns, are products of recent breeding efforts and are less well known.

Most domestic cats are no particular breed at all. Fewer than about three percent of cats in the United States result from matings planned by cat owners to produce offspring with particular traits.

Q: What are the main differences between breeds?

A: The most visible differences between cat breeds are in coat color, pattern, and length. Genetic analysis reveals that nearly

The world's first cat show was held in London's Crystal Palace in 1871. By the 1920s they were common in both Europe and North America. This show was held in Washington, D.C., in the 1920s.

all the differences between breeds of cats can be accounted for by mutations at approximately nine gene loci. At each of these are alternative alleles (variants of the same gene). Genes at these loci give instructions for a cat's color and pattern. The combination of alleles any cat inherits from its parents, together with how genes at different loci interact, determines what its fur, for instance, will look like. For example, the ancient striped markings and coloration that closely resemble the markings seen in the wild cats is called the striped or mackerel tabby.

The genetic instructions for the mackerel pattern are on the tabby allele, which is symbolized by the uppercase letter "T." A mutant allele, which is labeled t^b, holds the instructions for blotched tabby, but T will be dominant to it. This means that if T is paired with t^b, the instructions on the t^b allele will not be carried out; t^b is called a recessive gene. Because alleles come in pairs, if a cat inherits either two tabby alleles, TT, or one tabby and one blotched, Tt^b, the cat will be a typical tabby. If it inherits two blotched alleles, t^bt^b, it will be blotched. Each parent donates one allele to its young, so all their offspring will be blotched if both parents are t^bt^b, or about one in four offspring will be blotched if both parents have mixed Tt^b alleles.

Alleles at other gene loci that code other traits work in a similar fashion. In addition, genes at some loci influence or mask the effects of the genes at other loci. For example, the mutant dominant orange gene, O, masks the effect of both agouti black genes and thus converts a black or brown coat to an orange coat.

Above left: Although new breeds are constantly being developed, there are a few long-established breeds. The Persian cat, for example, with its distinctive round eyes, short broad nose, and long, flowing coat is recognizable to almost everyone.

Below left: White tigers, because of their lack of color and their blue eyes, are sometimes mistakenly considered to be albinos. They are not, however, albinos. White tigers occur when both tigers that mate carry a very rare recessive gene for white coloring.

In the Genes

Right: Siamese cats are known for their distinctive "points": the darker fur coloration of their extremities. Chocolate-point Siamese have creamy white bodies and chocolate-brown legs, tail, mask, and ears.

Q: What genes determine coat color, length, and pattern?

A: The chart on the facing page shows the gene loci most important for variation in the color, pattern, and length of the fur of domestic cats, and common alleles associated with each loci.

Q: How does temperature affect fur color?

A: Temperature or other environmental variables do not affect fur color, with one major exception. The color verses albino allele, c^s, produces a temperature-sensitive gene for an enzyme related to pigment production called tyrosinase. This gene is inactive at the cat's core body temperature, leaving the fur on most of the body a pale brown or cream, but is active at the cooler tips of the feet and ears, where it produces a normal amount of pigment. This is what creates the Siamese's points. The c^b allele is also temperature sensitive, but less so; therefore cats with this variant have uniformly darker coats.

The domestic tabby, with its striped markings, inherits its wild-type coloration from its wild ancestors.

COAT COLOR GENE CHART

A = Agouti Versus Non-agouti

- A is the dominant wild type, producing agouti color; this means that individual hairs have bands of different colors
- a is a mutant recessive; aa produces non-agouti, or solid-color hairs

B = Black

- B is the dominant wild type, producing black or very dark brown fur
- b is a recessive; b^b reduces black to dark brown or chocolate
- b^l is recessive to both B and b; $b^l b^l$ produces light brown or cinnamon color

O = Orange Versus Non-orange

- O is a mutant dominant that produces all-orange pigment; it influences the expression of the black locus, turning black or brown to orange, and also hides the expression of the agouti locus so all orange cats are tabby.
- o is the wild type; oo results in no orange pigment

T = Tabby

- T is the wild type, producing striped or mackerel tabby
- t^b is mutant recessive; $t^b t^b$ produces blotched tabby
- T^a is a mutant dominant; TT^a or $T^a t^b$ produce ticked or Abyssinian pattern, which is faint striping on the face or tail.

C = Color Versus Albino

- C is the wild type, producing full color
- c^s is a recessive; $c^s c^s$ reduces color to the points, as in the Siamese cat
- c^b is codominant with c^s and recessive to C and causes less color reduction than c^s; $c^b c^b$ results in Burmese coloration; $c^b c^s$ in Tonkinese
- c^a is recessive to all of the above; $c^a c^a$ produces albino cats with pale blue eyes
- c is recessive to all of the above; cc produces albino cats with pink eyes

L = Short Hair Versus Long Hair

- L is the dominant wild type, producing short hair
- l is a mutant recessive, producing long hair

W = All-white Versus Normal Color

- W is a mutant dominant; it overrides all other genes for pigmentation and also affects hearing
- w is the wild type, producing normal color and hearing

S = Piebald (white spotting versus non-piebald white spotting)

- S is a mutant incomplete dominant; SS produces piebald with very large white spotting
- s is the wild type, producing no piebald white spotting; Ss produces some white spotting

Fellow Travelers

Q: How did domestic cats spread around the world?

A: The Egyptians tried to keep cats for themselves and made it illegal to export them to other countries. Their embargo seems to have been surprisingly effective. There is little unequivocal evidence of domestic cats outside Egypt until 500 BCE in Greece, where a marble block depicts a leashed domestic cat squaring off with a leashed domestic dog. Earlier evidence of possibly domestic cats outside Egypt, including bones and footprints dating to 2100 to 2500 BCE from the Indus Valley's Harrappa culture in what is now Pakistan and western India, may represent local domestication or captive wild cats. Harrapan feline figurines depict cats with collars, but figurines of rhinos and other species that were captive and not domestic show them with collars, too. An ivory statuette of a cat from 1700 BCE Palestine and a fresco and head of a cat from 1500 to 1100 BCE Crete are better evidence of domestic cats outside Egypt. Both Palestine and Crete had trade connections with Egypt, but the very scarcity of cat artifacts suggests that domestic cats remained confined to their center of domestication for millennia. And even when they did begin to appear more often in Europe, they attracted little fanfare. It appears likely that there was no active trade in cats, but rather that the emigrants largely moved themselves, in the words of Konrad Lorenz,

"from house to house, from village to village, until they gradually took possession of the whole continent."

It has also been suggested that the movement and expansion of cats followed that of the black rat, which was native to Asia, and the brown rat, native to eastern Asia, and the house mouse, from southern Europe and Asia. Cats moved from

Movements of cat populations may have followed those of rats and mice in Asia and Europe.

Greece to Italy in the fifth century BCE and spread with the Romans through Europe via imperial routes. Cats reached Britain by the fourth century and had penetrated all of Europe and Asia by the tenth century. Surprisingly, cats were not known as ratters and mousers until the fourth century in Rome—both Greeks and Romans employed domestic polecats (a type of weasel) and ferrets as rodent catchers—and Romans did not even have a word to describe a domestic cat specifically until that time.

The movement of cats along established trade and travel routes, including maritime routes, may owe more to human intervention. Historically, cats were popular shipboard companions, where they were valued as rodent-killers and were considered good luck. Shipboard

The ancient Egyptians revered cats. This statue is only one example of the feline images that pervade Egyptian art.

cats reached remote islands and other far-flung spots on the globe during the Age of Exploration, from the thirteenth through the eighteenth century, when Europeans sailed the world and began to settle in foreign lands. Cats accompanied human migrants to the New World, for example, and few of even the most isolated uninhabited oceanic islands escaped colonization by domestic cats that quickly went feral.

Q: What can domestic cats tell us about human migration patterns?

A: It is possible to show the genetic linkages between the domestic cats in various parts of the world and movements of people around the globe. For example, domestic cats in various parts of the New World are genetically similar to the domestic cats of the native lands of the majority European immigrants. Domestic cats throughout New England are fairly similar genetically, while the domestic cats of New York City stand out as distinctly different. Why? Because New York was first settled by the Dutch and New England by the English, and both groups brought their own local cats with them. Even today, the cats of New York are more like those of Holland than those of New England, where the cats in turn are more like those of England. To cite another example, the distribution in Europe of orange cats, which are most common in Asia Minor, follows the path of Viking sailors, who took orange cats to Spanish Mediterranean islands and the north and west coasts of Scotland.

By the sixteenth century, domestic cats were common in Europe, as evidenced by their inclusion in Konrad Gesner's *Historia animalium,* published in 1551–87.

Viking sailors helped distribute the cat's orange coat on their travels to Spain and Scotland, where it then spread farther by trade and sea routes.

Breed Characteristics

Q: What are the largest and smallest breeds?

A: Most pedigreed cats weigh in on average at 10 to 12 pounds (4.5–5.5 kg). Smallest among the pedigreed cats is the Singapura, with females in the range of 5 to 6 pounds (2.3–2.7 kg) and males from 5 to 8 pounds (2.3–3.6 kg).

The Siberian forest, Norwegian forest, Maine coon, and Ragdoll cats are among the largest pedigreed breeds. The first three are believed to be descended from "natural" breeds—ones that evolved their large size and long thick fur coats as adaptations to their cold northern environments. The Ragdoll, in contrast, is entirely the product of human selection. This breed originated in the 1960s in the United States with a mating between a white Persian female (or possibly an Angora) and a male Birman, a large, powerful longhaired breed that originated in Myanmar (Burma). Maine coon males usually reach 13 to 18 pounds (6–8 kg), with females normally weighing about 9 to 12 pounds (4–5.5 kg). Neutered Ragdoll males reach 20 pounds (9 kg), with females comparatively smaller.

Q: What are the most unusual breeds?

A: Among the most unusual of the old breeds—ones that are definitively known from earlier than about the mid-1800s—are the tailless, or nearly so, cats: the Manx, which originated on the Isle of Man in the Irish Sea, and the Japanese bobtail. Scientists agree that the Manx's tailless condition is likely the result of a random mutation that became fixed in the population because of inbreeding on the isolated island. Cats with short stumpy tails existed in various parts of Asia but became known as Japanese bobtails because Japanese nobility chose them as their exclusive pets. They appear prominently in Japanese art. The Manx and the bobtail are not believed to be related,

The Ragdoll breed of cat was created by artificial selection in the latter half of the twentieth century. Ragdolls are known as affectionate, gentle, and tolerant, and they make great family pets.

although one legend has it that ancient Phoenicians, renowned seafarers, brought these cats to the Isle of Man from Asia.

Modern breeders have created several breeds with novel fur texture or appearance. The fur of the Selkirk rex is long and curly, for instance, while that of the Cornish rex is short and wavy. Breeders have also produced cats with odd ears. The Scottish fold's ears fold forward and rest on the head, while the American curl's ears fold backward at the tips.

Q: Why is there less variation among cat breeds than among dog breeds?

A: Domestic cats all fall within a small range of sizes, and no breed shows the extreme morphological or behavioral features that occur in some dog breeds. There are no cat equivalents of tiny Chihuahuas or massive Saint Bernards. Neither are there cat breeds specialized to hunt rabbits and or catch fish, although both of these

specializations occur among the felids. Lynx, for instance, specifically hunt rabbits and hares, while fishing cats fish. The simple reason for this could be time and human interest: Dogs were domesticated earlier than cats, perhaps as long ago as 15,000 years or more, and people began selectively breeding dogs for particular purposes early on. In contrast, selective breeding of cats began in earnest only about 150 years ago, and then only for aesthetically pleasing or unusual traits, not for practical purposes. It could be that dogs were already providing people with the useful services that might potentially have been offered by cats, so people had no need to try to create cats that herd sheep or pull sleds. We do not know that it is impossible to create more diverse breeds of cats, because the experiment has not been performed.

Scottish folds are bred for their forward-folded ears. The ancestry of members of this breed can be traced back to a single cat born in 1961 in Scotland.

Cats are not as varied in appearance as dogs, although there are some differences, both naturally occurring and artificially bred. For example, modern cat breeders have selected for various fur textures and lengths, such as the short, wavy fur of the Cornish rex.

Origins of Breeds

Q: When and where did most of the breeds appear?

A: For most of the history of domestic cats there were no breeds, or at least no deliberately created breeds. Over time, as cats spread throughout the world, differences emerged among the domestic cats predominant in various areas. This resulted in part because of what biologists call the founder effect, in which the particular individuals that reached an area first were by chance already somewhat genetically distinct from others in the general population. In addition, isolated populations adapted to local conditions through natural selection, or changed when a chance mutation for some trait became fixed—did not die out—in a population. From time to time, people may also have exerted

some selection for a novel or attractive fur color. It wasn't until the middle of the nineteenth century in England that cat fanciers began to show cats and thus took an interest in selectively breeding them for particular qualities and importing exotic cats from afar. Of the 80 pedigreed breeds listed by Desmond Morris, only 16 were recognized before 1800.

Place names attached to breeds may or may not reflect their geographic origins. Those that do are the names of some of the old breeds that emerged before cat fanciers began their experiments. The origins of the longhaired Persian cat are obscure (like those of most old breeds), but this breed is believed to have arisen in Persia (modern Iran), just as Angoras originated in nearby Turkey. The Siamese cat was first known in Siam (modern Thailand), and the Siberian forest cat is a product of frigid Russian winters. On the other hand, the Russian blue may be called Russian only because the first of its sort to reach Britain came

Right: The Russian blue breed has been given many names, including Archangel blue, foreign blue, and Russian shorthair. Its current name was chosen in the 1940s, long after it had become a popular show cat.

Below: The Siberian forest cat originated in frigid northern Russia, and it is well suited to the climate.

from Archangel, a Russian seaport. The Kashmir cat was created in North America and was so named because it is related to the Himalayan cat, as Kashmir is related to the Himalayas. The Himalayan cat is not from the Himalayas either; it is a cross between a Persian and a Siamese cat, and it was named after the Himalayan domestic rabbit, whose coat is similar in color.

Q: How are new breeds created?

A: In the mid-1800s, British cat fanciers divided domestic cats into two categories: the British (also called American or European) and the foreign. The British cats are cold-adapted, robust, stocky animals with large heads, short ears, and thick fur; they resemble the European wildcats, with which they sometimes interbreed. The foreign cats are a hot-climate form, with slender bodies, long legs, large ears, and short fur; they most resemble the African wildcat. In addition, cats are divided into shorthaired and longhaired types, with the Persian cat being an example of the latter. Today's breeds are largely the result of crossing British and foreign-type cats and shorthaired and longhaired cats, with additional selection for fur color or eye color.

Pedigreed cats owe their distinctive modern appearances primarily to human intervention, but variations in coat color, in particular, seem to have ancient origins. The ancestral coloration is that of the African wildcat: mackerel tabby or striped. But black, blue, orange, white-spotted, and white cats are found worldwide, suggesting that this diversity was present when cats first began to leave Egypt.

A few breeds are the result of chance genetic mutations for which breeders then consistently selected. For example, the hairless Sphynx breed originated from a hairless kitten born in 1966, and the curly-furred LaPerm from a kitten born in 1982. A few other breeds trace their origins to recent crosses with wild cats. The Bengal, for instance, may have sprung from mating a domestic cat with a leopard cat, a species native to parts of Asia. The leggy Savannah is a cross between a domestic cat and a serval, a tall, big-eared cat of the African plains. Some cat fancy governing bodies refuse to recognize breeds created through the interbreeding of wild and domestic cats.

Bengal cats are a mix of wild and domestic. Among domestic breeds it is considered large; males can weigh as much as twenty-two pounds.

Selective Breeding

Q: Are some cat breeds abnormal?

A: The cat breed most often cited as abnormal is the Sphynx. These surprisingly robust cats appear to be naked—they lack an insulating coat of fur and are covered only in very short, fine down hairs that are nearly impossible to see. They have no whiskers, large ears, and long, naked, ratlike tails. Sphynx cats obviously cannot survive outdoors, where they suffer from sunburn and chill.

Hairless so-called mutant cats had previously been recorded from many parts of the world, but these mutants never left a lasting mark. A pair of hairless cats found in 1902 in New Mexico were claimed to be the last of an ancient Aztec breed—but there is no credible evidence for this. And "ancient" is surely an exaggeration; there were no domestic cats in the Americas earlier than 1492. Some cat breeding associations deem abnormal a recently developed short-legged breed called the Munchkin, the feline version of a dachshund. The Munchkin's front legs are no more than three inches long, and its hind legs only a bit longer, but its body is average size. Short-leggedness is the result of a random, natural mutation that appears from time to time in domestic cats. Some of these cats cannot jump, and are clumsy. Many cat lovers find the Munchkin's appearance an affront to their ideal of a cat.

When considering abnormal cats, the Sphynx is often the first named because it is hairless.

Q: Do cats of different breeds have different personalities?

A: No cat owner doubts that his or her cat has a distinctive personality or temperament, and cat fancier associations and countless books on cats describe the personalities of the various breeds. The scientific study of individual differences in personality among animals of the same species is relatively recent, but emerging results for cats and other animals support what everyone already knows: Individuals may be shy or bold, curious or aloof, calm or nervous, friendly with people or hostile to them.

Careful studies also reveal that the environment in which a kitten is raised contributes significantly to its adult personality. For instance, cats that are not

" Time spent with a cat is never wasted. "
—COLETTE

handled by people when they are between two and seven weeks old are forever less friendly to people. But environmental influences on personality cannot account for the reported differences between breeds, which would have to have a genetic basis. So what is the evidence? One study compared Siamese, Persian, and nonpedigreed house cats by both surveying the perceptions of the cat owners about their cat's personality and observing interactions between cats and their owners in their natural home environment. The result bore out the conventional belief that Siamese cats are more playful, active, vocal, and demanding than Persians or house cats. Persians are cleaner, and both Siamese and Persians are more affectionate toward their owners and friendlier to people than generic, nonpedigreed house cats. In other studies, kittens whose fathers were judged friendly were more likely to be friendly too; because fathers were absent during the kittens' development, this suggests that personality may be inherited.

Studies of the relationship between a cat's coat color and aspects of its personality further support a genetic basis for breed differences. Black cats, for example, appear to be more tolerant of and less aggressive toward other male cats than orange cats are. Scientists are unsure what links coat color to personality. It could be that genes controlling coat color are near those that influence some aspect of the nervous system (and thus how the animal responds to the world), and that these genes therefore tend to be inherited together. Alternatively, coat color genes may help regulate both pigment production and the production of chemicals, such as dopamine, that affect brain activity.

Below left: Even though it expresses typical feline curiosity, a kitten that is raised without human contact will always be wary of humans.

Below right: Siamese cats are often chosen as pets for their affectionate and playful personalities.

Playing Favorites

Q: What is the most common breed and the most popular?

A: The most common domestic cats are nonpedigreed cats, which may be called alley cats, moggies, house cats, or simply cats. The most popular pedigreed cats, as measured by registrations with the Cat Fanciers Association in 2004, are Persians, with Maine coons a distant second, followed by exotic shorthairs, Siamese, and Abyssinians.

Above: The Maine coon is the second-most popular pedigreed cat in the United States—and also one of the largest domestic breeds.

Right: Estimates of the world population of domestic cats, both house pets and feral cats, reach as high as 800 million individuals.

Q: How many domestic cats are there?

A: According to a 2005 survey conducted by the American Pet Products Manufacturers Association, nearly 38 million U.S. households, or about three in ten, have at least one pet cat, and together these households own more than 90 million cats. The British charity Cats Protection League reported 7.5 million household cats in the United Kingdom. Another 40 to 50 million or so free-ranging, or feral, cats are estimated to live in urban, suburban, and rural habitats in the United States, and about a million in the United Kingdom. Estimates of the world population of domestic cats vary, but it may be in the range of 800 million.

Q: Are cats more popular than dogs?

A: Dogs enjoyed a long reign as man's best friend, but in recent years cats have wrested away the title—at least in the United States. A survey by the American Pet Products Manufacturers Association in 2005 found that although slightly more U.S. households own at least one dog (43.5 million) than own at least one cat (37.7 million), the number of dogs owned—about 74 million—is substantially lower than the number of cats, which is 90 million. Moreover, many people feed stray or feral cats they do not own, which is rarely true for less numerous feral dogs. Surveys in the United Kingdom suggest a similar and growing preference for cats over dogs. Changing lifestyles, with ever-busier people living mostly in urban

environments, likely account for this. Cats are generally less demanding pets than dogs—they do not need to be walked, for example—and are generally better suited to staying indoors much of the time.

Q: Do wild cats make good pets?

A: Many people are taken with the idea of living with a wild cat. By some estimates, as many as 10,000 or more large cats, mostly tigers, lions, and pumas, are privately owned in the United States, kept in backyards, rural properties, and even in city homes. In the fall of 2003, for example, police were called to extract a tiger from a Manhattan apartment he shared with a young man and other assorted animals in a tiny urban menagerie. Clearly, big cats do not make good pets, as most people who succumb to the temptation of purchasing a charming little cub soon learn. No matter how

"tame" they appear, wild cats are dangerous animals, and keeping them poses a risk to owners as well as to neighbors. Very often too, these inappropriate pets are abused, depressed, and poorly nourished because of the steep cost of adequately feeding a big cat.

People have tried to tame just about every species of wild cat, but with few exceptions wild cats cannot be coaxed into living comfortably with people. European wildcats, despite being a sister subspecies to domestic cats, are both shy and fierce, and attempts to tame them are largely unsuccessful, even when they are hand-reared. Even domestic cats that have not been properly socialized to people as kittens may never make good pets. Some people report success in making good pets of servals and ocelots, but there seems little reason to do this. There are plenty of domestic cats that need good homes, and these wild animals belong in the wild.

More households own dogs, but many cat owners house more than one cat, or, as in this case, one of each species.

Although some people try to tame large cats and keep them in or outside of the home, they are taking large risks.

CHAPTER 3

THE CAT'S BODY

The food writer M. F. K. Fisher wrote: "First we eat, and then we do everything else." So it is with cats. Cats are exceptionally specialized carnivores. Their bodies and their behaviors are adapted for their stealthy hunting and the explosive rush or pounce to deliver their killing bite. Their vertebrate prey comes as complete nutritional packages for them. The most distinguishing anatomical features of cats are connected to their exacting predatory behavior. Otherwise, cats are more generalized anatomically than humans. Cats are typically mammalian in their cells and tissues, in their development, in their organs and body systems, and in their body plan, so much so that cats are used to teach introductory mammalian anatomy and physiology to students. There is little that is unusual about their skin and fur or in their reproductive, cardiovascular, respiration, excretory, and endocrine systems. It is in the cat digestive, locomotor, and nervous systems, sense organs, and skeleton that we discover the specializations reflecting their hunting and feeding style. What we see in our cats is a vast amount of complexity, and that bundle of complexity endlessly fascinates us.

Above: The domestic cat is similar to its ancestor, the African wildcat *(Felis silvestris lybica),* in anatomy and behavior.

Left: The bodies of big cats are strong and powerful, exhibiting the traits that make all species of cats superb predators.

A Range of Sizes

Q: How big are cats?

A: The average measurements given for domestic cats are 6.5 to 8.75 pounds (3–4 kg) in weight, and 15.75 to 23.5 inches (40–60 cm) in head and body length, with a tail length of 9.75 to 13.75 inches (25–35 cm). These measurements, however, hide a great deal of variation.

Cats typically range in weight from about 5 pounds to about 20 pounds (2.3–9 kg)—a fourfold difference from heaviest to lightest. (Curiously, the range of size variation in individual wild cat species often reflects a fourfold difference. The largest tigers, for instance, are about four times as big as the smallest.) Some individual cats may be much heavier, but these are often obese cats that have been overfed and receive little exercise.

Above right: The rusty-spotted cat is one of the smallest of the wild cats. It weighs only 2 to 4.5 pounds (1–2 kg).

Below: Domestic cats weigh 6.5 to 8.75 pounds (3–4 kg) on average, but the range is far larger. Domestic cats can weigh as little as 5 pounds and as much as 20 pounds (2.3–9 kg).

Neutered cats grow heavier than their intact counterparts, and the largest cats reported for a breed are usually always neutered animals. In one recent study, six male cats and six female cats were neutered and compared with five intact males and six intact females. The cats were weighed before they were neutered and again three months later. Both the males and the females that were neutered gained significantly more weight after three months than the intact cats, and added the weight as fat. The males increased their food intake after being neutered, while the metabolic rate of neutered females decreased. Comparable effects of neutering on weight have been found in feral cats as well.

Attempts to breed miniature cats in the size range of the smallest wild cats, such as the rusty-spotted cat of India and Sri Lanka, which may weigh in at as little as just over two pounds (1 kg), have thus far met with little success. Dwarf cats appear from time to time, but they usually suffer from pathological conditions. Some breeders have attempted to create miniature lines of standard breeds by selectively mating the smallest of animals that appear. Problems arise, however, when a miniature mother produces normal-size babies, which are too big for her to deliver normally.

Q: Are male cats bigger than female cats?

A: Although male and female cats are very similar in external appearance, except for visible sex organs, in most species of cats males are usually bigger than females. In feral domestic cats, males are, on average, about two to four pounds (1–2 kg) heavier than females, a relatively small amount of dimorphism compared to that of leopards, in which males may be one and a half times the weight of females.

Among the pedigreed breeds of cats, where each breed has its characteristic size range, a male Singapura, for example, will virtually always be smaller than a female Maine coon. But within any single breed, the size differential is small enough that an individual male may be smaller than an individual female.

Biologists think that larger body size in the males of many species evolved because of its advantage in winning male-to-male combat, thus increasing a large male's mating opportunities. Larger males may win more contests, but females may also choose larger males to breed with because they appear stronger, suggesting that they are the fittest. This is called the sexual selection hypothesis. Female body size, on the other hand, is driven by the size of her young and by the energy demands of pregnancy and lactation. The average size of a female is one that works best in the habitats in which her species live.

When male cats fight one another, the larger has a greater chance of winning. This, along with females choosing larger males for their apparent fitness, may have led to a size difference between males and females.

Bones and Muscle

Q: How many bones does a cat have?

A: The classic treatise on the anatomy of the domestic cat states that a cat's skeleton is composed of from 230 to 247 bones. The number of bones varies with a cat's age. A young cat has more bones, some of which fuse together as it gets older. But this number does not include several small bones called sesamoids, most of which are found in the feet, in tendons, and between the joints of the feet bones and the toe bones, and a few others called chevrons, which are found in the tail. The cat's skeleton has 52 spinal vertebrae, of which about 20 are in the tail, and 13 pairs of ribs. In contrast, the human skeleton has 200 bones, again not including sesamoids, and half the number of spinal vertebrate of a cat—just 26. The greater number of vertebrae accounts, in part, for a cat's amazing flexibility.

The skeleton of the domestic cat has between 230 and 247 bones. Its design allows amazing flexibility and speed.

Q: What are the special design features of a cat's skeleton?

A: Most of a cat's skeleton is designed for speed and power. A cat has long leg bones, and even walks on its toes to extend the length of its limbs. Long legs and this "digitigrade" stance increase stride length—how much ground is covered with each step. The spine is also very flexible because the articulations of the vertebrae are smooth and rounded and allow rotation along the length of the spine. As a result, a cat can flex and arch its back to increase speed. This flexible spine also enables a cat to twist and turn easily. Another adaptation to increase stride length is a small clavicle (collarbone). This allows freer movement of the front legs. And, free from the shoulder joints, the shoulder blades further extend forelimb length. The small clavicle is also what enables a cat's body to squeeze through very tight openings.

Overall, a cat's body is slender and fairly elastic, allowing it to move smoothly and gracefully. The long, flexible tail, with about 20 caudal vertebrae, acts like a rudder to improve balance. The hind limbs are generally longer than the forelimbs; the hind limbs provide more force than the forelimbs and are important for acceleration and jumping.

Different cat breeds exhibit some variation in skeletal characteristics. Persian cats, for example, have relatively short, heavy leg bones that support their wide, short bodies, while Siamese cats are long and slender. Angoras have relatively delicate bones. Japanese bobtails and Manx have

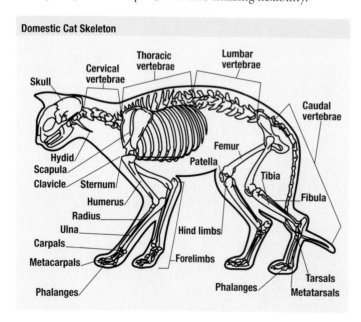

Domestic Cat Skeleton

Skull

Cervical vertebrae

Thoracic vertebrae

Lumbar vertebrae

Caudal vertebrae

Hydid
Scapula
Clavicle   Sternum
Humerus
Radius
Ulna
Carpals
Metacarpals
Phalanges

Femur
Patella

Tibia

Fibula

Hind limbs

Forelimbs

Phalanges

Tarsals
Metatarsals

no tailbones or a greatly reduced number of them. In several breeds, including the Siamese, the skull is small and wedge-shaped, while that of Persians is large, broad, and short.

Q: Does a cat have strong muscles?

A: In a healthy, fit cat, it is possible to see muscles rippling along its long body as it moves. A cat has large and strong leg muscles that give it great power for running and for pouncing on prey. The muscles that power its jaws are also very strong. Back and abdominal muscles make up a large portion of a cat's weight and are important in flexing the back as a cat runs.

Cat fanciers have selected to emphasize some muscle groups over others in developing breeds. For instance, Manx cats have particularly strong hind limbs, Turkish Vans are noted for muscular shoulders, and Maine coons and Norwegian forest cats are especially well-muscled overall.

Q: What are the internal organs of a cat?

A: A cat has a typical mammalian complement of internal organs: brain, heart, lungs, bladder, kidneys, and liver. The most distinctive feature of a cat's internal anatomy is its short, simple digestive tract, which relates to its strict diet of meat. Felids in general have relatively large lungs. A cat breathes faster than a human does, and its heart beats faster as well.

Above: A Manx cat is born with an abbreviated tail, or no tail at all. Breeding two tailless Manx together can create a kitten with a fatal spine defect, and is therefore discouraged.

Left: The long and thin cheetah is built for speed. The swift cheetah is the world's fastest cat.

Teeth and Jaws

Q: How many teeth does a cat have?

A: Most cats, including domestic cats and their wild ancestors, have 30 teeth, but some short-faced cats (the four species of lynx, the Asiatic golden cat, the African golden cat, and the caracal) have 28. The domestic cat's dental configuration is, on each side of the jaw, three upper and three lower incisors, one upper and one lower canine, three premolars on the upper jaw and two premolars on the lower jaw, and two upper and two lower molars.

Q: What do the different kinds of cats' teeth do?

A: A cat's teeth are specialized for different purposes. Long, stabbing canines are used for the bite that kills prey. A cat uses its canines to pierce the nape of its prey and break the cervical vertebrae. The canines are endowed with receptors that

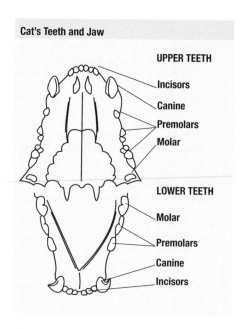

Cat's Teeth and Jaw

UPPER TEETH

Incisors

Canine

Premolars

Molar

LOWER TEETH

Molar

Premolars

Canine

Incisors

Right: The teeth and jaw of a cat.

Below: A domestic cat has 30 teeth. Certain ones are specialized for shearing meat off bones and others for plucking feathers or fur from prey.

detect pressure, and the jaw muscles fire very rapidly, so a cat can effectively feel when its canines are in the proper place and quickly deliver the killing bite. Behind the canines is a gap, which leaves room for the canines to sink deeply into the prey's neck during the killing bite. The canines of cats are also broader and more robust than those of other carnivores, helping to ensure that they do not break. Bladelike premolars on the upper jaw and molars on the lower jaw, called carnassials, are designed to work together like the blades of scissors for shearing meat off bones. Other molars are flattened and designed for crushing, but these are relatively unimportant in cats. Small incisors—the front teeth—lie in a straight line and help grab hold of prey and do fine work such as plucking feathers from a bird carcass. A cat cannot move its jaws from side to side, and hence it does not chew as humans do;

instead, using just one side of the mouth at a time, it cuts and tears its food into chunks it can swallow whole.

Q: How strong are a cat's jaws?

A: A cat's skull has short, powerful jaws, with attachments for large jaw muscles, which are needed to kill and eat the animals it preys on. Natural selection has optimized the design of a cat's jaw for the most powerful killing bite and cutting action, coupled with a reasonably wide gape. The shorter jaw length gives the muscle that closes the jaw, called the temporalis, extra strength. This muscle is attached to the side of the braincase. There is room on the skulls of many small cats for this large muscle to attach, but not on the skulls of bigger cats. Large cats have bony ridges, called sagittal crests, to provide more surface area on the skull.

Q: How are a cat's teeth and jaws different from a dog's?

A: A cat's teeth and jaws are similar to but more specialized than those of a dog. The first, most obvious difference is that a cat's jaws are shorter than a dog's; a cat has only 30 teeth compared to a dog's 42. A consequence of the shorter jaws is that a cat has the greatest power at the front of the mouth, where it is needed to deliver a single killing bite. In contrast, the jaws of a dog are most powerful toward the back. A dog's canines are not specialized to kill prey with a single bite; instead, its longer jaws give the shearing carnassials greater power to rapidly deliver shallow, slashing bites that wear prey down. Molars behind the carnassials in dogs are adapted to crush bones, which cats generally do not do. From the human perspective, a practical difference is that dog bites crush bones, muscles, nerves, and tendons, while cat bites are usually deep puncture wounds. For this reason, cat bites are more likely to cause infections because their teeth act like hypodermic needles to inject bacteria deep into the wound.

A tiger, as do all other species of cats, uses its canines to kill its prey. Canines are sharp and contain receptors that let the cat know if its teeth are positioned correctly.

Feet and Paws

Q: How many toes does a cat have?

A: All cats typically have five toes on their forefeet and four on their hind feet. But cats often exhibit the results of common genetic mutations that produce additional toes, a condition called polydactyly, from the Greek words meaning "many fingers." In most cases, the extra toes do not pose a hardship for the cats that possess them. Cats with six or seven toes on each forepaw are most common—the condition appears less often on the back paws—but as many as ten toes per foot have been reported. The most frequent mutation producing polydactyly is inherited as a single dominant trait that is not sex-linked; therefore, if one parent of two parents has it, about half their offspring will, too. Polydactyl cats are sometimes called Hemingway cats. Writer Ernest Hemingway kept a large colony of cats on Key West, a small Florida island. He received a six-toed cat from a passing ship's captain (cats with extra toes were considered good luck by seafarers), and this cat bred with others on the island. Eventually about half of Key West's cats had six toes. Polydactly is also particularly common in domestic cats of New England. Boston is believed to be where the mutation first appeared, either spontaneously or as a result of a cat arriving there aboard a ship from southwest England, perhaps with the Puritans in the 1600s. In either case, the mutated gene spread with people as

Polydactyly cats have extra toes; six or seven on each forepaw are most common. They are also called "Hemingway" cats because polydactyly cats on Key West, Florida, can be traced back to the author's cat colony.

"I am the cat that walks by himself and all places are alike to me."
—Rudyard Kipling

they moved about the eastern seaboard. Certain breeds of cats are also more prone to polydactyly than others. As many as 40 percent of Maine coon cats were once polydactylous, but the trait has been bred out of the pedigreed population.

Q: How does a cat walk?

A: As noted above, a cat walks in what is called a digitigrade stance. Its equivalent of our hands, the metacarpal bones, and feet, the metatarsal bones, are elevated, and only its phalanges—the fingers and toes—touch the ground. Further, only four of the five digits on the cat's forefeet touch the ground; the "thumb" is short and usually remains elevated. The effect of the digitigrade stance is to increase the effective length of the limbs, which contributes to a cat's ability to run fast. The toe shoes worn by ballet dancers work in essentially the same way.

Q: How does a cat walk so quietly?

A: The underside of a cat's paw is a marvel of design for sure and silent

locomotion. The paw has seven soft, spongy pads, separated by fur: one at the tip of each toe, called a digital pad; a large one in the center, called the plantar pad; and a small one at the wrist, called a pisiform, or pea-shaped, pad. Like shock absorbers, these pads cushion the cat's foot when it is running and dampen the sound of each footfall. The pads, and the ridges on the plantar pad, also provide traction for stopping without skidding and for climbing.

The pads on a cat's paws muffle the sound of walking and jumping. They also provide traction.

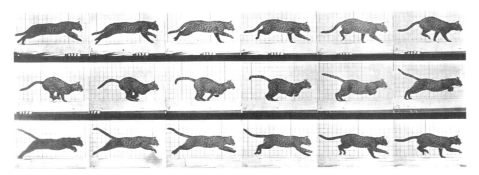

In his classic study of movement, *Animal Locomotion,* Eadweard Muybridge used time-lapse photography to break down the movements of humans and other animals, such as this cat, shown running and pouncing.

The Claws

Q: What are claws?

A: A cat has long, curved, needle-sharp claws (the equivalent of our fingernails and toenails) on each of its toes. The first claw on the forefoot, called the dewclaw, is very small and does not touch the ground. (Cheetahs are exceptional in this regard: The dewclaw on the forefoot does not touch the ground, but it is long. A cheetah uses it to snag and drag down prey.) A cat uses its claws to help grab and cling to prey and as weapons in fights. It uses them to scratch itself and to keep clean. Its claws can also close around objects, much as our fingers can. Claws are useful for climbing up trees, acting like a mountain climber's pitons, but are less useful for climbing down—one reason a cat may climb a tree and then refuse to come down. To protect these tools from wear and tear and keep them sharp, the cat usually keeps its claws hidden, retracted into sheaths of skin on its toes.

Q: How do claws retract?

A: When a cat needs to snare prey, climb a tree, or lash out at a competitor, the claws spring out, sharp and ready for action. When the claws are retracted, a spring ligament contracts and surrounding muscles relax; this holds the claws inside their sheaths. When the claws are again needed, the muscles contract and the spring ligament stretches to extend the claws beyond their sheaths. The mechanism is similar to the one that opens a jackknife.

It is a common misconception that cheetahs cannot retract their claws. While they lack the skin sheaths that in other cats usually conceal the retracted claws, cheetahs can nevertheless slightly retract their claws, although they remain exposed and visible. For cheetahs—the world's fastest cats—claws give traction while in hot pursuit of prey, just as the spikes on the shoes of runners give them traction.

A cat extends its claws to snag prey, climb a tree, or swipe at an enemy. The movement can be compared to the spring mechanism of a jackknife.

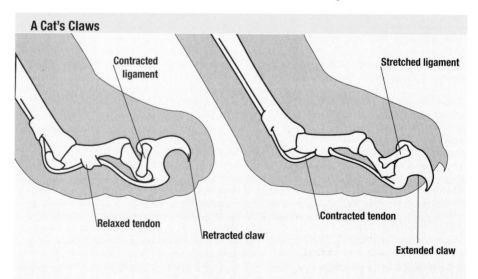

A Cat's Claws

Contracted ligament

Stretched ligament

Relaxed tendon

Retracted claw

Contracted tendon

Extended claw

Q: How does a cat keep its claws sharp?

A: Although claws are protected when not in use, they can become dull through wear. To keep them sharp, a cat runs its claws across tree trunks and other objects in its environment; in human homes, this usually means furniture, drapery, or other fabric. The cat is not actually honing its claws, as people would shape their nails with a file; rather, it is removing worn-out layers of its claws to expose fresh, new sharp ones underneath. And it does not scratch objects with the claws on its hind limbs. It keeps these claws sharpened by chewing off the old, covering layers.

A cat will look for rough textures in its environment upon which to sharpen its claws. Here, a lion turns a tree into a scratching post.

Q: Should a pet cat be declawed?

A: Some cat owners resort to declawing their pets in order to protect valuable home furnishings from scratches. Only the front claws are removed in a surgical process that involves removing both the claws and the first bone of each toe. The decision to declaw a cat should not be taken lightly—a cat without its claws is a seriously impaired animal. It will have a harder time grooming itself. It will be unable to climb and thus unable to escape from an aggressive cat competitor, an angry dog, or other potential predators such as coyotes or raccoons. Similarly, because claws are also defensive weapons, it will be unable to defend itself in a fight. Finally, a cat without claws will be unable to hunt, since claws are essential to its ability to seize prey. For all these reasons, many cat organizations, including the Cat Fanciers Association and the Canadian Cat Association, are adamantly opposed to declawing. Only if you always keep your pet cat indoors and plan to care for it until its death should you consider declawing it, and then only as a last resort, after all attempts to train it not to scratch your furniture have failed.

A cat's claws serve many functions, from grooming tools to offensive and defensive weapons. Because claws are essential to a cat's ability to take care of itself, the decision to declaw a pet should never be taken lightly.

A Cat's Fur Coat

Q: What is the function of a cat's coat?

A: Virtually all cats wear beautiful fur coats. Fur, or hair, protects the skin, enhances the sense of touch, and insulates the body from temperature changes. A cat's coat is composed of three different kinds of hairs. Short, thin, soft down hairs are closest to the skin and are the ones that best provide the coat's insulating properties by trapping heat lost through the skin. Down hairs are the most numerous of the three types. The top coat, hairs farthest from the skin, are called guard hairs. Guard hairs are long and thick, and their primary role is to protect the fur underneath from water and to protect the skin from abrasions and other assaults from objects in the environment. Guard hairs are the least numerous.

In between the down hairs and the guard hairs are the awn hairs. These hairs are intermediate in softness and length, as well as in relative number, and their role is intermediate too: they both insulate and protect. The very large, stiff vibrissae, or whiskers, are a fourth type of hair, specialized as sensory organs (see chapter four).

Variations in the coats of modern pedigreed cats are the result of human selection, and cats of some breeds do not have all three hair types, or one of them is emphasized over others. The Cornish rex, for example, has no guard hairs, while certain shorthaired breeds have no down hairs. The Sphynx cat appears hairless because it has extremely little fur, or at most a short fuzz over its body, and no whiskers.

Q: How long or short can a cat's fur be?

A: Among wild cats, species living in the coldest climates, such as Eurasian and Canada lynxes and snow leopards, have the longest, most densely furred coats, as would be expected—although there is seasonal variation. Conversely, species from hot climates have the shortest, sparsest coats. A similar relationship appears within the wildcat ancestors of domestic cats, with European wildcats living in cooler climates having longer fur than African wildcats that live in hotter climates.

Among the old, or natural, breeds of domestic cats, those originating in hotter climates, such as the Siamese, have short fur, while those from cold climates, such as the Norwegian forest cat, have long fur.

Three different kinds of hairs layered together create the cat's coat. Not all cats have all three layers, and the layers they have varies among breeds.

In the Norwegian forest cat, the very long outer coat resists water from rain or snow, while a very dense, thick down undercoat insulates it from the cold. A Russian blue is a shorthaired cat but with fur adapted to cold environments: Its coat is very dense and soft, and the hairs are uniformly short and thick. A Russian blue's coat has been compared to the fur coats of seals, which are designed to keep them warm in cold water.

Modern pedigreed cats have hair qualities and lengths unrelated to the thermal environment in which they live, and some have trouble coping with extreme outdoor temperatures. Persians, with soft, dense fur and a heavy top coat of guard hairs that can reach six inches (15 cm) in length, may suffer in the heat, while the Cornish rex, with short fur and very few downlike guard hairs, suffers in both hot and cold temperatures.

Q: Why does a cat shed?

A: Just as a human constantly loses and replaces hairs, so does a cat. Shedding gets rid of old, worn hairs and lets fresh new ones grow in to replace them. A wild cat, or a domestic cat that spends most of its time outdoors, usually sheds twice a year: in the spring, so that it can grow in a lighter coat for the warm summer months, and in the fall, in preparation for growing a heavier winter coat. Shedding occurs in response to changes in the photoperiod, or the relative amount of daylight in a 24-hour period. Increasing day length triggers shedding in the spring, and decreasing day length triggers the fall shed. A domestic cat kept mostly indoors is not subject to these natural changes and tends to shed throughout the year. Some breeds, such as the Cornish rex, are often touted as nonshedding. They do shed, but their short, fine hairs are simply less noticeable to human caretakers.

Canada lynx are known for their thick, dense coats. They are found in Canada and Alaska, where thick coats help them endure the deep cold.

With very short wavy fur, the Cornish rex is an unusual-looking breed. They are playful and affectionate pets.

Caring for Coats

Q: Why does a cat groom itself?

A: All cats groom themselves, and spend a significant amount of time each day doing so. Scientists call this behavior autogrooming (*auto* meaning "self") to distinguish it from one animal grooming another one, called allogrooming (*allo* meaning "other" or "different"). A kitten begins to perform grooming behavior when it is just three weeks old, even though its mother is still grooming it.

A cat autogrooms to keep its fur clean and to remove ectoparasites, which helps keep it healthy. There are, however, other, less obvious, functions of autogrooming. Autogrooming is important in maintaining the ability of a cat's fur coat to provide protection from extreme temperatures and moisture. Licking ruffled fur smoothes it down close to the skin, which enhances the insulating qualities of the coat. A cat does not have sweat glands all over its body, so applying saliva to the fur in hot weather helps keep it from overheating. As the saliva evaporates, it cools the body, just as evaporating sweat cools hot human bodies. As a cat vigorously licks its fur, it also stimulates the skin glands at the bases of hairs to produce water-repellent oils that protect it from rain.

Other functions of autogrooming are related to communication. Saliva carries chemical information, and applying it liberally to the body may maintain or enhance a cat's odor signature. Very often a cat licks itself after being handled by a human, and this may serve to cover up the odors that human hands leave on its fur. At the same time, the cat may be obtaining scent information, which is tasted through the vomeronasal organ, about the person who handled it.

Q: How does a cat groom itself?

A: The adult cat's grooming sequence is stereotyped and predictable, occurring in ten discrete steps: Lick the lips. Lick the side of one paw to wet it. Use the wet paw to rub the side of the head, including the ear, eye, cheek, and chin, on the same side of the body as the wet paw. Lick the side of the other paw to wet it. Use that wet paw to rub on the

Below right: There are ten discrete steps to the cat's grooming sequence.

Below: Even a kitten whose mother still grooms it, will go through grooming motions. There are many purposes for a cat's autogrooming, including removing dirt and ectoparasites, keeping itself from overheating, and enhancing the expression of its own odor.

Owners can help their cats by grooming them regularly, especially if their pet is a longhair. Longhaired cats need to be brushed daily to help prevent hairballs.

other side of the head. Lick the front legs and shoulders. Lick the flanks. Lick the genitals. Lick the hind legs. Lick the tail from base to tip. Along with licking, a cat nibbles away with its teeth at snarled clumps of fur and bits of dirt lodged in the fur and between the toes. Scratching parts of the body with the claws of the hind feet is also part of autogrooming.

Q: Why do people groom their pet cats?

A: While wild and feral cats groom enough to keep themselves as clean as they need to be, as do many domestic cats, pet owners frequently groom their cats as well. Fanciers who show cats are especially devoted to combing, brushing, and bathing their pets to remove dirt and keep fur shiny and untangled. While shorthaired cats that stay indoors may need little grooming from their owners, the fur of longhaired breeds must be groomed by hand daily to prevent matting and tangling. Grooming by hand, in which the human caretaker's combing or brushing removes most loose hairs, also helps to reduce hairballs. Hairballs are formed when a cat swallows its own fur as it grooms itself. The hair clumps up in the cat's stomach and the ball is eventually vomited, but occasionally the balls become impacted and require veterinary intervention to remove them from the gastrointestinal tract.

Colorful Coats

Q: Why does fur color and pattern vary?

A: Scientists believe that a cat's coat color and markings are designed primarily for camouflage, although they may also play

Above: A tiger's bold striped markings, as seen on this Sumatran tiger, help it blend into its forested habitat.

Right: Black cats may be more resistant to certain infections than the typical spotted cats.

a role in thermoregulation and communication. A cat must conceal itself while stalking prey, and in most species must also conceal itself from animals that prey on it. So while the markings of some cats, such as the bold stripes of tigers, may seem conspicuous when we see the animals in photographs or in a zoo, these same markings enable the animals to blend into their natural habitat, rendering them nearly invisible.

Species of cats with very large geographical ranges that may encompass many diverse habitats often display considerable variation in coat colors and patterns. The background color of the fur generally corresponds to the predominant colors of the natural landscape. Depending on the uniformity of the landscape, the fur may be plain or lightly marked, or it may be striped, spotted,

or blotchy to break up the outline of the body. In contrast, more boldly marked cats tend to be denizens of forests and woodlands, and many are completely or partly arboreal. Wildcats, the ancestors of domestic cats, tend to have heavier and darker markings when they live in forests and less pronounced and lighter markings when they live in open savanna.

Q: Why are some cats all black?

A: Known as melanism, black fur in domestic cats is the result of a single recessive gene at the agouti locus for coat color, which produces unbanded hairs of a solid color, coupled with the dominant B allele at the black locus (see chapter two). This also accounts for black versus spotted leopards. In both species, black background fur obscures the stripes or spots. Melanistic, or black, individuals appear in many, if not all, species of cats. There is some correlation between climate and the abundance of black individuals in

a particular population of a species, with black or darker individuals being more common in hot, moist rain forests.

Recently, evidence has emerged that suggests that genes for blackness, or darkness, may make their possessor more resistant to infections. Genetic analysis revealed that the gene that makes domestic cats black is different from the one that makes jaguars black and jaguarundis dark, and that both of these are different from genes for melanism in five other cat species. This suggests that mutations that make cats black evolved many times, and any trait that has multiple origins and persists over time in related species is likely to be adaptive. The jaguar and jaguarundi gene linked to melanism is similar to other genes that code for certain receptors on cell walls—receptors through which, in humans, viruses such as HIV sneak into cells and take them over. Certain mutations make these receptors more resistant to invasion, however, and give humans with these mutations some immunity from HIV. Thus, melanism mutations may give cats resistance to a virus or viruses. Along with a black cat's greater tolerance for living among other cats, its greater disease resistance may account for its high frequency in urban environments.

Q: Why are male calico cats rare?

A: Calico cats, also called tortoiseshell cats, have black and orange splotches of fur. Calico cats are almost always female, for reasons related to coat color genes in cats residing on the X chromosome. As in

Tortoiseshell cats are rarely males. They are so named because their coat patterns can resemble the patterns on the shells of tortoises or turtles.

all mammalian species, females have two X chromosomes, while males have one X and one Y chromosome. Calico females carry a gene for orange fur on one X chromosome and a gene for black on the other. During development, one of the X chromosomes in each cell of a female is turned off, but not every cell turns off the same one. In the calico cat, this leads to a mosaic of cells, some with genes that code for black fur and others that code for orange. Males, on the other hand, have a gene on their single X chromosome for either orange or black fur, so they are either orange tabby or black. The rare male calicos result from a genetic accident that give these cats both a Y chromosome and two X chromosomes; these males are sterile and exhibit feminine behavior.

Cats exhibit an incredible variety of colors and markings, from the classic marmalade tabby to a blotched pattern that combines both orange and gray tabby stripes.

CHAPTER 4

HOW CATS SENSE THE WORLD

Our pet cats may share our lives, responding to sights, sounds, and smells that are familiar to us; nonetheless they really live in a sensory world that is very different from ours. As are all mammals, a cat is born with five senses: vision, audition (hearing), gustation (taste), olfaction (smell), and proprioception (touch). But its sensory capabilities mean that it perceives the sensory stimuli differently than we do. A cat hears sounds that

we cannot hear, sniffs out scents that we are oblivious to, and possesses a sense of touch that extends beyond its body. On the other hand, its vision is poorer than ours, and it cannot taste at all one of our favorite flavors, sugar.

We may never fully comprehend how a cat perceives the world; the sounds and smells and other sensations that envelop it are beyond our ability to capture. But with technology, scientists are making progress in being able to see the world as a cat does. As a cat sees it, a human face, for example, looks like a grainy, black-and-white image from an old home movie.

Above: We may never know what the world smells like to a cat.

Left: Cats possess the same five senses that humans do—vision, hearing, taste, smell, and touch—but have different perceptions based on their unique sensory abilities.

A Cat's Eyes

Q: **How well does a cat see?**

A: A noticeable feature of a cat skull is the large eye sockets placed well forward on the face. Large sockets indicate, of course, that the eyes themselves are large, which suggests that a cat has good vision. Large eyes gather more light than small eyes, an advantage in low light conditions. Evidence from domestic cats shows that they can see in light one-sixth as bright as humans can. The primary reason for this is that the retinas of cats are mostly made up of light receptor cells called rods, with a smaller number of cells called cones. Rod cells are very sensitive to low levels of light, while cones respond to high light levels and also detect colors, which are lights of different wavelengths.

While cat vision is very sensitive at low light levels, cats have gained this sensitivity at the expense of acuity—the ability to resolve fine details. At low light levels, a cat must devote many more light receptor cells to stimulating a smaller number of optic nerve cells, and because fewer nerve cells are stimulated, the perception of the image will be less clear.

Large eye sockets placed well forward on a cat's skull reveal that a cat has large eyes and binocular vision.

The visual acuity of a cat is different from ours in another way, too. A human has a very high concentration of visual cells at a small spot in the center of the eye; this is where vision is most acute. Instead of forming a central spot in a cat's eye, however, these cells form a horizontal bar, known as the visual streak. This means that a cat's vision is most acute on a horizontal plane, matching the movement of its prey across the landscape.

Q: Why do a cat's pupils change size and shape?

A: A cat cannot see in complete darkness, but it is able to take advantage of far lower levels of ambient light than a human can. The size of the pupil determines the amount of light that enters the eye and hits the light-sensitive retina. It may seem logical then that the bigger the pupil, the better for a cat active and hunting in the dark. But a cat may be active during the day, too, so its pupils cannot be so big that it is blinded by daylight. In humans, pupil size varies in response to changing light levels: Pupils enlarge in low light and contract in bright light. (This is why we are briefly blinded if we go directly from a dark movie theater to the sunny sidewalk.) A cat's pupils do the same thing, but more so, growing very large and very small depending on the ambient light. The domestic cat and its close relatives have a unique muscular arrangement that closes the pupil almost completely to two tiny pinholes at either end of a vertical slit. In contrast, a big cat has elliptical pupils that appear round when dilated in the dark but are long and narrow in the light.

Above: The pupils of a domestic cat contract to slits in bright light.

Above left: The pupils of a tiger remain oval in bright light.

Q: Why do a cat's eyes shine in the dark?

A: Another adaptation for night vision is a structure called the *tapetum lucidum,* which lies behind the retina. Like a mirror, the tapetum lucidum reflects back through the retina the light that hits it, thus producing a brighter image. Basically, the same light gets used twice. This is what causes the glowing eyeshine you see when you catch a cat in your car headlights at night.

A golden cat's eyeshine, like that of all cats, results from light reflecting off a mirror-like structure behind its retina.

Q: How does a cat focus on prey?

A: The placement of its eyes, on the front of its face, gives a cat binocular vision—the ability to focus both eyes on a single object at the same time. Binocular vision allows a cat to judge distances, which is important for pouncing accurately on prey. Among the Carnivora, cats have the greatest degree of binocular vision, although it is less than that of humans. This means, however, that cats have a wider visual field than ours— 295 degrees versus 210 degrees—giving them better peripheral vision than we have.

Able to focus both eyes on its prey at once, a cat can tell how far away it is and adjust its pounce accordingly. Many predators have this ability, called binocular vision.

The nictitating membrane of a cat, known as the third eyelid or haw, is usually visible only as a pink or white bump in the corner of the eye nearest the nose. If the haw covers all or part of the eye, the cat is probably ill. This cat's haws are shown peeking from the inner corners of its eyes.

Q: What is a cat's "third eyelid"?

A: Many mammals and other vertebrates have a third eyelid, known technically as a nictitating membrane. Usually translucent, this membrane moves horizontally from the inside corner of the eye to cover and protect the sensitive surface without the instants of blindness that accompany blinking. In some species it is used very often; in flying birds, for example, it keeps the eyes moist and dirt free. In general, a cat closes the third eyelid only when it is ill. Humans have a nonfunctional remnant of this membrane, the small pink bump in the corners of our eyes.

Q: Do cats have "color vision"?

A: A cat's eyes have a relatively small number of the cones needed for color vision, and these cones are sensitive to either green light or blue light, but not to red. This is called dichromatic vision and lets cats see some colors during the day. Nonetheless, cats do not seem to pay attention to colors —perhaps because a green animal is no easier to catch in the dark than a blue one.

To see well in the dark, cats sacrifice both color vision and a certain amount of visual acuity. Splotches of dappled sun and shade playing on the forest floor—to us, a beautiful setting for a sinuous striped or spotted cat—are just gray blurs to the cat itself.

High-pitched Hearing

Q: How well does a cat hear?

A: Domestic cats have long been subjects in studies of hearing. A cat can hear the same sounds we can, and it can hear things we cannot. A cat's hearing is far more sensitive to high-pitched sounds than ours is, and is even more sensitive than that of a dog. While the upper limit of our hearing is about 20 kilohertz, a cat's is about two octaves higher, or up to 60 to 70 kHz. A dog's upper limit is between 35 and 50 kHz.

Below right: All cats have fairly large and mobile external ears, as does this domestic cat.

Below: The serval's ears are relatively the biggest of all cats' ears. These African cats hunt almost entirely by listening for mice and rats.

Measuring the responsiveness of auditory nerves reveals that a cat can hear tones up to 100 kHz, but such tones have to be so unnaturally intense, or loud, that this sensitivity is not useful to it. A domestic cat can also detect very low-frequency sounds—0.2 kHz—that we cannot hear. Like that of humans, however, a cat's hearing diminishes with age.

A cat's extraordinary sensitivity to sounds is one reason our pets sometimes seem clairvoyant—or their behavior inexplicable. But for a predator that hunts by stealth, moving very quietly itself as it listens for the soft calls and the sounds of small movements by prey, excellent hearing confers a big advantage.

Q: Why does a cat move its ears?

A: A cat's sensitivity to high-pitched sounds enables it to detect the squeaks and chirps of rodent prey, which use ultrasounds in the range of 20 to 50 kHz to communicate. The only problem is that these rodent calls are also very quiet.

This cat appears to be anxious about something, but the cause of its agitation is a mystery. Superb hearing means a cat may hear sounds humans cannot, making their responses to these sounds hard for us to understand and interpret.

A cat therefore has relatively large external ears (pinnae), with additional surface areas created by convolutions on the inside of the pinnae to collect the sound waves. The pinnae are also highly mobile, each controlled in the domestic cat by 30 muscles, as compared to 6 such muscles in humans, so that a cat can move its external ears to better register the sounds. Servals that hunt rodents scurrying through the tall grass of African savannas possess relatively the largest external ears of any cat so that they can detect their prey entirely by sound rather than by sight. Servals can even hear rodents moving through underground burrows so that they can nab them when they emerge.

Q: Can a cat detect vibrations?

A: The ability to sense vibration is related to both hearing and touch. Sound is composed of cycled air vibrations that hit the eardrums in a particular way, while other vibrations are detected by receptors deep in the skin. Cats are said to be quite sensitive to substrate vibrations—which may account for the idea that their behavior may predict an impending earthquake as they supposedly detect tiny preliminary tremors deep in the earth. There is no scientific evidence, however, that the behavior of cats, or of any animals, can be used to predict earthquakes or similar natural events.

The Sense of Touch

Q: **Is a cat sensitive to touch?**

A: A cat's skin is quite sensitive to touch, and specialized sensory hairs occur all over a cat's body. Very little is known about how these are used, however, except for the whiskers. Feline whiskers, or vibrissae, are coarse, stiff hairs that essentially extend a cat's sense of touch beyond the surface of the skin. Richly endowed with nerves, the vibrissae detect even the most minute variation in air currents caused by objects in the environment.

A cat usually has 24 long whiskers, 12 on each side of the muzzle, that are arranged in four horizontal rows.

Q: **What do whiskers do?**

A: Whiskers are found in three sites on a cat's face: on the cheeks, above the eyes, and on the muzzle. Whiskers enhance a cat's ability to move accurately, especially in the dark. Muzzle whiskers reveal this function. A resting cat holds its whiskers to the side, a sniffing cat holds them back against its cheek, but a walking cat fans them forward, in the direction in which it is moving. Whiskers are also fanned forward as a cat pounces on prey. They help the cat judge exactly where to deliver a killing bite. A blindfolded cat can even orient itself to kill a mouse with a neck bite using input from its whiskers. A cat also has vibrissae on its wrists or carpal joints to assist it in placing its feet correctly without looking when stalking. Areas of the cat's brain that process visual signals and areas that process tactile signals are similarly mapped and adjacent to one another. This suggests that the two senses act in a coordinated way to enable a cat to navigate a complex world.

Squared off for a fight, these cats move their whiskers to better detect tiny movements that may signal the opponent is about to launch an attack.

Q: Why does a cat like to be petted?

A: Mother cats lick their kittens repeatedly, and some scientists speculate that a hand stroking or petting a cat's fur simulates, or substitutes for, the licking of a fond mother cat. Even when fully mature, a domestic cat that as an infant was well socialized to humans seems to act as a kitten in its relationship with its human caretakers; it even seems to beg for this maternal attention. A kitten raised without contact with people will often mature into an adult that positively dislikes being petted.

In one study, scientists determined that a cat being petted by its owner most liked to be stroked near the temporal gland on the upper cheeks between the eyes and the ears, and least liked, even disliked, being stroked near the caudal gland on the back near the base of the tail.

Above: A cat may enjoy a child's stroke because it reminds it of being licked all over by its mother as a kitten.

Left: Many cats enjoy their owners petting and rubbing their cheeks.

The Taste Buds

Q: What tastes does a cat perceive?

A: The sense of taste does not seem important in cats, which possess fewer than 500 taste buds, compared to our 9,000 or so. Taste buds are absent from the center of the cat's tongue, where the papillae, the small protuberances on the surface of the tongue, are modified to be strong, backward-pointing, and rough, like a rasp, and serve to scrape bits of meat off bones and fur or feathers from prey. A domestic cat perceives, in order of importance, sour, bitter, and salt.

A cat's low sensitivity to salt may be related to the fact that its typical meat diet is high in sodium; it therefore does not need a taste for salt to stimulate it to seek out this essential compound. A cat will largely avoid sour-tasting and bitter-tasting food and water. It is especially sensitive to bitter quinine, refusing to drink it in solutions far

Above right: As carnivores, cats have specialized taste buds that respond to the taste of meat.

Below: Spiky papillae, not taste buds, cover the center of a cat's tongue. A cat uses its rough tongue like a rasp to scrape meat off bones. The texture also helps hold water that a cat laps up with its tongue.

more dilute than those that rabbits and hamsters, for example, would drink. In addition to sour, bitter, and salt, the taste buds of a cat respond to amino acids. Amino acids are the building blocks of the proteins found in meat, so it's not surprising that taste buds sensitive to amino acids predominate in cats. A cat responds more to some amino acids than to others, however, and this may enable it to discriminate between meat of varying quality or state of decay. The meaty taste receptors were discovered relatively recently. This taste's quality is called umami, from the Japanese word for savoriness.

Q: Why does a cat ignore sugar?

A: A cat is unusual in its indifference to sweet-tasting foods. Omnivores, herbivores, and even some carnivores, such as bears, appreciate and seek out sweet treats, but a cat does not. In fact,

a cat cannot even discriminate between plain water and sweetened water. Further, when scientists stimulated the taste nerve fibers of cats with sucrose and other sugars, they recorded no response, in contrast to a cat's strong responses to salty, bitter, and sour substances.

In 2005, scientists figured out why cats have "sweet blindness." In all mammals, receptors for sweet tastes are formed of two proteins, referred to as T1R2 and T1R3. Two different genes code for (direct the production of) these proteins. It turns out that cats have a defect in the gene that codes for the T1R2 protein, such that the protein cannot be made. With only half its parts, a cat's sweet-receptor does not work. The same defective gene was also found in a tiger and a cheetah, suggesting that all cats are sweet-blind. Being sweet-blind may make cats more sensitive to the taste of amino acids in meat, and this may account for their strict meat-eating habits.

Above and right: A cat begging for a bite to eat will be happier with a bowl of dry food than with a cookie. Cats do not have the ability to taste sweet flavors.

Cats seem to go on the principle that it never does any harm to ask for what you want.

—JOSEPH WOOD CHURCH

The Sense of Smell

Q: What organs do cats use to smell?

A: A cat uses two organs to smell, or more broadly, for olfaction, which means the sensing of chemicals. One includes the chemical receptors on the interior lining of the nostrils and is what we usually think of when we talk about smell. The olfactory mucosa that lines the nasal cavity in a cat contains some 200 million specialized olfactory receptors, about half the number that a dog has. Similarly, the olfactory lobes, the area of the brain that processes information from the receptors inside the nostrils, are relatively smaller in a cat than in a dog. A cat's sense of smell, although not as acute as a dog's, is estimated to be about 30 times better than a human's. The other way a cat detects chemicals is through the Jacobsen's or vomeronasal

organ. This organ consists of two tiny openings on the roof of the mouth through which chemicals send messages to parts of the brain concerned with sexual behavior. Whether this organ exists and is functional in humans remains controversial, but it is found in most mammals.

Right: This cat's grimace, called flehmen, helps chemical messages get to the brain, where they influence sexual behavior.

Below: A cat's olfactory system includes the hypothalamus and olfactory lobes in the brain, and parts of the nose and mouth.

A Cat's Olfactory System

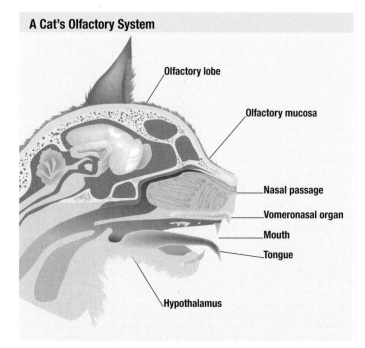

Olfactory lobe

Olfactory mucosa

Nasal passage

Vomeronasal organ

Mouth

Tongue

Hypothalamus

Q: Why does a cat curl its lip after sniffing certain things?

A: A male cat performs a behavior called flehmen, in which it curls its lip into a grimace after sniffing a female to detect whether she is in estrus (receptive to mating). Flehmen may serve to draw chemicals into the vomeronasal organ, an organ that is particularly important in the gathering of scents related to sex.

Q: For what purposes does a cat use its sense of smell?

A: Unlike many other carnivores, a cat does not generally use smell to hunt. Its olfactory abilities are not as acute as those of a dog, for example, which does rely on smell to track prey. This is reflected in the size of the brain area devoted to olfaction. In a dog, the olfactory lobes form about 5 percent of the brain volume, while in a cat they form less than 3 percent. Olfaction is important in the social and sexual life of a cat, however, and most communication between cats is via scent marks.

Q: Why do some cats love catnip?

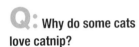

A: Catnip (genus *Nepeta*) is an herb native to Asia and Europe and now widespread in North America. Domestic cats, it is well known, can go wild with a whiff of catnip—a fact that sells a lot of cat toys. Less well known is that catnip, or catmint, sends only about half of domestic cats into a frenzy of rolling, rubbing, and head shaking; the other half are indifferent to the herb and its active ingredient— the chemical nepetalactone. Whether or not a domestic cat responds to catnip is determined by a dominant gene; but why this herb induces a state that most closely resembles a female cat in estrus—although both male and female cats respond the same way—remains a mystery.

Plant chemicals other than nepeta-lactone are now known to produce a similar ecstatic response in domestic cats. For instance, actinidine, found in silver vine *(Actinidia polygama)*, a kiwi relative, works even better than catnip to send a cat into a frenzy.

Q: Do any odors repel cats?

A: A cat detests the smell of vinegar, onions, naphthalene (the chemical in mothballs), and strong citrus scents. Many commercially available cat repellents include oil of citronella, orange, or lemongrass, and a sprinkling of lemon or orange peels may briefly keep a cat out of a garden, as will mothballs. A cat will also avoid rue, a shrubby herb with a strong, nasty odor.

The smell and taste of the herb catnip, as well as a few other plants, send some domestic cats into a frenzy, but no one knows why.

CHAPTER 5

DOMESTIC CATS AS PREDATORS

Cats are often described as perfect hunters, but they miss kills surprisingly often. Cats have evolved to find and kill prey, but prey has evolved to foil predators. Cats hunt where they know they can find food, and they alter their hunting behavior with changing circumstances. They stalk or wait in ambush for their prey, then rush or pounce and deliver the killing bite. They become more efficient hunters with experience.

Domestic cats readily revert to a feral state. Your bedside tabby can be a very efficient hunter roaming about your neighborhood, and free-ranging domestic cats have a striking impact on wildlife. Our domestic and feral cats descended from wildcats that are efficient small-rodent and bird predators. The flexibility in their hunting technique enables them to kill a variety of prey from tiny mice to good-sized ducks. As strict carnivores, cats have nutritionally balanced diets because their prey is nutritionally interchangeable. They do not have the same capability to live on a mixed diet of vegetables, fruits, and meats that sustains our omnivorous domestic dogs. Pet owners must provide for their cats a diet that copies the animal diet that felines are adapted to consume.

Above: A kitten stalking in the grass. Young cats learn much about hunting from observing and imitating their mothers and through practice.

Left: Even a well-fed domesticated cat instinctively hunts and kills prey such as birds.

The Domestic Cat Diet

Q: What are a cat's favorite foods?

A: Cats are strict carnivores, eating small mammals, birds, reptiles, and fish. A domestic cat is a superb hunter, developing its hunting skill with experience. Even a house cat that is fed moist or dry commercially prepared cat foods will still be a successful hunter. A cat's prey depends on what is available at different times of the year, and the time of day the cat hunts. Detailed studies of the diets of feral cats and cats associated with households but having extensive access to outdoor feeding areas have been conducted on four continents and on many islands. On continents, cats mainly feed on small, ground-dwelling mammals. Deer mice, voles, house mice, and young rabbits make up about 70 percent of the diet of a free-ranging cat. Cats kill young rats and avoid adults. Ground-feeding birds make up about 20 percent of the diet, and these may include small songbirds, as well as game birds as large as pheasants.

The remainder of cats' wild food comes from a variety of species. Lizards and nonvenomous snakes are frequently killed in southern climates. Frogs and fish are recorded in some studies but are not frequent in the free-ranging cat's diet. Invertebrates, including insects, spiders, crayfish, and mollusks, are frequently recorded but are a very low percentage of the diet. In Australia, reptiles make up about 33 percent of the cat's diet, as compared to less than 2 percent on the other continents. On islands without seabirds, cats feed on small mammals, birds, and reptiles in about the same frequency as they do on continents. On islands with seabirds, birds make up about 60 percent of the diet. Reptiles make up 20 percent of the diet on islands without seabirds and 12 percent where seabirds are present.

Q: How many meals does a cat need a day?

A: Cats have evolved to hunt small meals on an opportunistic basis. Observers have watched free-ranging domestic cats depart to hunt immediately after eating at home. The numbers of meals provided by a household usually does not influence

Above: Offering a pet cat plentiful kibble or cat food may not stop it from hunting.

Right: Small prey such as mice, birds, and young rabbits make up a significant portion of a free-ranging cat's diet.

the number of prey brought back to the owner by free-ranging cats. Studies have shown that when cats are offered unlimited food over a 24-hour period, they may eat 8 to 16 discrete meals.

Q: Why does a cat sometimes reject its food?

A: If your cat walks up, sniffs the food bowl, and declines the food you offer, do not take it personally—as long as the food is fresh and appropriate. To understand this rejection, consider how its free-living relatives might respond. Is sex in the air? Cats become much less attentive to food when hormone levels rise and mating becomes a priority. Have you presented the meal in a place where the cat feels

safe and secure? If not, move the food bowl away from a busy, noisy, brightly lit area to a more secluded spot. Is the meal too large? Domestic cats are specialized mouse-catchers and prefer their meals in small packages. Food offered in portions that are too large may be unmanageable for the cat, so it will take its time and not eat too much at once, returning several times to finish. Are you offering the same meal over and over without any variation? In the wild, cats can become specialized hunters, but they also have to generalize and take a variety of prey so as not to become dependent on a prey type that will disappear seasonally. You also may not be the only one offering a food dish in the neighborhood. Is a neighbor feeding your cat? Perhaps your cat is making the neighborhood rounds and has enticed others to feed it.

Left: Unlike a dog, a cat may not devour all its food in one sitting. When given a choice, most cats prefer to eat many small meals throughout the course of a day.

Below: A mouse catches the attention of a free-ranging cat. Mice are the perfect size for these specialized carnivores.

Cats know how to obtain food without labor, shelter, without confinement, and love without penalties.

—*W. L. George*

Hunting and Killing Prey

Q: **How do domestic cats hunt?**

A: We know that cats carefully select their prey, and different prey types, a bird versus a mouse, for instance, usually require different hunting techniques. Cats have evolved a concealed hunting style and search strategies that place them within the vicinity of prey. Cats have excellent memories, and experience directs them to potentially good hunting sites. Cats are also attracted to recently disturbed areas such as a new forest clearing, a harvested grain field, or newly mowed field—places where the lives of their prey have been disrupted.

Cats use both visual and acoustic (sound) cues to find prey. Once a prey is located, they stalk and pounce. A cat usually pauses just before it pounces, as if it is processing all available sensory information. The sensory center for a cat's predatory prowess resides in the superior colliculus, a part of the midbrain that acts as a multisensory relay system to receive visual, tactile, and other sensory information and relay it to the spine via the tectospinal neural tract. Nerve cells in this tract are larger and more numerous in cats than in their prey, enabling the cat to react faster than its prey can.

With experience, adult cats can locate prey at close range by sound alone. Kittens are innately attracted to scratching noises and high-pitched mouse calls.

With experience, cats can also recognize and attack immobile prey. Cats attend to and move toward a potential prey that is not too large or moving too fast, and preferably moving in a straight line. Cats do not seem to possess an innate ability to identify a specific object as prey nor any particular species of animal as prey; cats learn what is prey through experience. Cats are generalist predators and learn to take a wide range of prey, readily switching from one to another. They also take food they have not caught themselves; they learn to do this through

Left: A cat can be a patient creature, waiting in a likely place for prey to appear. This sit-and-wait strategy is known as the stationary or S-strategy.

Right: The typical cat has four canine teeth, two at the top and two at the bottom of the jaw, with which it delivers the killing bite to its prey.

experience or by watching their mothers scavenge. When they accept household food, they are in effect scavenging.

Cats do not roam randomly to seek out prey. They use at least two different search strategies: the mobile or M-strategy, and the stationary or S-strategy. In the M-strategy, cats move rapidly between productive hunting areas, and once within a productive area they move through it slowly and deliberately, systematically searching. In the S-strategy, cats move to a potentially productive site and then sit and wait for a small mammal or a songbird to appear. For instance, a cat may sit or crouch at the entrance to a mouse burrow. When the mouse emerges, the cat tenses attentively until the mouse moves away from the burrow, and then pounces without a preceding stalk. In contrast, birds, many of which have virtually a 360-degree visual field, must be stalked, and cats use all available cover to sneak up on birds before pouncing. When the bird is preoccupied or obscured by

cover, the cat moves forward, then freezes, and repeats this until it can pounce. If a cat fails to capture after a pounce, it moves on to another site. It may hunt a number of sites within one hunting patch or move on to another area. Cats repeatedly return to sites where they have hunted successfully.

Q: How does a cat kill prey?

A: The canine teeth are a cat's all-important killing tool. Cats deliver very precise killing bites to prey's neck vertebra. Dogs and many other carnivores grasp and shake their prey as part of the predatory sequence. Cats also shake their prey sometimes, but it is more of a shaking-off than a death shake. They may also toss a prey animal before making the killing bite. During the killing bite, the canine teeth are inserted between the vertebrae, acting like a wedge to force them apart and partially or completely sever the prey's spinal cord.

Preparing to Eat

Q: Where does a cat takes its prey to eat?

A: A big cat, such as a puma or tiger, that kills deer as large as or even larger than itself, usually walks around the immediate vicinity after killing and before dragging its prey into a secluded spot where it settles down to eat. A leopard may drag its kill up into a tree where it can eat out of the reach of a tiger, lion, or other potential predators that might steal its kill. A cat the size of a domestic cat also has to be concerned about a rival—another cat, large dog, or large hawk, for example—trying to take its kill, so rarely does it start to consume its prey immediately. Instead, a domestic cat puts its prey down, looks around or explores the area, and then picks up the prey again.

It may play with the dead prey. It may do some grooming. And it may repeat these behaviors several times. A prey animal that is stunned and motionless but not dead may awaken and try to escape while the cat is taking its break. If the cat detects this movement, it rushes back immediately to kill the prey. This "taking a walk," as scientists have called it, is part of the normal predatory sequence, even for a very hungry cat, and gives the cat an opportunity to look for a place where it can be concealed while eating. If a concealed place is available, the cat will take the prey to it, and then eat. If not, a cat may begin eating on the spot.

Q: Why does a domestic cat bring its prey "home"?

A: This puzzles and surprises cat owners, who may find themselves stepping on a dead shrew their tabby left on the floor by the bed. There are multiple reasons for this. If there are kittens at home, then the function is simply to provide food for them. The renowned cat biologist Paul Leyhausen suggested that when kittens are not present, the human cat owner may be treated as a "delegated kitten" the cat wants to feed. This makes sense for females, but males and neutered cats also bring prey home, although males take no part in feeding or caring for kittens. Cats sometimes cache, or store, prey to eat later, and a cat may carry its prey back home for storage. "Home" may be the protected place cats like to retreat

A leopard goes to considerable lengths to avoid sharing its meal with—or losing it to—other predators, such as climbing a tree to eat its kill.

A house cat may use prey to "gift" its owner. Cat biologists speculate that one of the reasons cats bring prey home is that they see their human caretakers as "delegated kittens" in need of food.

to with their prey before eating it. A cat may also be in a conflicted situation in which it does not know what to do with its prey animal. For example, some prey species, such as shrews and moles, are unpalatable and less likely than other species to be eaten after a cat kills them. Studies in Europe have shown house cats kill and bring home these species, but they are not found in the stomach contents of feral cats that were shot. House sparrows are also prey that are frequently brought home and left uneaten. They too may be unpalatable.

Q: How does a cat prepare its food?

A: A cat starts eating small birds headfirst or at a wing joint and spits out the feathers as it eats. After eating the head, a cat plucks birds pigeon-sized and larger by gripping the feathers with the teeth, placing the forepaws on the prey, and pulling; it spits out the feathers while shaking its head. A cat cleans feathers off the tongue by drawing it over the incisors in a special licking movement. A cat eats small mammals headfirst, but for larger mammals and plucked birds, it begins by opening the body cavity using its carnassial teeth.

A cat follows a typical sequence of behaviors when eating each of its different prey species.

Puzzling Hunting Behavior

Q: Why does a well-fed cat still hunt?

A: In mammals generally, a feedback mechanism prevents further eating once an animal is full, while hunger usually triggers searching behavior. In cats, the different behaviors that make up the entire predatory sequence are relatively independent of one another, and searching for prey and hunger may be disconnected. The domestic cat's wild ancestors are the specialized predators of small birds and mammals, and it takes several kills each day to provide the sustenance they need. Thus, cats are programmed to hunt frequently for relatively small meals and may begin a new hunt even though they have just eaten and are full; however the intensity of the hunt following a full meal may be lower. This is also why providing several meals over a 24-hour period best serves a domestic cat, even if it is troublesome for the owner. While well-fed domestic cats still hunt, one study showed that home-fed cats spent half as much time hunting as feral cats that did not have access to human-provided food but lived in otherwise comparable situations. Also, home-fed hunting cats ate a smaller number of the prey that they killed than the feral cats did.

Q: Why does a cat sometimes kill more than it can eat?

A: This behavior is sometimes called surplus killing, and it usually occurs when a cat finds itself with many prey that cannot escape, such as in a chicken coop.

Surplus killing makes little biological sense at first: It has little survival value, and it seems a waste of effort. The answer to this puzzling hunting behavior lies in the loose linkages between the different behaviors that make up the entire predatory sequence. When a cat is surrounded by prey, the search and detection part of its hunting behavior is no longer necessary, and somehow the seizing and killing parts go into a loop without cycling through the consumption part of the sequence. In other words, killing does not lead to eating; instead the cat does more killing. This behavior is adaptive because if the cat finds itself in a

Above: Even a sated cat may leave its food bowl to go out to hunt, although perhaps not as vigorously as a hungry one.

Below: When presented with an abundance of easily caught prey, a cat may kill more animals than it can eat.

position to kill several prey quickly, it will do so, and eat the carcasses later. But this is rarely possible under wild conditions.

Left: Cat toys often mimic mice or other prey. An indoor house cat often pounces on or shakes its toys as it would live prey in the wild.

Below: A cat with a bird. "Playing" with prey is not a cruel act on the part of a cat. Trapping and releasing gives a cat hunting practice and also tires out its quarry.

Q: Why does a cat play with prey before killing it?

A: Cats play with both dead and live prey. Watching your cat pounce repeatedly on a mouse, batting it into the air with its paw and pouncing on it again and again, can be upsetting. Your cat is not being cruel to the mouse. If your cat has little experience with live prey, catching a mouse is a major event. Or perhaps your cat has killed live prey before but only infrequently. As noted above, the hunting drive is only loosely linked to the hunger drive. When the cat repeatedly traps and releases a mouse, it is holding back the killing bite and prolonging the hunt. Inexperience may play a role, but your cat may also "play" with prey with great exuberance, seeming relieved to have a chance to perform these behaviors. It appears to be caught up in capturing over and over and not yet motivated enough to deliver a killing bite. Ambivalence may also be involved. An experienced cat may play with a shrew, for example, which it knows from experience to be distasteful. A different set of what appear to be playful behaviors results from your cat simply not being sure of itself, or even overreacting. If your cat has little experience with a mouse or rat, it may be intimidated and engage in hit-and-chase behavior because the cat fears retaliation from the prey. This behavior also tires the prey, reducing its ability to defend itself. It is prudent behavior for the inexperienced cat.

Prey Versus Hunters

Q: Are cats perfect hunters?

A: Hunting cats have to work for their meals, and often miss them. Potential prey animals frequently slip past them undetected. Cats may detect a prey animal but calculate that, given the circumstances, it is uncatchable and ignore it. It is not easy to determine how often a cat misses a prey; a target may have detected the stalking cat and silently escaped. Using just pounces as a measure of hunting success, scientists report that it takes hunting feral cats about two pounces for each mouse captured, three pounces for each insect, more than three pounces for each bird or lizard, and five pounces for each rabbit. Domestic cats are behaviorally and morphologically adapted to catch small prey and are less inclined to take on larger prey. In a Baltimore, Maryland, study, the rats that alley cats most often captured were less than half grown, averaging 3 ounces (100 g) in weight, while most of the rats the scientists captured in live traps weighed 9 to 12 ounces (300–400 g).

The time it takes to capture prey is another measure of hunting success, and this varies with a cat's experience as well as with changes in the seasonal abundance of prey species. In one study, mother cats took, on average, 1.6 hours to capture a rodent, while nonmothers of both sexes took on average more than 11 hours per capture. In autumn, when rodents were most abundant, it took cats 40 minutes per capture, compared to 70 minutes in spring when rodents were least abundant. Dominant cats may also exclude subordinate cats from productive hunting areas, thus reducing the success rates of subordinates.

A cat's hunting success rate varies due to many factors, including its previous experience, its relationship to other cats in its hunting area, and the seasonal availability of different prey species.

Q: How does the hunting of wild cat species compare with that of domestic cats?

A: The tiny black-footed cat is in the same lineage as the domestic cat. A biologist followed several habituated black-footed cats on hunts and learned that they had a 60-percent success rate. Servals studied in Tanzania were successful in about half their pounces on rodents and insects but only in about one quarter

Q: Why does a cat chatter its teeth when it sees a bird through a window or twitch its tail when trying to approach a robin on an open lawn?

A: A cat watching a bird at a feeder outside the window knows that it cannot get to it. It tenses up and its teeth begin to chatter. Scientists call this a vacuum activity. The cat is trying to deliver a killing bite on a bird it cannot reach. A robin hopping about on the lawn seeking worms is equally enticing. Cats use cover to approach a prey animal, but mowed lawns are too open for a successful approach and pounce. The inexperienced cat approaches anyway, even though it knows it is exposed, because it wants to kill the bird. So the cat is conflicted: It wants to crouch and to rush forward at the same time, and its tail starts wagging frantically. If the robin had not seen the cat before, it does now, and effortlessly moves on. Hunters by nature, domestic cats in human care frequently find themselves in frustrating circumstances.

Practice makes perfect, a study of Serengeti cheetah has found, with hunting success rates of 100 percent for adult cheetahs preying on gazelle fawns. A mother cat is less successful while her cubs are still with her.

A house cat keeps an eye on a bird feeder. By chattering its teeth, a cat may just be showing its excitement at spotting potential prey, or venting its frustration at seeing potential prey that it cannot get to.

of pounces on harlequin quail. Namibian leopards had an overall success rate of 38 percent, with one kill for every 2.7 hunts. Serengeti lions had a success rate of 24 percent, but success rates varied in different cover types: 41 percent in heavy cover and 12 percent in light or no cover. Lions were more successful at night than they were during the day, and success was higher on moonless nights than on moonlit ones. Not surprisingly, cats improve their hunting success rates with experience, as shown by a detailed study of cheetah in the Serengeti. Adults improved at catching baby gazelles and hares, eventually reaching a 100-percent success rate. Cubs tagging along lowered a mother's success rate. Adolescents and young adults tended to be seen by prey far more often than were adults.

Cats Are Not Vegetarians

Q: Do cats receive sufficient nutrition from a vegetarian diet?

A: No. Both dogs and cats must acquire their energy, protein, water, minerals, fatty acids, and vitamins from their environment. Unlike omnivorous dogs, which can live on a mixed diet of meat, fruit, seeds, and vegetable, cats are strict carnivores. But cats cannot survive on a diet of only lean muscle meat. They are adapted to eat their whole prey, flesh as well as heart, liver, and other organs. Therefore, cats must eat other animals whole or have diets that substitute what a diet composed of other animals would provide. The cat's body does not synthesize some of the essential molecules that are needed by virtually all species, so these must be obtained from food. These include vitamins, essential amino acids, and some unsaturated fatty acids. Dogs have diverse metabolic pathways to digest their food. Cats, as strict carnivores, have a narrow range of metabolic pathways by which to digest food and obtain these essential molecules. For example, most mammals, including dogs, can convert linoleae to arachidonae in their livers, but not cats. These essential fatty acids are essential for proper growth, normal skin and coat, reproduction, and blood clotting. The richest source of these essential acids is the organ meat cats eat.

Below: Although your cat may enjoy chewing on corncobs, such vegetable matter does not provide the nutrients felines need.

Right: Dog food does not contain the ingredients that meet the very specific nutritional needs of cats, including taurine, needed for a cat's visual and heart health.

Q: Should you feed cats dog food?

A: No. Cats rapidly become seriously ill on an omnivore diet. Commercial dog foods, for example, are formulated to meet an adult dog's need for about 4 percent protein in its diet. Adult cats, in contrast, require at least 19 percent protein in their diets. To try to force your cat to eat dog food or a vegetarian diet is abusive. Indeed, much of what we know about the nutritional requirements of cats has come from the problems that arise when owners feed

Eating grass provides the minute amount of folic acid that a carnivorous diet does not provide.

their pets deficient diets. A by-product of protein metabolism is ammonia. Cats need an essential amino acid called arginine in their diet in order to convert ammonia to urea; lack of arginine leads to immediate ammonia toxicity in cats.

Cats are unusual among mammals in that they need a dietary source of taurine; cats fed synthetic diets devoid of taurine lose their ability to resolve visual detail. Most mammals also produce their own vitamin A, which is necessary to change beta-carotene into retinol, a step in the production of light-absorbing pigments in the retina. Cats do not produce their own vitamin A or beta-carotene, and without dietary sources, they suffer night blindness. Cats appear to have no dietary requirement for carbohydrates, although these are important sources of energy for dogs. Cats lack the liver glycolytic enzyme that dogs and other mammals have to digest carbohydrates. Cats, like all animals, require glucose as blood sugar, but a cat's glucose is produced from protein.

Q: Why do cats eat grass?

A: Cats are strict carnivores, yet we have all watched cats eat grass on occasion. Because they do so at times does not mean that cats can be converted into vegetarians. Grass eating has puzzled cat owners and scientists alike, giving rise to much folklore and speculation. That grass acts as a laxative, or helps the cat vomit up hairballs, or adds roughage to the diet are examples of folklore. Scientists now believe that by eating bits of grass, cats are obtaining very small quantities of folic acid they cannot obtain from meat. Folic acid is required for the production of hemoglobin, essential for good health. When a cat is deficient in folic acid, it becomes anemic and its growth suffers.

Cats and Water

Q: How much water does a cat need?

Below: A cat takes a sip from a kitchen faucet. Fresh water—not milk—should be in your cat's bowl; many adult cats are lactose intolerant and cannot digest milk.

Below right: If your local drinking water is chlorinated, your sensitive-nosed cat might opt for other than the "fresh" water in its bowl.

A: Domestic cats squat over a water bowl and steadily lap up water. The cat curls the tip of the tongue back, spoonlike, and flips water into its mouth, swallowing every few licks. Water constitutes 99 percent of all molecules within an animal's body. Cats obtain their "free water" from the water in their bowls, and from puddles, streams, and the like. Wild cats obtain what scientists call preformed water from food that is metabolized into energy. Metabolic water is a product of oxidation that occurs during metabolism. The cat's kidneys are about 2.5 times more efficient than those of humans in ridding the body of waste and retaining water. Fed a dry commercial cat food, cats drink about one tablespoon of water for every ounce of dry food (1.5 to 2 ml water per 1 g dry food). Domestic cats need to drink little free water if they are fed other animal tissue. When given a choice, cats are most likely to select moist food over dry because it is easier to ingest, but experiments have demonstrated that cats adjust their water intake to compensate for lack of water in their diet.

Q: Why does a cat drink dirty water?

A: The water bowl set on the kitchen floor, filled with what seems to be clean, fresh water, may be ignored while a cat saunters right out the door and drinks from a puddle. To the cat, the water in the bowl may not be as appealing as it appears to be to the cat's caretaker. The surface of the bowl may retain some slight residue of detergent that a human cannot detect but repels a cat, for example. Tap water designated as safe drinking water for people is often heavily treated with some form of chlorine and has a chemical smell that cats can detect. Thus, a cat may prefer the water in the puddle even if it does have a lot of

microbes swimming around in it that would make people queasy. The problem with puddles and other natural water sources is that, aside from rotting vegetation and swimming microbes, they may be polluted with poisonous pesticides, insecticides, or herbicides, and cats have a greater sensitivity to these kinds of poisons than do humans. A cat should be regularly provided with clean water it finds palatable. Clean its water bowl carefully, rinsing it to be sure all detergent has been removed. Let the tap water stand for a time before offering it, or use bottled water whose taste is acceptable to the cat.

Q: Do cats learn to avoid toxic water and foods?

A: Cats do learn rapidly to avoid foods that are toxic or lacking in certain nutrients such as arginine and thiamine. For example, cats given a single meal of food containing lithium chloride refused to eat that food three days later, and remembered this for at least 40 days more. Cats frequently reject foods they have not encountered before, a behavior that scientists call neophobia. Cats also have a preference for foods they know but have not encountered for some time, a behavior called neophilia, or the novelty effect. Yet, even a small dose of a toxic substance may overcome a cat's system before any learning can protect it. If a cat has access to the car garage, people need to be particularly careful about keeping leaking antifreeze from the cat. Antifreeze seems to have an attractive taste to cats, and they will lap it up, but even a little of the ethylene glycol in antifreeze may cause the cat irreversible liver damage. The cat may fall into a deep coma and die.

Domestic Cats and Wildlife

Q: How do hunting domestic cats affect birds and other wildlife?

A: Domestic cats first surfaced as rodent catchers for early farmers, and today cats are still kept to combat agricultural pests. Domestic cats have lost none of their predatory instincts over time, and predation by feral cats has a significant effect on the numbers of rodents (rats and mice), lagomorphs (rabbits and hares), and birds in an area. Their strongest effect has been observed on islands, but is felt on the continents as well. The Global Invasive Species Specialist Group of the World Conservation Union (IUCN) included the domestic cat on its list of 100 of the world's worst alien species. Cats are believed responsible for, or at least involved in, the extinction of more bird species than anything else except habitat destruction. In one notable example from 1894, David Lyall brought his cat with him while he was lighthouse keeper on Stephens Island, a small, uninhabited island off New Zealand. Within a year the island's unique flightless wren was extinct. All the specimens of this wren known to science were brought to Lyall by his cat.

Domestic and free-ranging cats live at higher densities than wild predators because people protect domestic cats from disease, predators, and competition; people provide a dependable supply of supplemental food; and their densities are not limited by territoriality. In Great Britain an estimated 9 million cats kill 300 million wild animals each year. An estimated 90 million pet cats and 40 to 50 million free-ranging cats live in urban, suburban, and rural habitats in the United States. More than a billion small mammals and birds are taken each year by rural cats alone. Reducing rodent numbers may be a service to humans, but cats also take staggering numbers of songbirds. In Wisconsin, nearly 40 million songbirds are killed by cats each year. Many of these species

Its predatory behavior affects wildlife populations, unless a feline is exclusively an indoor cat. For example, each year the 9 million cats of the United Kingdom kill 300 million wild animals.

are already in decline because of habitat loss in North America as well as in Central and South America where many of these birds winter. Cats are implicated in the decline of least terns, piping plovers, and loggerhead shrikes in the United States. Only 100 to 300 Lower Keys marsh rabbits are thought to remain in existence, and each year 53 percent of the deaths of these rabbits are attributed to feral cats.

Q: Does belling your cat help birds?

A: Restricting a cat's outdoor movements is one means of reducing its impact on wildlife. Belling a cat—making it wear a collar with a small bell attached to it—has been suggested and used as another deterrent. The tinkling of the bell presumably alerts a potential prey to the cat's presence. In two Australian studies, however, in which kills were measured by the number of prey delivered to owners over a fixed time, bell wearing had no marked impact on a cat's predation of wildlife. In a third study, bell-wearing cats

While one bell on a collar may not decrease a cat's kills, the verdict is not yet in on two bells.

actually killed more wildlife. (Amphibians apparently have a poor ability to detect high-frequency sounds and would not be alerted by the bell.)

In a fourth study conducted in England, bell wearing did lead to a reduction in the numbers of prey that cats delivered to their owners, but did not affect the relative number of mammals, birds, or amphibians the cats delivered. What is unclear in all of the studies reported to date is if the cats become familiar with the bell's sound and therefore adjust their predatory tactics to compensate. Some authors have suggested placing two bells on the cat's collar instead of one, making it more difficult for the cat to adjust its moves to silence a bell.

Other ways to help protect wildlife from roaming domestic cats include locating bird feeders away from any objects that may provide cover for a cat's approach and keeping cats indoors at night.

Because amphibians cannot hear high frequencies, they do not hear the bell on a cat's collar.

CHAPTER 6

SOCIAL LIFE

Domestic cats are independent but live rich social lives. Only where food is abundant in a small area are feral cats found living together in colonies. Typically, finding and killing small birds and rodents is most efficiently done by a single cat, and a carcass is a valuable commodity not to be shared with other cats except a female's own offspring. Like all mammals, the female cat feeds her kittens directly through her mammary glands. Males are unnecessary for females with young; females care for their kittens by themselves. In fact, females often avoid adult males to prevent potential infanticide (killing of young) and competition for food. Even so, independently living cats need to communicate their intentions and moods to one another, and they do so with their postures, tail movements, eyes, ears, and vocalizations. With the scents they deposit, cats communicate through messages that we cannot decode. With posture and sounds, cats efficiently convey their mood and intention to potential predators—a dog, for example. And they communicate with their housemates—humans— or rather, they teach humans to respond to their needs.

Above: When cats rub against each other they exchange scents and create a common odor that denotes kinship or enhances familiarity between nonrelatives.

Left: Free-living or feral domestic cats sometimes live together in colonies with distinct social networks.

Group Living and Solitary Living

Q: Why are most wild cats predisposed to solitary living?

A: Female wild cats are accompanied by dependent young for 80 percent of their adult lives. In this respect, females are group living. But in nearly all wild cats species, adult males and females do not live together or cooperate, and are solitary living. Only 10 to 15 percent of all carnivores live in groups outside the breeding season. Most carnivores hunt more efficiently alone, and most mammals do not need two parents to care for young. Group living has several other disadvan-tages: It increases the risks of being detected by a predator; it increases the risk of disease and parasite transmission; and it increases the chance of aggression and injury, which a hunting carnivore cannot afford. Living at low density at the top of the food chain and being an obligate carnivore, or one that eats only meat, predisposes most cats to live alone.

Cats are obligate carnivores that hunt most efficiently alone, so adult wild cats of most species, such as pumas, are predisposed to solitary living.

The wild relatives of our domestic dogs, along with wolves and other wild canids, do live in pairs and even large groups. Males and older offspring, called helpers, bring food back to the den to provision the female and the young, and wild canids hunt large prey efficiently together. Female lions, male lions, and male cheetahs also cooperate and live in groups. Male lions and cheetahs, living

Female lions live with their female kin in groups called prides. The pride members hunt together to kill large prey, protect recent kills from scavengers, and care for and protect their young from potentially dangerous adult male lions.

in groups called coalitions, have a breeding advantage over single males or smaller coalitions. Group-living male cheetahs control territories that are rich in prey and denning sites to attract females. Female lions live with their close female relatives in groups called prides. These groups live where prey is abundant in open environments, but where other lions can easily detect them. Female lions can kill large prey animals by themselves; they also cooperate to kill large prey. But once they have a kill, they do not want to lose it to a stranger; pride members help protect these kills. Pride members also band together to protect their young from infanticidal males.

Q: Do wild cats have social lives?

A: Most prey of free-living wild cats are too small, relative to body size and the effort expended in the hunt, to share with other cats. Also, wild cats are generally intolerant of one another. This intolerance toward other cats of the same species seems to be hardwired, so that individuals' home ranges or territories are often mutually exclusive or only marginally overlap. Still, neighboring cats communicate, and generally each knows what the others are doing. In addition, scientists have learned that even though young males leave their mother's home range or territory, not all daughters do. Eventually daughters and granddaughters take over more of the area, until the older female cannot survive and is "squeezed out."

Q: Why do some free-living domestic cats live in colonies?

A: We do not know if human selection during domestication led to greater tolerance among domestic cats. We do know that free-living domestic cats surviving on wild prey such as rabbits and rodents tend to live solitary lives. They may have greatly overlapping home ranges but do not form groups. Domestic cats with substantial clumped and rich food resources, such as those found on farms or at dumps or docks, however, do live in groups, called colonies. These are not simple aggregations of cats as first thought; these cats have complex social lives. Adult females form the core of cat colony society. Related females and their kittens maintain their own social groups within colonies. Males are usually more peripheral and are not permanently associated with female social groups.

Male domestic cats are marginal members of a cat colony and are not permanently associated with the female groups at the core of the social network.

Purring Cats

Q: Why do cats purr?

A: Purring conveys contentment: "All is well." It is a pleasurable sound. Yet, cats that are in labor, chronically ill, or in severe pain purr continuously; such cats are obviously not well. Scientists believe that purring acts as a "manipulative" contact-soliciting or care-soliciting signal with its roots in kittens' communicating with their mothers. Purring signals a friendly social mood and acts much like a human smile. Dominant cats purr when approaching a submissive cat, and submissive cats purr when approaching a more dominant one. Very young kittens even purr without interrupting nursing. Mothers purr when lying with their kittens. Mothers purr when approaching the nest box. Purring is a close-range communication and cannot be heard more than a few feet away. This presumably protects a purring cat in a den from being detected by a predator. Purring can go on for minutes while the cat inhales and exhales. Because cats purr when their bodies are in contact with others, scientists believe that the body surface vibrations also act as a tactile signal that is as significant as the auditory message.

Q: How do cats purr?

A: The purring sound of a cat is made by the sudden separation of the vocal folds generated by a buildup and release of pressure as the opening (glottis) between the vocal folds is closed and then opened. The muscles that move the vocal folds to open and close the glottis in the larynx are driven by a free-running, neural oscillator that generates contractions and releases about every third of a second (300–400 milliseconds). Except for a brief transition pause, purring is produced during both inhaling and exhaling and sounds like a continuous vocalization. Purring is nearly ubiquitous among the cats, although it is not heard in lions and tigers.

Q: What other sounds does a cat make?

A: Cats make calls while experiencing fear and pain, during aggressive and defensive encounters, sexual encounters, mother-young encounters, and cat-human interactions. Cats purr and chirrup or trill with the mouth closed. These are "contact calls." The mother

A purr is a pleasant sound that usually conveys a cat's contentment. A cat may also purr to solicit care and attention.

Left: A cat's meow is derived from the mewing sounds made by kittens. A cat meows at its human caretakers to solicit food or something else it wants. Cats seldom meow to communicate with other cats.

Right: A frightened or defensive cat spits and hisses with an open mouth. When attacked or caught off guard, a cat shrieks abruptly to startle the predator or attacker.

uses the trill to call her kittens, or a cat may use this soft call to greet a human. With the mouth open and gradually closing, cats meow in greeting, males meow and females cry to advertise their sexual readiness, and both howl during aggressive encounters. With the mouth held open, cats spit and hiss when on the defensive and growl and snarl when aggressive. Cats yowl when frightened and shriek in fear and pain. Kittens less than three weeks old can purr, spit in defense, and emit a distress call similar to the meow. The familiar meow call, derived from the mewing sounds kittens make, is seldom used to communicate with other cats. The meow is learned and usually associated with food solicitation from the human or in other situations when a cat wants something. We all can distinguish between the begging meow and the demanding meow.

The abrupt shriek that a cat makes in pain or fear startles the attacker. The low pitch of the growl and long duration of the yowl convey the size and strength of the cat. The high intensity of male and female sexual calls advertises fitness as a sexual partner. Lions, tigers, leopards, and jaguars roar. Small cats do not have these long-distance, advertising calls in their vocal repertoire. Small cats chatter or click their teeth when they see a potential prey animal but cannot get at it. Some observers of felines have suggested that this sound may have its origin in a sound used by females that are training their older kittens to hunt.

A meow massages the heart.
—STUART McMILLAN

Body Language: Eyes and Ears

Q: **What can you tell by looking into a cat's eyes?**

A: Eyes are said to be the window to the soul. The "evil eye" is a warning. You know the way someone, or your cat, looks at you is an important part of your encounter. Humans relate to the gaze of the cat, perhaps more than that of other pet species, because we both have forward-set eyes that generate our binocular vision. Prey animals judge a predator's intention by watching its eyes. Some species of moths and butterflies have evolved eye-shaped patterns, called eyespots, on their wings as an effective way to deter their rodent and bird predators; the eyespots resemble the eyes of feline predators that prey on rodents and birds. Pet cats look at the cupboard where their food is stored or at the door when they want to be let out. Cats learn through association that they can gain our attention by looking and vocalizing.

A cat's long stare with wide-open eyes is an aggressive, threatening gesture. If you stare back and lock eyes with your cat, you are being intimidating. So, when your cat stares at you, do not stare back. Blink. Cats perceive blinking as friendly, so a blink signals that your stare is not hostile. When your cat's pupils suddenly enlarge, and there has been no change in light intensity, it is experiencing a strong state of emotional arousal. This may be a pleasant experience, such as when food arrives, or unpleasant, such as the sight of a dog or rival cat. When your cat contracts and narrows its pupils, it is in an aggressive, dominant mood. A cat's eyelids also signal its mood. When they are fully opened, a cat is on alert; when

Left: An aggressive cat gazes at an opponent with wide-open eyes and a long stare, and may also contract and narrow its pupils.

Right: Heavy, half-closed eyelids signify a contented, relaxed cat that is completely at ease in its surroundings.

A cat's facial expressions and the position of its head indicate mood and intention. When feeling calm and comfortable, a cat's ears point forward and slightly outward.

half-closed, it is relaxed. By learning to interpret your cat's moods by watching its eyes, you can adjust your own actions to make the cat feel more at ease.

Q: What can you tell by a cat's ears?

A: The cat's gaze is one of the facial expressions that direct and inform another's attention. The ears, nose, and tilting and shape of the entire head indicate mood and intention. A relaxed cat's ears point forward and slightly outward. When the cat is alert, the ears are fully erect and point directly forward. When conflicted or agitated, it nervously twitches its ears. A defensive cat rotates and flattens its ears against its head so they are invisible when viewed straight on. An aggressive cat rotates and half flattens it ears so the backs become fully visible.

When on the verge of aggression and considering whether or not to pounce, a cat may have one ear slightly raised and the other flattened.

This says: I am ready to attack. But the ears are in a position such that they can easily flatten into a defensive mode. By watching a cat's ears, you can detect its mood shift. A relaxed cat might bring up just one ear when it is aroused. A cat teetering on the brink of aggression and defense might have just one ear slightly raised and the other flattened. Or one ear might threaten and the other signal indifference.

Body Language: Tail

A cat's tail is an expressive body part. For example, a cat wags its tail to express inner turmoil, such as when it wants to do two or more things at once. Once the conflict is resolved, the cat stops wagging its tail and takes action.

Q: When does a cat wag its tail?

A: At a distance, a cat's eyes and ears may not be visible, so larger body postures and movements signal mood and intentions to others. When a cat enters or leaves a social group it raises its tail, signaling it is relaxed and friendly. When a cat wags its tail it is in a state of inner conflict because it wants to do two things at once. When it resolves its conflict and decides to take one action or another, it stops wagging its tail.

Q: What can you read from a cat's body posture and tail?

A: Tail positions are usually changed in tandem with body postures. A relaxed cat walks with its back flat and its tail down and curved up at the tip. When the cat becomes interested in something, its tail rises slightly and curves up at the tip. An erect tail with the tip bent over signals a reserved, friendly greeting. A fully erect tail coupled with nearly flat back is a greeting with no reservations. This is how a kitten greets its mother; there is an element of subordination in this display and an invitation for others to sniff its rear. The tail held erect and quivering is a more intense greeting, usually between a cat and its human, indicating personal recognition.

A cat signals a submissive mood when it crouches and lowers it tail, tucking it between its hind legs. A fearful cat arches its back and lowers and fluffs its tail. When the tail is swished

A cat adjusts the position of its tail along with its overall body posture to convey its mood. When something captures the interest of a cat, its tail rises and curves up at the tip.

fiercely side to side, a cat is about to attack; the more vigorous the tail lashing, the closer the cat is to launching the attack. When a cat is lying in wait, just the tip of the tail may twitch with growing tension as the decision to pounce nears. If a cat's tail is held still and only the tip twitches on meeting another, it means mild irritation. The stronger the twitching, the more imminent the paw swipe. A female in heat holds her tail to one side when she is ready to be mounted by the male. Stiff legs signal aggression. An aggressive cat approaches another with stiff legs and flat back, and the tail is held straight and fully bristled.

Free-living domestic cats that share a common area may approach each other with tails bent slightly at the tips, signaling a reserved but friendly greeting.

Q: Why does a cat fluff up and arch its back when it sees a dog?

A: Fluffing up the fur is called pilo-erection. When threatened by a strange dog, a cat fully stretches its legs, arches its back, raises its tail, bristles its fur, and turns broadside, all to make it look larger than it really is. Looking larger may deter the enemy. In this display, the cat hisses or growls if it senses an attack is imminent—the best defense is often a good offense. An experienced cat may lash out at the dog, adding an explosive spit to the hiss. If the cat turns and runs, it sets off the predatory sequence in the dog. Better to stand tall, hiss, and spit.

A frightened cat hisses, arches its back, lowers and fluffs its tail, and bristles its fur to make itself appear larger than life and possibly deter an attacker.

Marking Behavior

Q: What is scent marking?

A: All cats leave scent marks in their environment that convey information about their sex, reproductive status, identity, and occupation of a particular area, and perhaps their age and dominance and health status. The odorous substances involved in this marking are in urine, feces, and saliva and are also produced by special glands on the tail, lips, cheeks, and feet.

Right: The substances that give scent marks distinct, pungent odors are found in urine, feces, and saliva and are also produced by glands on the tail, lips, cheeks, and feet.

Below: A confident cat often repeatedly sprays the same objects and specific areas in its home range to advertise its occupancy of the area.

One function of the claw-raking that so annoys cat owners is to deposit scent from the feet glands and to provide a visual signal that the scent is there. Cats do not deposit scent marks at random. Marking is most frequent at boundaries of territories, along well-used paths, at intersections of paths, and on particularly prominent habitat features such as tufts of grass, trees, fence posts, shrubs, and walls. Scent marks, unlike vocal or visual signals, persist in time and are uniquely suited for communicating about the past. A fresh scent mark reveals that it was laid down very recently and the cat that made it is nearby. Old, faded scents tell the opposite story. Cats crisscross their home ranges regularly to keep track of what is going on in their area by reading the odoriferous messages left by their neighbors and strangers and to leave messages of their own.

Q: Why do cats spray urine?

A: Spraying irks cat owners, but it is an important part of cats' scent communication behavior. Spraying is the sign of a confident cat. Cats squat to spray or stand and spray on vertical surfaces, called erect-spraying. When squatting, the cat makes several treading movements with its hind feet, lowers its hindquarters, and sprays as its tail quivers. When erect-spraying, the cat holds its hindquarters high, and its tail is held at a 40 to 90 degree angle. One or both hind feet may leave the ground briefly. All reproductive males and most reproductive females spray. Even neutered cats spray. The

Cats deposit scent marks on grass, trees, shrubs, and other objects within their home ranges and on territorial boundaries. Marks convey information about a cat's sex, reproductive status, and dominance to neighboring cats.

urine that males spray has a penetrating, pungent order, while that of females and neutered cats is much less so. Spraying indicates to others that the cat has passed by, and cats repeatedly respray the same objects in their home range. It functions to reduce contact between individuals by revealing a cat's occupancy of an area so that others stay away, but females also spray to advertise that they are in estrus.

Q: Why do cats bury their feces?

A: A cat digs a hole, defecates, at times also urinates, sniffs it, covers it, and sniffs it again. A cat refrains from advertising itself when it buries its feces and thus reduces its odor display. It is a subordinate action. Burying does not eliminate all the scent, but buried urine and feces do not come across as a serious threat to other cats. Dominant feral males do the opposite; they place their feces on raised grass tussocks or mound up some dirt with their forepaws and

defecate on top. This is advertising their dominance. When house cats bury their feces, they do so because they are acting in a subordinate way to their dominant humans. House cats, male and female, bury their feces at home but may not bury them when they are farther afield.

When a domestic cat digs a hole and buries its feces in a litter box, it is diminishing the scent. In doing this, the cat is acknowledging that his owner is dominant in the home environment.

Rubbing and Rolling

Q: Why do cats rub heads with other cats and rub against people?

A: Cats rub their heads and many other parts of their bodies against each other and against objects in the environment. They rub their heads, cheeks, chins, and necks against urine and other marks left by other cats and sometimes roll their entire bodies in urine, rotten meat, and other strong-smelling substances on the ground. The lips, chin, and tail have glands that produce fatty secretions, and cats rub them primarily to mark objects. Head and tail rubbing are used to mark other cats and people. Cheek rubbing is most often seen between breeding pairs and between females and kittens. In rubbing, cats both apply their scents and pick up their partner's or offspring's scents and scents from the environment. Exchanging odors with social partners, either directly or indirectly by rubbing in their urine marks, may enhance their relationship, because familiar odors may reduce tensions when they meet

Cheek rubbing is an intimate scent-exchanging behavior most often seen between breeding pairs and between females and their kittens.

Cats head rub to exchange scents with other cats and with their human companions.

face to face. A common odor may be an olfactory badge denoting kinship. In making their odor more like that of the environment, cats also camouflage their own scent, which makes it more difficult for prey to smell their approach.

Females rub their tails on objects and their humans in the early stages of estrus, but they also tail rub when not sexually motivated. When our pet cats rub against us, they are leaving their scent on us and picking up our scent. Domestic cats rub their humans often. This is a behavior that would normally be directed by young cats toward their mother and is indicative of a relaxed, noncompetitive relationship. In feral cats, this behavior is directed by a subordinate cat toward a dominant one. It is a behavior similar to the tail-wagging, fawning behavior a dog directs to its owner.

Q: Why do cats stand on their hind legs to greet people?

A: Head rubbing is an indispensable greeting between familiar cats. Kittens approach their returning mother with a hop to try to reach and rub her head. Humans are so much taller than cats that hopping up to head rub is impossible. A cat might leap up on a piece of furniture to get itself into position for a head rub with a person, or it may perform a little stiff-legged hop,

raising its front feet together off the floor. Scientists call this an intention movement. It is a greeting that has its origins in the head-to-head rub.

Q: Why do cats roll on their backs when greeting you?

A: The relationship between a person and his or her cat is usually relaxed and noncompetitive. A cat rolling over on its back and exposing its belly is placing itself in a subordinate position. It is also placing its most dangerous weapons— paws and claws—in positions to do real damage. As inviting as a cat's belly might seem to stroke, it is not advised that you try to do so unless you and the cat have a very high degree of familiarity.

When a cat lies on its back and exposes its belly—whether to its owner or another cat— it is expressing familiarity and comfort in the relationship.

A cat sometimes raises its front feet together off the floor or leaps up onto a piece of tall furniture in an attempt to give its owner a friendly head rub.

Socializing with Cats

Q: Do cats care about their human owners and caretakers?

A: Probably not. Cats seem to interact with humans as if we were a particular kind of cat. Kittens raised around people will, when they grow up, more easily socialize with people. Handling kittens while they are growing increases their friendliness and attachment. Kittens not handled during this time will be very difficult to socialize later and probably will never really adjust to being handled. Later in life, cats learn from their experience with people how to react toward them. If a cat's experience with people has been positive, it will tend to respond positively, if always a bit standoffishly. Unpleasant experiences with people can lead to behaviors that make cats unapproachable,

as well as personalities we judge to be neurotic, because cats have learned to treat people as enemies. Not so long ago, the wild ancestors of domestic cats were fierce hunters living solitary lives; domestic cats easily slip back into the wild life and are by nature very independent. What is more, cats sense the world differently than we do and respond accordingly. They can hear sounds at frequencies that we cannot. They can see in light levels that we cannot. They are sensitive to vibrations that we cannot feel. And there are probably other environmental stimuli that they can sense and we cannot. Successful human-cat relationships come from remembering that a cat, after all, is a cat, not a person.

Q: How have people learned to interact with their cats?

A: Scientists have pondered the human-cat bond: Do we keep cats because we have a tendency to adopt and nurture young or sick animals? Do we form attachments with our pet cats as we would

Below: Although their wild ancestors were solitary hunters, domestic cats can be very sociable with people. Feral cats, however, usually fear and avoid people.

Below right: Kittens that are handled frequently and raised around people grow up to be friendly and affectionate adult cats.

The human-cat bond is most rewarding when we appreciate cats for what they are without expecting them to share human values.

offer social support to other human beings? Do we keep cats because we perceive that they offer social support to us? The answer appears to be that there is some of each of these in our relationship with pet cats, depending on the different personalities of both cat owners and cats. People nearly always have expectations about their pet cats. Some people dislike cats because they are independent and not easily trained or controlled. Other people value their cats for just these very traits. Inevitably, people treat pet cats as if they were people too. We empathize with them and attribute human intentions to them. And we are surprised when cats do not act in predictable ways or perform behaviors that seem "inhuman." For example, cats kill and, with a little practice, become very good at it. But this is neither good nor evil—it is what cats do. We may feel sorry for the mouse but should not accuse the cat of wickedness. A cat is not being disloyal when its human family moves and it, instead of settling into the new home, finds its way back to its "home" and settles in with the new owners without missing a beat. The cat is simply returning to its own home range, where it feels most comfortable and where it can live with an efficiency and predictability that it does not have in a strange place. This is more important to the cat than its human social partners. We can most enjoy cats when we accept them for what they are without expecting that they share human values.

For a man to truly understand rejection, he must first be ignored by a cat.

—*Stuart McMillan*

Describing the Breeds

Pedigreed cat breeds are described by variations in a set of ten features: origins, body morphology, head shape, eye shape, tail type, ear conformation, fur pattern, length, and color, and eye color.

Bengal

ORIGINS

Natural

These are old breeds, whose defining traits are believed to have evolved naturally in response to local environments or as a result of chance founder effects. Modern cat fanciers, however, have refined these breeds so that they may be quite different in appearance from their pro-genitors. Example: Turkish Van are descendents of working cats from around Lake Van, a mountainous region of Turkey near the border of Iran, that were adapted to hot summers and cold winters, and to enjoy swimming.

Hybrid

Also called man-made, these breeds resulted from deliberate crossing of established breeds to produce novel combinations. Example: Ocicat is the result of interbreeding Abyssinian, Siamese, and American shorthair to produce a domestic cat resembling an ocelot.

Spontaneous mutation

From time to time, a chance mutation results in an unusual trait in a kitten or kittens. The breeders then selectively breed individuals with this trait to produce a new breed; other features of the founding cat may be retained. Example: Devon rex originated with a kitten with curly fur, perhaps fathered by a curly-furred feral cat. This cat had big ears, large eyes, and short nose—features retained in the breed.

Wild hybrid

A few breeds, not recognized by some cat fancy associations, stem from crossing domestic cats with wild cats. Example: Bengals are a cross between leopard cats, native to Asia, and shorthaired domestic cats.

BODY MORPH

Cobby

Also called British, these cats are robust, stocky, and broad-chested, with relatively short legs. Example: British shorthair

Foreign

Also called Oriental, these are slim, svelte, elegant cats with relatively long legs. Example: Siamese

Intermediate

Cats with body morphs in between cobby and foreign. Example: Abyssinian

HEAD SHAPE

Wedge, or triangular

Example: Siamese

Round

Example: Persian

Rectangle

Example: Havana brown

EYE SHAPE

Round

Example: Burmese

Almond, or oval

Example: American shorthair

Slanted

Example: Siamese

EYE COLOR

The color of a cat's eyes is genetically linked to its fur color.

Blue eyes

Pointed cats, such as the Siamese, always have blue eyes. White cats and cats with many white markings may also have blue eyes.

Green, gold, or copper eyes
For cats other than pointed cats, some shade between green and copper is the typical eye color, including some white and white-marked ones. Some cats have been bred for intense eye color, producing deep green or shiny copper eyes; more often, eye color tends to be less intense, in the greenish-yellow to gold range.

Odd-eyes
Some white and white-marked cats have one blue eye and one green or gold eye.

American bobtail

Siamese

TAIL
Cat breeds exhibit a range of variation in tail length, thickness, and amount of fur. Examples: Tails range from the Japanese bobtail, with a short, stubby tail like a rabbit's, to the short, thick tails of Persians covered with long fur, to the slender, long tails with short fur of Siamese.

EARS
Ear size, shape, and placement vary greatly among the various breeds. Examples: Sphynx cats and Selkirk rex have very large ears, Persians, very small ones. The ears of Scottish folds are small and bent forward.

FUR LENGTH
Long
Long may mean very long fur all over the body, or just some parts of the body. Shorthaired breeds selected for long hair often have intermediate length, but are called longhaired. Examples: The classic longhaired breed is the Persian. Balinese is the longer-haired version of the Siamese, with intermediate length fur.

Short
Shorthaired cats may have a single or double coat. The fur may be straight, wavy, or curly. Examples: Siamese are shorthaired with a single coat and straight fur. Manx have a double coat. Cornish rex have short wavy fur.

Classic red tabby

FUR PATTERN

Tabby

Tabby is the original pattern of domestic cat fur and comes in four varieties:

- Classic, in which markings are dense and clearly defined dark colors on a lighter ground color. Markings are barred on the legs and form rings on the tail. Upward-pointing markings form the letter "M" on the forehead.
- Mackerel or blotched, similar to classic, but thinner vertical stripes go around the body.
- Spotted, in which broken stripes look like spots.
- Ticked, or agouti, in which the tip of each hair has a band of color darker than the rest of the hair.

Pointed

In the pointed pattern, the face, ears, legs, feet, and tail are darker than the rest of the body. Siamese are the classic example, but there are many variations on pointed.

FUR COLOR

Cats come in a bewildering array of colors, which basically overlap and sometimes hide their patterns. The interaction between the cat's ground color and the color of its stripes or points determines the cat's color, and both may vary from black to gray (also called blue) to red (or orange) to cream and white. Among some breeds, coat color is integral to the breed's definition. Havana browns, for instance, must be brown, and Russian blues, blue. In contrast, other breeds may display many different colors. The American shorthair, for instance, may come in 80 different colors. (For information on the genetics of coat colors and patterns, see pages 24–25.)

SOLID COLORS

Most solid colors result from the tabby pattern being suppressed.

Recognized colors are:

- White
- Black
- Cream
- Red
- Blue
- Chocolate
- Lilac
- Golden
- Cameo
- Brown
- Silver
- Fawn
- Cinnamon

Shaded colors

Each of a cat's hairs may be shaded, called ticked, or solid. In shaded colors, hairs are colored at the tips and lighter below, closer

Chinchilla

to the skin. Shading can be added to solid colors, as in smoke, as well as to most other colors and patterns, as in shaded silver tabby. Shaded colors are:

- Chinchilla, with light ticking as well as light solid color on the rest of the hair; the tabby pattern is suppressed, so that chinchilla cats often appear nearly solid colored.
- Shaded, similar to chinchilla but with greater contrast between the ticked and solid part of the hairs; the tabby pattern is suppressed as well.
- Smoke, with a white or near-white coat below solid color hairs.

Tabby colors

The color names of tabbies usually refer to the ground color of the cat. Thus, a brown tabby has black stripes on a brown to gray ground color. With each color class, the shades may vary. For instance, the black stripes on the brown tabby may be very dark black or lighter.

- Brown tabby, black stripes on brown to gray.
- Blue tabby, gray stripes on gray.
- Red tabby, red stripes on cream.
- Cream tabby, cream stripes on lighter cream.
- Silver tabby, black stripes on white, but stripes may also be blue, cream, or red, always on white.

Point colors

Although the seal point of Siamese is the most familiar, cats may display a variety of point colors, even white.

- Seal point, dark brown points on pale, brownish to ivory body; chocolate and lilac point are variants.
- Blue point, gray points on a light gray or tan body.
- Lynx point, tabby points of any tabby color.
- Tortie point, tortoiseshell points.

Patchy colors

Cats may have patches of different colors, generally referred to as tortoiseshell. Cat fanciers distinguish between tortoiseshells with white patches and those without.

- Tortie, patches of red, black, and cream.
- Blue tortie, patches of blue and cream.
- Brown patched tabby, patches of brown tabby and red tabby.
- Blue patched tabby, patches of blue tabby and cream tabby.

- Tortoiseshell and white, small white areas.
- Calico, largish white patches mixed with red tabby and solid black patches.

Tortoiseshell

- Dilute calico, largish white patches mixed with cream tabby and solid blue patches.
- Torbie and white, varying amount of white patching on a patched tabby.

The Breeds

The breeds described here are those recognized by the Cat Fanciers' Association (CFA); other organizations recognize additional breeds as well as additional colors of established breeds.

ABYSSINIAN

Origin

An old or natural breed, the Abyssinian is strikingly reminiscent of the African wildcat. Its name arises from the location—modern-day Ethiopia—reportedly from which the first of this breed was imported to England. More likely, however, these cats originated on the coast of the Indian Ocean and Southeast Asia, introduced elsewhere by people traveling from the Indian Ocean port of Calcutta.

Description

An elegant cat, with a lithe, muscular body between foreign and cobby, with large ears and almond-shaped eyes set in a slightly wedge-shaped head. Its soft, short fur is ticked, with no tabby markings. Colors include ruddy, red, blue, and fawn.

Personality

Intelligent, gentle, high-spirited and playful, an "Aby" is a good companion but not a lap cat.

Similar breed

The Somali is a longhaired Abyssinian, the result of selective breeding of Abyssinians carrying a recessive gene for long hair. It is otherwise very similar in body form and personality, and comes in the same colors.

AMERICAN BOBTAIL

Origin

This cat, only recently accepted by the CFA, arose from a natural mutation in an American cat for a short bobcat-like tail.

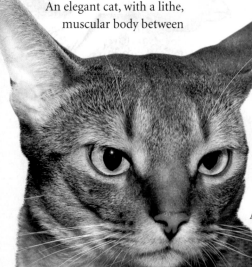

Abyssinian

Description

Medium to large in size, well muscled and athletic, it closely resembles a bobcat, with a powerful aura of the wild in its demeanor. Its water-resistant coat ranges from thick shorthair to medium-length longhair, and comes in all colors and patterns. Its head is a broad, modified wedge, with medium-sized ears and large, near-almond shaped eyes.

Personality

Despite its wild aura and hunter's eyes, this cat is adaptable, quiet but playful, with near doglike devotion to the people it bonds with. Bobtails may take two to three years to fully mature.

AMERICAN CURL

Origin

All American curls are descendants of a stray, longhaired black female kitten, found in California in 1981, with a natural mutation for backward curled ears.

Description

A perky-looking cat, the American curl is medium-sized, elongate without being svelte, with a modified wedge-shaped head and round eyes. Its curled ears are relatively small. It comes in all colors and patterns, and with short or long hair.

Personality

American curls are kittenish throughout their lives. They are playful, curious, and friendly, with even tempers, and strong loyalties to their owners.

AMERICAN SHORTHAIR

Origin

American shorthairs trace their ancestry to the working domestic cats that arrived with early European settlers, perhaps even on the *Mayflower*. This is your basic domestic cat, now carefully bred to maintain its basic cat-ness.

Description

Medium to large in size, these cats are robust and well muscled with round head and eyes and medium-sized ears. Their short, thick, coarse coats may be any one of more than 80 colors and patterns.

Personality

Healthy, friendly, easygoing, and intelligent, American shorthairs are also independent.

Similar breed

The American wirehair is very similar to the American shorthair, differing mainly in its wiry coat: Every hair, even the whiskers, is crimped, hooked, or bent in some way. Wiry fur appeared as a spon-

Birman

taneous mutation in a farm cat born in New York in 1966.

BIRMAN

Origin

An old breed, the Birman's origins are in Burma, where it was a cat sacred to priests. Pedigreed Birmans in the West owe their existence to a pregnant female secretly sent from Burma to France in 1919. With a single founder, however, the breed was out-crossed with other breeds so that it could be maintained.

Description

A large, stocky cat, with a round, broad head and round, blue eyes, the Birman has long, silky hair, and a fluffy tail. Its fur is pointed, with the unique distinction of having white "gloves" on all four feet.

Personality

The Birman is gentle, active, playful, but independent enough to ignore busy owners.

BOMBAY

Origin

The Bombay was created in the United States in the late 1950s and 1960s by crossing Burmese with black American shorthairs, to produce a cat evocative of a black leopard. It took years of careful breeding to consistently produce Bombays.

Description

Always solid, shiny black, with short fine fur, the Bombay is medium sized, and heavier than its lithe body suggests. Its head and eyes are round, its ears medium sized. Deep gold to copper-color eyes are characteristic.

Personality

Very people-oriented and easy-going, Bombays will even play fetch with their human companions, but they rarely vocalize other than to purr. They do well with children, and with dogs and other pets.

British shorthair

Description
Very heavy for their medium size, Burmese are stocky, round, and muscular. The head is a rounded wedge, with large eyes full of expression. Its coat is short, fine, and, in the United States, comes in only four solid colors: sable, champagne, blue, and platinum.

Personality
Burmese are so people-oriented, playful, and trusting that it is recommended that they not be allowed outdoors because they lack instincts for survival. Charming and intelligent, they have soft voices.

Similar breed
The European Burmese originated with an American Burmese sent to the United

BRITISH SHORTHAIR
Origin
Descendents of the domestic cats of Rome brought to Britain during the Roman Empire, this is the oldest English cat breed, noted for strength and hunting prowess as well as loyalty, serenity, and endurance. Its original color was blue.

Description
These cats define cobby: robust, stocky, and broad-chested, with relatively short legs. Their head is round, as are the eyes, and ears are medium. Its short, dense fur now comes in most colors and patterns except pointed.

Personality
Not acrobatic, but intelligent and easy to train, British short-hairs are calm, undemanding, and can be aloof cats.

BURMESE
Origin
This modern hybrid breed was founded in the 1930s by an oriental-type cat with brown fur imported to the United States from Burma and a seal-point Siamese. It has been selectively bred to look more like the husky Burmese ancestor than like the Siamese; the Siamese points were bred out.

Burmese

Kingdom, with further crossings to Siamese cats there. Apart from being slightly more svelte than their American cousins, European Burmese come in a greater variety of colors, thanks to the introduction of genes for red fur.

CHARTREUX
Origin
Similar in appearance to a blue British shorthair, the Chartreux is a natural breed that was described in French documents as early as the 1500s. Legend says that they were kept by the French monks who created Chartreuse liqueur, and hence, their name. Other evidence suggests that they were named after Spanish wool, for their woolly fur that is the texture of sheep's wool.
Description
Robust, even chunky, these are solid, powerful cats with round broad heads, powerful jaws, small ears, and round, gold to copper eyes. The round head tapering to a narrow muzzle gives the impression that these cats are smiling. The Chartreux comes only in shades of blue, with each hair tipped in silver.
Personality
Quiet, intelligent cats that softly chirp rather than meow,

Chartreux form deep, doglike attachments to a family.

CORNISH REX
Origin
This rather strange-looking cat with short, soft wavy fur all over its body, originated from a spontaneous mutation in a litter born in Cornwall, England, in 1950.

Chartreux

Description
Very slender and lithe, with a cheetah-like conformation—its back is arched, it has a narrow waist and stout chest, and its head is small and oval. Despite its delicate appearance, it is muscular and acrobatic, aided by strong hips and long legs. Eyes are set far apart, as are the very large ears. Cornish rex cats may be

any color or pattern so long as the fur is characteristically wavy.
Personality
Affectionate and people-oriented, these cats make lively, playful companions, retaining a kittenish friskiness throughout their lives. They enjoy fetching as well as tossing small objects in their paws.

DEVON REX
Origin
Similar in appearance to the Cornish rex, the pixie-like Devon rex originated from a spontaneous mutation for wavy and curly fur in a single kitten born in 1959 in Devon, England. The mutant gene is different from the one that produced the Cornish rex.

Description

These are small to medium-sized cats with small heads, very large ears, and large, oval, wide-set eyes. The body is long and slender but well muscled, and the legs are long too, making them good jumpers. The blunt-ended tail is rather thick. The wavy hair is highly variable, but is thin and not dense, so they seek out warm spots. Devon rex cats may be any color or pattern, including pointed.

Personality

Energetic cats with happy dispositions, Devon rex are playful, people-oriented cats that constantly seek out human interaction.

EGYPTIAN MAU

Origin

A natural breed with origins in Egypt (*mau* is an Egyptian word for cat), the breed began with two of three cats imported to the United States from Cairo in 1856. The only old breed to naturally sport spots, the Mau looks like the first domesticated cats pictured in Egyptian art.

Description

Graceful, slender but strong and muscular with long legs, Maus have smallish, rounded-wedge-shaped heads with medium to large ears and large, rounded almond-shaped eyes that slant toward the ears. The shiny coat is medium length. Black to dark brown spots and markings appear on four ground colors: silver, bronze, smoke, and black.

Personality

Only moderately active, Maus are highly intelligent and extremely loyal to their owners. Their voice is soft and melodious, and rapid tail wiggling expresses contentment.

Devon rex

HAVANA BROWN

Origin

The Havana brown, possibly named for the color of a Havana cigar, boasts a solid warm-brown coat. This breed is hybrid, the result of many years of selective crossbreeding beginning in the 1950s with a match in England between a chocolate-point Siamese and a black shorthaired cat with a trace of Siamese. Once in the United States, Russian blues, other Siamese, and a black shorthair with a recessive gene for brown were added to the mix to produce the only all-brown breed.

Description

In the United States, the Havana brown is medium-sized, with a well-muscled body that is neither cobby nor svelte. Its head is unusual, longer than it is wide, with a broad, beaky nose and flat cheeks behind the whiskers. In Europe, the head is more like that of a Siamese. The fur is medium length and smooth.

Personality

Intelligent, easily trained, and highly adaptable, Havana browns are described as more like dogs than cats. They purr very loudly, but are not very talkative compared to Siamese.

Japanese bobtail

JAPANESE BOBTAIL
Origin
A natural breed known in Japan for many centuries, the first three Japanese bobtails were imported into the United States only as recently as 1968. In the United States, all bobtails are descendents of these three. Bobtails appear frequently in Japanese art, especially as symbols of good luck.
Description
The short tail varies in length, but standards dictate it be no longer than three inches; otherwise, size, shape, orientation, and flexibility vary. The body is medium-sized, long and slender, but not narrow. Long, bent hind legs are longer than the forelegs. The head is softly triangular, with large ears and large, oval eyes. Bobtails may have short or long hair, in a variety of colors and patterns, but the most popular and traditional are tricolor (called Mi-Ke)—black, red, and white—and black, cream, and red tortoiseshell. The eyes may be blue, green to gold, or odd.
Personality
Maturing earlier than some other breeds, Japanese bobtails are active and playful from the start. Intelligent and adaptable, they enjoy travel and are strong and healthy. Talkative, their voice is soft and musical.

KORAT
Origin
A rare natural breed with ancient origins in Thailand, the Korat, named for a province in Thailand, is defined by its blue fur, tipped in silver so that it appears to shimmer like a halo. Thais consider it a sign of good fortune. A male and female imported from Thailand in 1959 founded the U.S. breed.
Description
Medium-sized and semi-cobby, Korats have unusual heart-shaped heads, with large, round expressive eyes that are luminous green in the adults. Their coats are short and fine. They have extraordinarily sensitive hearing, vision, and olfaction.
Personality
Gentle, cautious cats, Korats dislike noise and must be carefully trained to accept handling. They are very calm and affectionate, however, and enjoy being petted.

LAPERM
Origin
Cats with soft, curly fur first appeared as a result of a spontaneous mutation in a domestic Oregon farm kitten, born bald and only later growing in its curly locks. Initially not selectively bred, the number of kittens born with this mutation, which turned out to be carried on a dominant allele, gradually increased and eventually attracted the notice of cat fanciers.

Maine coon

Description

LaPerms are medium-sized, with semiforeign bodies and medium-length legs. The head is wedge-shaped, with large, cup-shaped ears, and medium to large round to oval eyes. LaPerm's curly fur may be short or long, and fall in waves or in ringlets that vary from tight to loose and long. All color and patterns appear. Oddly, a molt may result in a cat losing its curls for life, leaving it with just a thin coat. Kittens may be born bald, or lose their baby fur at about two weeks of age, slowly regrowing their coats by four months.

Personality

Very active and inquisitive, but also gentle and affectionate, LaPerms are quite people-oriented and may begin to purr at the first sight of their human companions.

MAINE COON
Origin

The Maine coon is a natural breed of longhaired cat, believed to have acquired its long, thick fur to keep warm in the cold winters of Maine. The "coon" part of its name comes from the silly idea once touted that these cats resulted from cats mating with raccoons.

Description

One of the largest of domestic cat breeds, Maine coons are robust and well-muscled, with broad chests and long bodies. The large head is also broad, with a modified wedge shape. The large eyes, usually green, gold, or copper, are round but slightly slanted toward the base of the large, tufted ears. The tail is long and covered in flowing hair. Maine coons may display all colors and patterns except pointed and solid chocolate and lilac.

Personality

Reputed to be diligent mousers, these cats are good companions, with loving, calm personalities and impressive intelligence. They are talkative, but quietly so.

MANX
Origin

The Manx arose from a spontaneous mutation on the Isle of Man in the Irish Sea, where isolation maintained the mutation in the domestic cat population. Best known as tailless, Manx cats can also have a full tail, a short tail, or a rise where the tail should be. Crosses between two tailless cats usually result in deformed kittens that soon die.

Description

The Manx has a very short, robust round body; even its head is very round, as are its cheeks, eyes, and the tips of its ears. Its hind legs are much longer that its front legs, so that its back end sits higher than its shoulders, as if to advertise its tail or lack thereof. Manx may be any color or pattern and come in both shorthair

Manx

and medium longhair; the long-haired variety is sometimes called the Cymric.

Personality

A speedy runner that hops somewhat like a rabbit, the Manx is very playful and a surprisingly good jumper. Like a dog, a Manx may retrieve and bury toys.

NORWEGIAN FOREST CAT

Origin

A natural breed, cited in Scandinavian literature and legends for hundreds of years, the large, longhaired Norwegian forest cat is the European counterpart to the Maine coon, adapted to cold northern winters.

Description

Magnificently furred, these forest cats are noted for long, dense, water-resistant coats, with flowing ruffs or manes framing the faces of older individuals. Even the insides of their ears are furred to protect them from the elements. They are large brawny cats, with broad chests, heavily muscled, medium-length legs, and long tails. The head is triangular, with large, almond-shaped eyes. Forest cats come in most colors and patterns.

Personality

Its origins make this an excellent outdoor hunter, with intelligence and high energy. Kittens raised with loving, gentle humans make adaptable, people-oriented cats.

OCICAT

Origin

After a cross in 1964 between an Abyssinian and a Siamese unexpectedly produced a kitten that grew to be a large, spotted cat resembling an ocelot, these hybrids were selectively bred, with an admixture of American shorthairs, to maintain their wild-cat look.

Description

A medium to large cat with a hefty athletic body, ocicats have modified wedge-shaped heads and broad muzzles. Almond-shaped eyes, slightly slanted, and large wide-set ears set off the face. The tail is long and thin. Shorthaired, the ocicat is always a spotted tabby and comes in the range of tabby colors.

Personality

The ocicat's wild look belies its adaptable, social temperament, making these cats easy to train. Although not demanding of

Norwegian forest cat

attention, the ocicat prefers the company of its owners or other cats and even dogs.

ORIENTAL

Origin

The Oriental was founded in the 1950s with Siamese stock bred with Russian blues and other shorthairs to produce a Siamese-like cat but without color points. Through selective breeding for color and pattern diversity, the Oriental comes in more than 300 different colors and patterns, and also as a longhaired variety.

Description

The Oriental looks in all ways like a Siamese, but for the colors and points, and the eyes, which are most often green. Despite its delicate appearance, it is a muscular, hardy cat.

Personality

Orientals are demanding, curious, and intelligent, with a hint of mischief in their playfulness. They enjoy company.

PERSIAN

Origin

The Persian's origins are shrouded in mystery, but it is considered a naturally longhaired breed with origins in modern-day Iran. The modern breed, however, owes a great deal to selective breeding, including, in the United States, crosses with Maine coons and Angoras.

Description

The Persian's large body defines cobby: robust, stocky, and broad-chested, with relatively short legs. Its broad head sits on a very short neck. Its nose is short, wide, and flat; the eyes large and round; and the ears small and tilted forward. The soft, thick coat can reach to six inches (15 cm) in length, even on its long tail. Persians come in all colors

Persian

and patterns, including color-points, which are sometime called Himalayans.

Personality

Persians are languid, gentle, quiet cats, not given to much activity, that enjoy a peaceful environment where they get much pampering. They are best kept indoors. Their long fur requires constant grooming from attentive owners.

Similar breed

Exotics are Persians in almost every way except the coat is short, thick, and dense.

RAGDOLL

Origin

A medium longhaired hybrid breed created in the 1960s in California, the Ragdoll is the result of crossing a white Persian with a seal-point Birman and later a sable Burmese. Very large and docile, the Ragdoll gets its name

from its tendency to fall limp when picked up. Ragdolls are very slow to mature.

Description

Among the largest of the breeds, the Ragdoll is a heavily built, strong-boned, sturdy cat, with a broad wedge-shaped head and thick, medium-length legs. Its large, oval eyes are blue. The Ragdoll comes in a variety of colorpoint colors and patterns.

Personality

Loving and adaptable, Ragdolls are gentle, affectionate, people-oriented cats that tend to stick to the floor rather than jump about.

Similar breed

RagaMuffin is basically a Ragdoll that comes in a greater variety of coat colors, including tabby and blue, and its eyes may be in the green to gold range.

RUSSIAN BLUE

Origin

Considered a natural breed, the Russian blue may have originated in northern Russia. The first Russian blues to reach England may have come from the northern Russian port of Archangel.

Description

The Russian blue is noted for its solid blue double coat, which is so dense that it is compared to that of seals. The blue hairs are tipped with silver, so this cat practically glows. Its foreign body is reminiscent of a Siamese, but less tubular. The head is broader, and the face somewhat flattened. Its ears are large and very wide set, and its bright-green eyes are large and round. The tail is long and tapered.

Personality

Fairly shy, Russian blues are quiet and undemanding yet affectionate pets with soft musical voices.

SCOTTISH FOLD

Origin

All Scottish folds, characterized by small ears that are folded downward to

Russian blue

the head, can be traced to a white farm cat born in 1961 in Scotland with a spontaneous mutation for folded ears. They are often bred with American shorthairs in the United States, and with British shorthairs in the U.K. Kittens are born with normal, straight ears that may or may not fold at three to four months of age.

Description

This is a stocky, well-rounded medium-sized cat with short legs. It has a round head, prominent cheeks, and large, round eyes. The nose is broad and flat. Its short, dense coat comes in most colors and patterns except colorpoint and solid lilac and chocolate.

Personality

Hardy cats, Scottish folds are quiet, calm, and adaptable. They are not very talkative.

SELKIRK REX

Origin

These cats with curly hair originated with a spontaneous mutation in a female domestic cat found in a Montana shelter in 1987. She was crossed with a black Persian and curly-haired kittens were born. The breed is still being perfected, with outcrosses to Persians, exotics, British shorthairs, and American shorthairs.

Description

The Selkirk rex is being bred to resemble the British shorthair in body morph—large and heavy boned with a broad, round head and large round eyes. Hair is curly, even the whiskers, and may be either short or medium long. All colors and patterns are displayed.

Personality

Tolerant and patient, these sturdy cats are loving pets.

SIAMESE

Origin

A natural breed with Asian origins, likely Siam (modern-day Thailand), Siamese were once stockier, with rounder heads, than today's svelte, elegant cats with chiseled heads, although their colorpoint pattern, short fur, and blue eyes are characteristic. They first came from Siam to England, and then to America, in the late 1800s.

Description

Medium-sized, Siamese are everywhere slim and long: long, tubular bodies, long legs and tails, long, narrow, wedge-shaped heads, long noses, and tall ears. Eyes are almond-shaped, slanting upward toward the ears. Seal points, with dark brown to near black points on pale, nearly white bodies, were the first seen. Chocolate points, blue points, and lilac points came later.

Personality

Famous for their loud voices and talkativeness, Siamese are demanding, very active cats, playful, intelligent, and a bit high-strung.

Similar breeds

Colorpoint shorthairs are Siamese with points of colors other than the four listed above, such as lynx point. Balinese is a longhaired Siamese, bred after long hair appeared as a spontaneous mutation; it is less loud and talkative than Siamese but otherwise similar and bearing the same four point colors. Javanese is a Balinese with a greater variety of point colors. The names of these last two are fanciful and do not reflect origin.

SIBERIAN

Origin

A natural breed from Russia, Siberians are relatively rare elsewhere, first imported into the United States in 1990.

Description

Similar to Maine coons and Norwegian forest cats, Siberians are large and strong, with medium-long hair, triple coats, and ruffs, but

Singapura

tend overall to be rounder. They come in all colors and patterns.

Personality

Sweet and loyal with gentle dispositions, Siberians are good hunters, acrobatic, and capable of great leaps.

SINGAPURA

Origin

These small cats may be a natural breed, native to Singapore in Southeast Asia, but the U.S. breed was founded with the import of four cats from that small nation in the 1970s.

Description

Although very small, Singapuras are stocky and rather square, with round heads and short noses.

Their ears and almond-shaped eyes are large, the tail relatively long. The Singapura comes in only one shorthair color and pattern: ticked sepia (also called sepia agouti) with brown ticking on an ivory ground color.

Personality

Singapuras are outgoing, curious, intelligent cats that are very people-oriented and somewhat demanding.

SPHYNX

Origin

The modern Sphynx breed of hairless cats began with a hairless domestic kitten, the result of a spontaneous mutation, born in Canada in 1966. Sphynx have been carefully interbred with fully furred cats and then back to hairless ones to create a healthy, if strange, hybrid cat. Sphynx may be covered with fine down and sometimes hair appears on the nose, tail, and toes.

Description

Lacking fur, the Sphynx appear delicate, but they are actually sturdy, strong, medium-sized cats with broad chests and bulky, even somewhat beefy, builds.

The head is long, on a slender neck, and the ears and eyes are very large. They can be any color or pattern, but these are only seen as pigmentation on the bare skin. Sphynx need to be kept warm and risk sunburn if let outdoors.

Personality

Intelligent, energetic, curious, and demanding cats, Sphynx enjoy human company.

TONKINESE

Origin

Tonkinese are hybrids of Siamese and Burmese, developed at the beginning of the 1960s in Canada to combine the best features of these two breeds.

Description

As planned, the Tonkinese body is medium-sized and the morph is intermediate between that of its ancestors, and overall, it is a medium sort of cat from ears to fur length to tail. Even its aqua-colored eyes blend the bright blue of the Siamese with the green-gold of the Burmese. Color-pointed, but with less contrast between point color and ground color, the Tonkinese ground color is usually a dilute version of the same, darker point color. Siamese types, with blue eyes, and solid-color Burmese types with green-gold eyes also occur.

Personality

Tonkinese have strong personalities combined with somewhat noisy playfulness. They can be stubborn but always affectionate, and prefer not to be left alone, when they make mischief and look for ways to escape from indoors.

TURKISH ANGORA

Origin

A natural breed with a long history in Turkey, the medium longhaired Turkish Angora nearly went extinct before being revived in Turkey's Ankara Zoo. CFA accepts for registration only cats descended from Turkish ones.

Description

Medium-sized, long and lithe with fine bones, and a medium long wedge-shaped head, long nose, and almond-shaped eyes. The Angoras' coat is medium long and sports a long tail and ruff. The traditional and most popular fur color is solid white, accented by eyes of any color, including odd-eyes. It does come in other colors and patterns, however, except pointed and solid lilac and chocolate.

Personality

Highly intelligent and devoted to their owners, Angoras make charming, very playful pets.

Tonkinese

TURKISH VAN

Origin

Noted for its swimming abilities, the Turkish Van is a natural breed of working cats from central and southwest Asia. First imported to England in 1955, they did not appear in the United States until 1982. They are fairly rare.

Description

Turkish Vans are large, powerful cats, with long, broad, muscular bodies and deep chests, and long, full tails. The head forms a long, wide wedge, tipped with large ears. The eyes are round. In summer, its coat is short, but its winter coat is medium long and, like cashmere, is water-resistant. They come in only one color—white—and one pattern of color only on the head and tail, a pattern called "van" when other cats are bred for it.

Personality

A lively cat, whose natural aggressiveness has been bred out, Turkish Vans are not for everyone, especially those looking for an affectionate lap cat.

CHAPTER 7

MALES AND FEMALES

The life of a cat is driven by its need to find food to survive, but in an evolutionary sense, all that hunting and eating matters only if cats also mate and produce young, over and over again. A wild cat's success in life is measured by the number of offspring that carry its genes into the next generation and the next. Domestication changes this formula. People may alter their cat's food-finding behaviors by providing it with prepared foods and restricting its access to prey it can catch and kill. We also necessarily restrict its

Above: In the wild, a cat's existence centers on mating and producing young—when not searching for sustenance.

Left: Domestic cats do not usually have the same breeding opportunities as wild cats or feral domestic cats.

mating and kitten-rearing behaviors and opportunities. We may do this by keeping it confined and away from cats of the opposite sex, by providing prearranged breeding opportunities to produce the kittens we want, or by neutering it. When we deal with our cat's reproductive behaviors we usually are in the greatest conflict about our pet's lives. But while people ponder such concepts as fulfillment in life, a cat does not. It simply lives a day at a time, seeking to take advantage of the circumstances in which it finds itself.

Cat Breeding Season

Q: Is there a breeding season in domestic cats?

A: When the yowls of tomcats fighting and a queen's cries pierce an early spring night, the whole neighborhood is put on notice. Cats are mating. Yet there is surprisingly little synchrony among females living in the same neighborhood as they come into estrus, or heat, so the sounds of cats mating may well continue to spice the night through the spring and summer. Dogs come into estrus every six months or so. Cats are called poly-estrous, and if a queen is not impregnated during an estrous cycle, the cycle repeats two or three times or more from March through September. If a female loses a litter, she comes into estrus again shortly thereafter. The entire estrous cycle of a queen is two to three weeks, and she is receptive—in heat—to a male from one to several days during this cycle. During the winter months when daylight lasts less than eight hours a day, a female stops cycling and becomes what is termed anestrous during the winter. The estrous cycle is initiated in the queen's body when daylight lasts more than 12 hours. This registers in the cat's brain, which in turn sends a hormonal (chemical) message to the cat's ovaries and initiates the release in the ovaries and other glands of other hormones, which in their turn stimulate the cat's estrous behaviors. Because cats are also stimulated by artificial light, however, estrus can begin as early as January and extend to December in modern urban and suburban environments. Similarly, indoor queens, living in an environment with about the same amount light and dark throughout the year, may cycle all year if they do not mate and become pregnant.

In modern environments, female cats may come into estrus, or heat, at any time of the year, but spring and summer estrous periods pre-dominate. A queen may be receptive to a male's advances for up to several days during her estrus.

England in 1760. Its hero was a cat named Tom who enjoyed the favors of many females. The name stuck, and we also now apply it to many other dashing, male-oriented objects—Tomcat fighter jets, for example.

The custom of calling a male cat "Tom" likely originated with the book *The Life and Adventures of a Cat*, published in England in 1760.

Q: **Why are female cats called queens and males called toms?**

A: In England, cat breeders, perhaps with tongue in cheek, traditionally referred to their female cats as queens, and this custom has been accepted almost everywhere in the English-speaking world. *Queen* is from the Old English word *cwen*, which means "female ruler, wife, or honored woman." And female cats, in their independence, do seem to behave as though they lord over the households where they live. Cat breeders usually refer to their breeding males as studs. In England, Tom was a name that was used for male kittens for several hundred years. But the modern use of tom to refer to male domestic cats in general is reputed to have its origins in a popular book, *The Life and Adventures of a Cat,* published in

Q: **At what age are cats sexually mature?**

A: Although a domestic cat's muscles and skeleton are not completely grown until the cat is about a year old, both male and females can breed as early as five months of age, although puberty can also be as late as two years, depending on the breed and on the individual's nutritional state. Puberty can begin only when the hypothalamus area of the brain is mature enough to produce gonadotroprin-releasing hormone (called GnRH for short) to the pituitary areas of the brain, which in turn sends gonadotropic hormones through the blood to the cat's reproductive organs. This initiates the maturation of the sex organs—ovaries in females and testes in males—which also produce hormones that stimulate the production of the eggs and sperm, along with the behaviors, necessary for successful breeding and reproduction.

> "No matter how much the cats fight, there always seem to be plenty of kittens."
>
> —ABRAHAM LINCOLN

Cat Breeding Arrangements

Q: **Are cats monogamous?**

A: No. On the surface it seems that cat society is simply an aggregation around a resource: queens seeking food, or toms gathered around a queen in estrus. But scientists have been teasing apart the rules of cat society for the last half-century. Cat society is remarkably complex, more so because we, as owners, inject ourselves into it. Toms and queens both seek multiple breeding partners when they are available and are called polygynous or promiscuous breeders. Males provide no parental care and are out of the picture for most of a female's life. Strange males will even kill kittens, a behavior called infanticide. Some queens stay around their homes but grow more restless as the estrous cycle progresses. Other queens, if allowed to, roam widely during the phase of the estrous cycle just before full heat.

Some of the queen's courtship behavior attracts multiple males, to create a "may-the-best-man-win" competition among them and ensure that the highest-quality male available fathers her young. During peak estrus, a queen usually, but not always, mates with the most dominant tom present, which is usually the male that holds the territory they are on. She may also mate with other males that attend her during estrus. No tom, or mother for that matter, is sure of the paternity of the kittens produced. Scientists think there may be at least two kinds of benefits of this mixed or uncertain paternity. It may diminish the risk of infanticide by males because a male simply has no way of knowing for certain if the kittens are his offspring. And a female may increase her reproductive success by mixing her genes with those of different males.

Left: Both toms and queens may try to mate with multiple breeding partners. A queen's behavior during courtship may actually attract multiple males and foster competition among them.

Right: Scientists speculate that uncertain paternity may be a way of discouraging males from killing kittens because a tom has no way of knowing if the kittens are his or another male's.

Free-living domestic cats often live at such high densities in cities that the tendency for them to live apart in well-spaced territories is suppressed.

Q: How does cat society work?

A: Reproducing adults of wild cat species have individual home ranges where they hunt and mate and where females rear their young. In some wild cat species, such as tigers, both males and females defend these home ranges against other adults through fights and other displays. The defended area is called a territory. Male territories overlap female territories, and a male's larger territory overlaps the areas of several females. This is the extreme form of wild cat land tenure and social organization. And given the space and dispersed food resources, this is how free-living domestic cats live. Domestic cats living on the food we provide and what they can capture and scavenge in their neighborhoods live at higher densities than they could if no food was provided. So cat societies exist on a continuum from solitary to colonial.

Densities of cats living in cities can be several thousand per square mile, or more. In cities with high densities of free-living cats, the tendency for them to live on well-spaced home ranges is overwhelmed by their sheer numbers; cats still have their own places, but they live in a social order determined by their relationships with others and the social dominance networks they fashion. Adult females form the core of cat society, and groups of related females, or female lineages, are the building blocks. Males are not so tied down by their familial relationships. For pet cats, their territory is the human home and its immediate vicinity. When they are allowed to venture farther afield, conflicts and challenges arise over areas that two or more cats believe are their own. Some conflicts arise over food, but conflicts are especially intense among males competing for breeding opportunities.

Cat Fights

Cat fights establish the winners' social dominance, especially among tomcats vying for access to a female in estrus.

Q: Why do tomcats fight?

A: Tomcats sort out their social status through aggression, which is largely controlled by the male hormone testosterone. Toms compete most intensely for mating opportunities; fights among them are usually more frequent and severe when the toms are competing to mate with a female in estrus. The tom that wins passes his genes on to the next generation, so there is evolutionary selection pressure for a certain amount of male aggression.

When cats live on well-spaced home ranges, a male that holds exclusive rights to a territory he shares with several females usually has to contend with only one intruder at a time. Within his own territory, the owner is confident and usually dominant to intruders, but he acts less confident when he is the intruder in the territory of another male. The picture changes when cats live at close quarters, with little space to establish territories. Toms that know each other fight less than males making their first assessments of each other. When one tom has a decided size and strength advantage over another, fighting is less pronounced—the smaller, weaker cat knows it is best to avoid a losing battle—but fighting escalates when the opponents are of equal size and strength. Older toms tend to dominate younger ones, but size matters more. Apart from actual fights, males compete for dominance through vocal duels, chases, and threats.

An older tom tends to dominate younger males, but he may also carry the scars of his past battles.

Q: How do tomcats fight?

A: A fight between evenly matched toms may rouse the entire neighborhood. The great cat biologist Paul Leyhausen, the first to describe tomcat duels in the scientific literature, reported: "Their battle song swells and dies and the tips of their tails twitch more and more violently."

Dueling tomcats draw themselves up on their legs, with their heads stretched forward, their backs held straight, hairs on the back and tail puffed out, and tails held stiffly at a downward right angles, the tips twitching. Both hold their ears raised at a sharp angle and turned so far around that the opponent can see the backs of the ears. The movements of each cat mirror those of the other, as if they were shadow dancing. They face each other, eyes locked, for many minutes, motionless, only a few inches apart.

Suddenly, one tries to bite the nape of its adversary, and the other fends off the fangs with its forepaws while scratching violently with the hind paws, all accompanied by piercing shrieks. They separate, threaten again, and rejoin the battle. They repeat these behaviors until one tom shows he has given up by remaining motionless in a defensive posture, ears folded tight. The winner does not attack again, although it continues to threaten for a while, before turning away from the subordinate and sniffing the ground intensively. The defeated cat does not slink off until the dominant one quits sniffing the ground; only a completely defeated tom runs away immediately. The victorious cat now owns the ground on which the fight occurred. These same two cats may not fight again: Dominance rank has been settled until and unless the dominant male loses physical condition and becomes obviously vulnerable to being ousted from his place at the top.

Rival males squaring off for a fight may display identical expressions and postures before a fight begins. Equally matched dueling toms repeatedly threaten and fight until the subordinate male gives up by assuming a defensive posture.

Getting Ready to Mate

Q: How do female cats find mates?

A: Adult male cats routinely patrol all areas of their territories to check on the sexual status of females living there. But a female nearing heat also actively tries to attract males. During proestrus, the period just before a female comes into full estrus, she may increase her scent marking as she moves about her home range, although domestic females do not scent mark as lavishly as their wild counterparts do. Changes in the chemical composition of the urine she marks with correlate with the rise in estrogens that precede full estrus. She begins making loud caterwauling cries to attract males. The scent marks she makes are like road signs; the calls are like a loudspeaker announcement. The message is loud and clear: "Come find me, I'm ready to mate," and ensures that local males are well informed. Other behaviors a female performs more frequently as estrus approaches include rolling, cheek rubbing, and body rubbing; she may be generally much more restless but eat less. Anyone with a domestic cat in heat is familiar with these behaviors, because they are also directed at her human caretakers, whom she is treating as a "partner." This proestrus behavior can last for several days, becoming more intense the closer she is to estrus. Cat owners might find this mounting passion troublesome and succumb to the temptation of opening the door and just letting her out. Or, despite best human efforts, she may streak though a door barely cracked open, much to her owner's dismay. She will be back home in a few days in a much calmer state.

Q: How do cats court?

A: When cats of the opposite sex meet, there is always the chance, armed as they are with claws and fangs, that a false move on either's part will escalate into lethal combat rather than copulation. This constrains the courtship. Males are capable of mating at all times but are not always equally eager to mate. Experienced males, not surprisingly, are more proficient in the courting ritual than inexperienced ones. Males in unfamiliar surroundings may be

As estrus approaches, a female cat advertises her readiness to mate with behaviors such as scent marking and loud calling.

indifferent even to a fully receptive female, whereas males in familiar surroundings are interested immediately.

Head rubbing is an important part of male courtship in the early stages when he is trying to get a female to let him get close to her. She may engage in what scientists call "flirting chase" for a few days before she allows the tom to come close. She solicits his advances by walking sinuously by him, rolling in front of him, and touching him. She looks at the male or turns her backside toward him, holding her tail straight up to reveal her swollen vulva. Despite this flirtation, she remains coy, aggressively rebuffing the male's attempts to get close and mount her. The male gives way, only to try again and again. At times he will sit and lick his partially or fully erect penis. Over the course of a few days, courtship behavior intensifies, until finally the female becomes fully receptive and accepts the male's advances.

Left: When a female cat is in estrus, she rubs her cheeks and body more frequently, sometimes directing her behavior toward human caretakers.

Below: A female cat solicits the attention of a male by touching him or rolling in front of him, even before she is fully ready to accept his advances.

Mating Cats

Once a male cat successfully mounts a cooperative female, the act of copulation lasts from only a few seconds to less than a minute. But they may copulate many times in the next hours.

Q: How does a female signal she is ready to mate?

A: During courtship, between bouts of flirting and rejection, a female cat gives into episodes of mutual licking and rubbing with her attending male. After days of buildup, the moment of mating may arrive abruptly. While the female is crouching or even rolling around, the male approaches her from behind, loosely bites the nape of her neck, and steps over her, first with a forepaw and then with his hind paw. The female adopts a crouching posture, called lordosis, which makes her genitals accessible to him. At the same time, she rests her forelegs on the ground as far as the elbow, stretching her head out flat above them, and closes her eyes to a narrow slit with her ears lying slightly

A female cat in estrus licks and rubs her attending male as a build-up to copulation.

backward. The male then mounts. If she does not lift her vulva sufficiently, he treads on her back with alternating movements of his hind feet, until she is in the proper position and her tail is held off to one side. He then places his hind feet on the ground and inserts his penis into her vagina and copulates.

Individual copulations are generally brief, lasting from a few seconds to less than a minute. After a few thrusts, she begins to shriek and he begins to growl. Immediately after the male ejaculates, the female twists her body to dislodge him, often swatting at him with her paw. An experienced male knows this is coming and backs away to avoid the swat. The female then may lick her vulva and groom, as the male withdraws a short distance. Within a few minutes, mating begins again, but not with the elaborate, tension-filled displays that

preceded the first copulation. As soon as she wants to be mated, she assumes the lordosis posture; he mounts and copulates with her again. Over the next hours, this is repeated many times.

Q: **How do several male cats court a female cat?**

A: When circumstances permit, several male cats will simultaneously court a female cat in estrus. The highest-ranking male follows her most closely as she "flirt walks" in front of them. The other males form a peripheral ring around the courting pair; threats keep most peripheral males at a distance, although actual fighting does erupt among males during this courting phase. Threats and fights are more intense between the central and peripheral males than among the peripheral males themselves. The dominance situation is confused by the estrous female as she moves around. For instance, she may move from one male's territory to another's, giving a subordinate male the chance to rush in and take control. The central male generally performs all of the copulations, at least in the early part of the female's estrus, but he may leave while the female is still receptive, enabling a peripheral male to take his place. Scientists watching a very large cat colony in Rome found that often it was the less dominant and less aggressive males that were more successful in breeding females. While evenly matched dominant males were squaring off for a fight, a less dominant male would move in and mate with the estrous female.

When several males compete to mate with a receptive female, it is usually the dominant male that copulates with her as peripheral males form a ring around the mating pair.

Puzzling Mating Behaviors

When a male cat bites the nape of a female's neck as he copulates with her, she becomes immobile. This prevents the female from turning her teeth and claws on him.

Q: **Why does a tomcat bite the back of a queen's neck while mating?**

A: A tomcat may hold the back of the queen's neck between his teeth during mounting and copulating. A mother transports kittens by holding them in her mouth by the scruff of the neck. Kittens being held this way go immobile; they do not struggle in their mother's grasp. Adult cats never quite lose this response, so a tom may use the nape bite to immobilize a female while copulating with her. This serves to protect him from her claws and teeth should she try to turn on him.

Q: **Why does a female scream while mating?**

A: A tomcat's penis is covered with small, stimulating spines. Intromission or ejaculation stimulates a copulatory shriek from the queen and growls from the tom. Contrary to folklore, the queen's shriek is not the result of pain caused by the tom withdrawing his spine-covered penis. It is true, however, that the function of the spines is to stimulate the female's vaginal walls. Females in most cat species are induced ovulators (see next question) and copulatory stimulation is required for ovulation to occur. Scientists now believe that a queen's copulatory

A female cat is very vulnerable during copulation. Her shrieks may be defensive, preventing the male from attacking her as if she were prey.

shriek may be defensive. A female is in a very dangerous position when she is mounted, because the male could deliver a killing bite. The copulatory shriek may prevent him from switching from her lover to her attacking predator.

Q: What is induced ovulation?

A: Most cats are believed to be induced ovulators, most of the time. Induced ovulation means that the stimulation of copulation is required for a female to ovulate, unlike human females of reproductive age, who spontaneously ovulate about every 28 days even if no male is present. Waiting to ovulate until copulation ensures that opportunities for successful fertilization are not missed.

Ovulation occurs when eggs are released from the ovary into the oviduct, where the tom's sperm can fertilize them. Stimulation of the queen's vagina sends a nerve signal to the hypothalamus in the queen's brain. This signal causes the release of gonadotropin-releasing hormone (GnRH), which then stimulates the nearby pituitary gland to secrete luteinizing hormone (called LH for short). Traveling through the queen's bloodstream, LH reaches the ovary, where it stimulates ovulation and, later, the development of the progesterone-secreting corpus luteum in the ovary in the spaces where the eggs developed. This all happens very quickly. LH reaches the ovary within minutes of mating, and a female may ovulate within hours, depending on the concentration and duration of the elevated levels of LH. She may ovulate several eggs during this period, which, if they are fertilized, will result in multiple embryos.

Q: How often do female cats mate during estrus?

A: While a queen can ovulate after just one mating, the chances of her ovulating and being impregnated increase with the number of copulations. In laboratory studies, LH levels return to baseline in the queen's bloodstream within 12 to 24 hours after a single mating. After multiple matings that occur within less than two hours of each other, LH does not return to baseline for up to 38 hours. Usually, female cats copulate many times during their heat period. The queen's estrous period lasts just two to three days, and brief copulations continue night and day through the period. One study of free-living cats recorded an average of 15 copulations in 24 hours, while a laboratory study reported 8 to 12 copulations during the four hours following the first mating.

A female in heat may yowl constantly. Although a queen can ovulate after just one mating, her chances of becoming impregnated increase the more times she copulates during her estrus.

After Mating

Q: Do males and females stay together after mating?

A: No, tom and queen part company after the two- to three-day mating period. The only role that a father plays in caring for his young is to defend the territory so that another tom does not move in and kill them. Unlike wolves and some other canids, female cats raise their young without the assistance of mates or other helpers. Caring for young is solely the mother's job in all cat species except the lion and in some domestic cats living in colonies. These mothers may nurse each other's young and bring prey back to them.

Q: What happens after mating?

A: If, for some reason such as insufficient copulatory stimulation, a queen does not ovulate, her estrous behavior subsides and she goes into

Male cats play no role in raising young, which is strictly the responsibility of female cats.

what is called interestrus for a few days and then gradually returns to estrus. If it is late in the year and day lengths are less than about eight hours, she may go into anestrus, during which her ovaries become inactive for the winter months.

If a female does copulate and ovulate but no eggs are fertilized by the tom's sperm, this produces a different result. The corpora luteum, a mass of cells that forms from an ovarian follicle after the release of a mature egg, secretes the hormone progesterone, a steroid that supports pregnancy if fertile eggs are present but creates a pseudopregnancy if fertile eggs are absent. In pseudopregnancy, hormonal and other changes may be indistinguishable from those of a true pregnancy. Pseudopregnancy, however, lasts for 35 to 40 days, a little more than about half the length of a true pregnancy, before the queen resumes cycling.

Q: How long is gestation?

A: Gestation or pregnancy is the period when the kittens are developing in the mother's uterus. Gestation lengths are longest in the largest cats, and range from 100 to 114 days in lions to 66 to 70 days in the tiny rusty-spotted cat. The African wildcat's gestation period is about 58 days. Gestation in the domestic cat is about 65 days but varies from 58 to 72 days. This variation is caused by differences among individuals and also by environmental conditions. If your cat's pregnancy extends beyond day 70 or so, you should consult your veterinarian.

Q: How does a female's behavior change during pregnancy?

A: As your cat's pregnancy advances, she decreases her activity and does less climbing and jumping. In the last 20 days, her appetite and weight increase. She grooms herself more frequently, and she looks for and explores potential birth sites, preferring undisturbed areas with a soft surface. You may not actually see her doing this, and your pregnant cat may surprise you by giving birth in a closet where she never would go before. On the other hand, if your cat is very sociable and home-adjusted, she may have her kittens in some exposed place—on your bed, for example.

Q: What are the signals of impending birth?

A: During the last few days before a female gives birth, you may see the movement of the fetuses. But there are other signals, too. The female's vulva and mammae swell, and the mammae begin to secrete colostrum—a fluid produced late in pregnancy and for a short time after parturition (the process of giving birth). Colostrum is full of antibodies that give a boost to the immune systems of newborn kittens. She may use her incisors to pull out the hairs around her nipples. Just before parturition, she will probably become more irritable, defensive, and even aggressive, and engage in more self-licking. You may hear her cries and pants. She may urinate and defecate before seeking out her chosen birthing spot.

The rusty-spotted cat, the smallest wild cat species, has a short gestation of just 66 to 70 days.

As the mother cat's pregnancy approaches full term, she grooms herself more often and jumps and climbs less.

Neutering Your Cat

Q: Should domestic cats be spayed or neutered?

A: Owners neuter their cats to prevent unwanted kittens and to curtail behaviors associated with mating, such as fighting, urine marking, and wandering. Females are spayed (or ovariohysterectomized) by surgically removing, under anesthesia, the uterus and ovaries through a slit in the abdomen. Males are castrated by surgically removing the testes through a slit in the scrotal sac. These are medically safe procedures and have been performed by veterinarians millions of times. A cat can be neutered at nearly any time in its life. It is common practice to neuter cats before they become sexually mature, at about seven months of age. So-called early neutering is done when a kitten is about seven weeks of age. Both males and females become nonreproductive immediately after neutering, but it may take some time before males neutered after puberty stop performing unwanted behaviors. Most males neutered before puberty never engage in serious fighting with other males. When males are neutered as adults, 50 percent stop fighting immediately, and in another 40 percent fighting gradually declines. That last stubborn 10 percent never stop fighting with other males. Veterinarians have studied the effect of neutering done before puberty on growth rates. Neutering does not stunt growth, but it does change metabolic rate in cats. Neutered cats gain weight if food is always available to them, so only carefully monitoring and controlling a neutered cat's diet will keep it from getting fat. Generally, a cat will be calmer and more easygoing after it is neutered. A pet cat may spend more time with you, and neutered cats do not roam to breed. Their hunting abilities are not affected. Neutered males and females can both be expected to live two to three years longer than intact cats.

Q: How long do toms and queens breed in their lifetimes?

A: A queen can produce two or even three litters of kittens a year throughout her reproductive life if she is allowed to do so. (Her wildcat relatives produce only one litter a year. Domestic cats also produce more young per litter than wildcat females do.) A cat can be expected to live between 9 and 15 years, although cats in the protective care of their owners can live beyond 20 years of age, and there are

Neutering a pet cat prevents it from reproducing, and may also eliminate unwanted behaviors associated with sexual maturity such as fighting, scent marking, and wandering. To prevent a cat from licking or chewing the surgical incision line, the vet may send it home with a hard plastic cone that surrounds the head, known as an Elizabethan, or "E" collar.

that live in the same areas; preventing hybridization between domestic cats and European wildcats is therefore a high conservation priority. Programs to neuter feral cats are gaining popularity to prevent such hybridization as well as simply to reduce their numbers where they threaten birds and small mammals. So that feral cats retain the whole range of normal sexual and aggressive behavior, males can be made sterile by vasectomy (cutting the sperm ducts) rather than by castration, while females only need their fallopian tubes cut to keep eggs from entering the uterus for fertilization.

A domestic cat can produce two or three litters a year through her reproductive life, which usually lasts about 10 years.

Neutering feral cats helps to reduce their numbers, perhaps decreasing their impact on prey species. Neutering may also aid in the conservation of some wildcat species by preventing hybridization with domestic cats living in the same area.

documented cases of domestic cats living into their 30s. Most queens, however, stop reproducing before they are 10, and the oldest queen to reproduce was reported to be 12. From ages 8 to 12, the number of kittens produced in each litter declines. Toms have been reported to reproduce until they are as old as 16, but in free-living domestic cats, reproductive life may be over by 5 or 6 years because older animals are displaced by younger ones. The older animals have reduced access to food, and their risk of accidental death increases.

Q: Should feral cats be neutered?

A: Conservationists believe that the most serious threat to wildcats is hybridization with the domestic cats

"Kittens can happen to anyone."
—PAUL GALLICO

CHAPTER 8

BRINGING UP BABIES

Watching kittens grow up is a rewarding experience, but in kitten development there is no breather. Kittens grow rapidly and become adults before you realize it. At birth, they are blind, deaf, and trying frantically to get their back feet and front feet coordinated. They paddle to their mother, drawn by her warmth, and nuzzle her belly fur in search of her nipples and the milk that nourishes them. Their eyes open in their second week. In their third week their teeth begin to erupt and they take their first steps. Month-old kittens begin to play with one another.

At five weeks, they begin to practice their predatory behaviors and begin to eat solid food. They are weaned during their second month. By 10 weeks their coordination is fully developed, and clumsy kittens turn into skilled hunters over the next few months. As kittens grow to nutritional independence, their relationship with their mother changes dramatically. Usually by 10 months, our former kittens are sexually mature and begin their adult lives. And we will have more kittens, if we have not taken steps to prevent it.

Above: Kittens grow up very quickly. In just about 10 months, the blind, helpless babies are transformed into mature adults ready to have babies of their own.

Left: A kitten raised to maturity by its mother, but exposed to humans, develops into an adult cat well adapted to life among people.

Birth

Healthy queens rarely require human intervention when it comes to time to give birth. The best advice is to let nature take its course. A domestic cat typically gives birth to four to five kittens per litter.

Q: Where do cats give birth to their babies?

A: A pregnant female stops eating just before giving birth. Some owners want to help in the birth and, using their cat's loss of appetite as a signal, prepare a nice box where she can have her babies. She may cooperate. Just as likely, she has already selected the site where she will have her kittens: a warm, dark, secluded place. A healthy female seldom has difficulties with delivery, and doting owners should avoid disturbing her. Being disturbed may interrupt her normal birthing behaviors, and she may even eat her kittens. Just before the birth, she is very unsettled. There is a discharge from her vagina. She may both defecate and urinate. She may feed, lick herself, cry, pant, dig at the floor, roll, and do so repeatedly. There

is no fixed pattern to her preparturition behaviors, although they are localized in the vicinity of the birthing place.

Q: How many kittens are born at a time?

A: Domestic cats nearly always give birth to more than one young, with 19 the largest litter ever recorded, of which 15 kittens were reported to have survived. Typically, domestic cats give birth to four or five kittens in a litter. For their closest wild relative, the wildcat, as well as for most other wild cats, the typical litter is two or three. A mother gives birth to one kitten at a time. Parturition is complete when the entire litter is delivered. In a major study of birthing behavior in domestic cats, the interval between kitten births ranged from 32 seconds to more than 50 minutes. Moving, crying kittens are a critical stimulus for the mother, and stillborn kitten are usually eaten.

A pregnant cat seeks out a quiet, warm spot that is hidden from view in which to give birth. In this instance, it is the hollow of a tree.

Q: What takes place during birth?

A: During the births, the mother is responding to what is going on within her (uterine contractions and the passage of the kittens), to the by-products of the birth (fluids, placentas), and of course to the kittens themselves. One scientist remarked: "Parturition in the domestic cat cannot be viewed as a regular patterned flow of events; rather it is a series of sporadic episodes broken by other activities." After her somewhat frantic prebirth behavior, the female calms down and strains her abdomen, which looks similar to her straining to defecate earlier. In fact, uterine contractions have begun, during which she squats, strains, and crouches. Some mothers scratch at the floor, brace their body, roll, or rub, and may even go into lordosis. The female circles around as though she is trying to inspect her rear, because she perceives that something unusual is happening to her body, but out of her view. Her contractions soon come several minutes apart, and several minutes or more later a kitten emerges from her vagina. Some kittens emerge headfirst; others rear first. After each kitten and afterbirth (placenta) is delivered, she eats the afterbirth, chews and breaks the umbilical cord, licks and noses the kitten, licks her vulva, and laps up the birth fluids. Licking cleans the kitten and stimulates its breathing and movement. A kitten may get to a nipple and start to nurse even before the next kitten is born, although this usually does not happen until all the kittens have been born. With

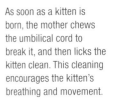

As soon as a kitten is born, the mother chews the umbilical cord to break it, and then licks the kitten clean. This cleaning encourages the kitten's breathing and movement.

the birth of the last kitten, the female goes into what scientists call the "period of rest," which lasts for 12 hours or more, during which time she simply lies quietly, her body encircling her new kittens. She normally remains with them nearly continuously for up to 48 hours, taking just short breaks away from them.

Kittens at Birth

Q: How big are kittens at birth?

A: Most of the kittens born in the same litter are about the same size at birth. Kittens weigh just under 4 ounces (100–110 g), or about 3 percent of the mother's weight, and are about 5 inches (13 cm) in length. Little difference is seen among the weights of kittens born in litters of one to four. Above a litter size of four, kittens are smaller: The more kittens in the litter, the smaller the kittens. First-time mothers also tend to have smaller litters than they do subsequently.

Top: Kittens rely on their mothers for food, protection, and warmth.

Bottom: A newborn kitten's eyes remain closed for 7 to 10 days.

Q: Why are newborn kittens helpless?

A: Young giraffes can run nearly as fast as their mother within a few hours after birth. They have to be able to do so to avoid being eaten by a predator. In the giraffe's case, the mother has invested a great deal of her energy in producing such a well-developed young. In contrast, female cats invest little in their young until they are born, perhaps because the demands of hunting preclude females' carrying very large babies. All cats have small, semi-altricial (mostly, but not entirely, helpless) young. Kittens are born fully furred, but their ability to maintain their body temperatures is poor, and they cannot move well. They rely on their mothers entirely for food and protection. They are born with their eyes closed, and they remain closed for 7 to 10 days after birth. They have a strong sense of smell but seem not to be able to hear for the first few days. It is not until they are a month old that kittens can move any significant distance from the nest and get back on their own.

Q: How do you tell male and female kittens apart?

A: Adult male domestic cats are usually considerably larger than adult females, but this size difference takes about two years to be fully expressed. Male and female kittens usually do not differ in birth weight, and they remain very similar in weight up until about six to eight weeks. Thereafter, male kittens grow faster and are soon larger than

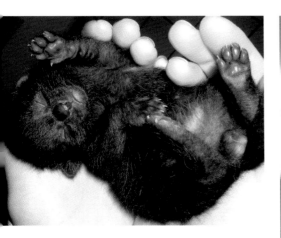

female kittens. In the days after birth, a cat owner can determine the sex of kittens by gently examining their rear ends. Of course a male has testicles and a penis and a female has a vulva, but it is surprisingly tricky for an inexperienced observer to identify these on a newborn kitten. The sex of many a kitten has been initially misdiagnosed.

Q: Is mother rearing preferable to human rearing for kittens?

A: Yes. Raising kittens in the absence of their mother and siblings has profound effects on their behavior that last into adulthood. Scientists have tracked the effects of early rearing experience on subsequent adult sexual behavior in domestic cats. Cats reared alone are suspicious, fearful, and aggressive toward other cats. Males raised alone have a reduced ability to copulate. When in estrus, human-reared females cheek-rubbed and solicited attention from their caregiver but were difficult to approach and handle. They responded with extreme aggression to any sudden motion. This is also how these females responded to males when they were in estrus. They were attracted to the male but did not have the social skills to deal with his approaches.

Top left: A male kitten has a penis and testicles; nonetheless, it is often difficult to determine the sex of a newborn.

Above: Although it is possible to hand-feed a kitten, one that has been reared by its mother experiences fewer behavioral problems as an adult.

An ordinary kitten will ask more questions than any five-year-old.
—*W. L. GEORGE*

Initial Kitten Care

Q: How do mother cats take care of newborn kittens?

A: Smells, touch sensations, and warmth fill the world of newborn kittens. Their first resting place is saturated with the smells of their mother and those created during their birth. The mother lies on her side with her stomach and mammary glands exposed to her kittens, with her fore and hind legs extended to form a circle around them. The warm, attractive, enveloping mother calms the kittens down. She purrs and licks the kittens and herself almost continuously. The newborn kittens right themselves and crawl slowly and hesitantly forward with paddling movement of their forelegs and uncoordinated pushing with the hind legs. They nuzzle into the mother's fur, climbing on her until they make contact with protruding nipples. There may have been some nursing during the birth period, but nursing begins in earnest when the last kitten has been delivered and the mother begins her resting time with them. The kittens may fumble at the nipples at first, but attachment and suckling usually begin within the first hour and nearly always by the end of the second hour. During the initial nursing, the kittens receive colostrum through the nipples; this fluid contains antibodies to kick start the kittens' immunity to various diseases. Earlier, the mother had ignored the kittens' calls, but now she begins to respond. The sight of a kitten not enveloped in her body with the others does not stimulate the mother to retrieve it, but she does respond to the displaced

Below right: Mother cats lick their kittens both to clean them and to reinforce the bond between them.

Below: Newborn kittens snuggle into their mother's fur and begin to nurse when the last littermate has been born.

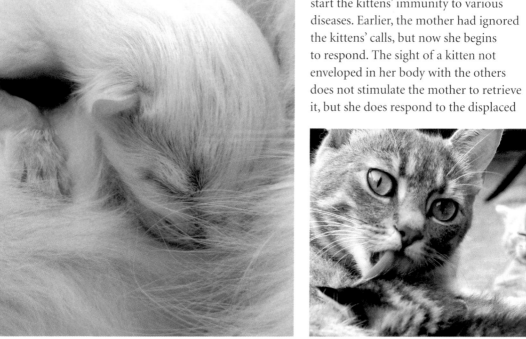

kitten's shrieks and quickly gathers it into her fold. Kittens' orientating skills gradually improve, however, and soon even still-blind kittens can find their own way back to their mother without resorting to crying for help.

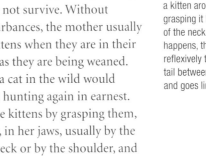

Q: Why do mothers lick their kittens?

A: Mothers lick their kittens to stimulate them and to transfer her own odors to them. This licking cements the mother-kitten bond. When a mother returns to her kittens after a brief foray out of the nest, she rouses them by licking them. She also licks their perineum (anogenital region), which stimulates them to defecate and urinate; kittens are five to six weeks old before they can eliminate body waste without their mother's stimulating licking. During the first 20 days of the kittens' lives, the mother initiates nearly all the feedings. She lies down and presents her mammae to them and facilitates the kittens' attachment and sucking by licking the accessible kittens.

Q: How do mothers move their kittens around?

A: If the new mother is disturbed, she may move her kittens from place to place. This is normal, but if it begins too soon

after their birth and happens repeatedly, the litter may not survive. Without external disturbances, the mother usually moves her kittens when they are in their fourth week, as they are being weaned. This is when a cat in the wild would have to begin hunting again in earnest. She moves the kittens by grasping them, one at a time, in her jaws, usually by the nape of the neck or by the shoulder, and carries them with her head held high. The kitten goes limp and tucks its tail between its legs. This is also how she retrieves marooned kittens, although she may initially be clumsy at it. With practice, the mother's retrieving techniques improve.

A mother cat moves a kitten around by grasping it by the nape of the neck. When this happens, the kitten reflexively tucks its tail between its legs and goes limp.

Milk

Newborn kittens spend up to eight hours nursing in their first day of life. A lost or abandoned kitten can be fed kitten formula from a bottle or with an eyedropper.

Q: **How many nipples does a female cat have?**

A: A female domestic cat has four pairs, or a total of eight nipples, which become enlarged by the stimulation of suckling kittens. The rear nipples, those closest to the mother's tail, are more accessible to newborns and are used more than the fore nipples. The forwardmost pair of nipples may not be functional in some mothers.

Q: **Do kittens fight for access to nurse?**

A: With an average litter size of four in the domestic cat, there are plenty of nipples to go around in most litters. Competition for nipples occurs when there are more than six or eight kittens born in a litter. Many kittens show a preference for a nipple or pair of nipples. Kittens in both small and large litters sometimes establish these preferences as early as the first day. In other litters, however, the preferences are less rigid. Kittens in larger litters display more competitive scrambling as they search for the nipples, but stable nipple preferences reduce this competition.

Q: **How often do kittens nurse?**

A: Suckling occurs both day and night, but it is not always easy to tell whether squirming kittens protectively encircled by their mother are actually nursing. Video analyses show that

the kittens nurse 4 to 8 hours in the first 24 hours after birth. Suckling is accompanied by the kittens' purring and treading against the mother's abdomen. Treading is thought to stimulate milk discharge. The amount of time the mother spends nursing her kittens decreases after the first two weeks and also varies with litter size. A mother of four kittens may spend 70 percent of her time nursing at day four, in comparison to a mother of two that spends only 40 percent of her time nursing four-day-old kittens. After two weeks, the time spent nursing levels off accordingly. A mother with two or three kittens spends 30 to 50 percent of her time nursing, while a mother with one kitten spends less than 15 percent of her time nursing over the next month. When the mother leaves the nest she may drag some of the kittens out still attached to her nipples. The kittens learn to return to the nest on their own within three or four days.

Q: What is in a mother cat's milk?

A: Cat milk contains proteins, sugars, calcium and trace elements, and vitamin A. The composition of milk varies among different species, and it changes over the course of lactation. Cat milk contains far more fat and protein and has about two and a half times more energy than cow or human milk. The mother on average produces about 4 percent of her body weight in milk each day she lactates.

Q: When do kittens begin to eat solid food?

A: Kittens' milk teeth (equivalent to human "baby teeth") start to erupt at about two weeks of age. The kittens shift from their mother's milk to solid food during their second month. Their permanent teeth start to replace their milk teeth at 10 to 12 weeks, and cats have their full adult complement of teeth by seven months of age.

Mother cats require two to three times their normal food intake during lactation, depending on litter size. They may require several feedings a day, and fresh water in a clean dish should be readily available.

Growth

It takes only a few weeks from birth for a cat's motor skills to develop, but in some breeds sexual maturity may be delayed for up to two years or longer.

Q: **How fast do kittens grow up?**

A: In the few weeks after birth, the kitten's motor skills, sensory perceptions, and physical and social development come together to form the mature cat. Cats may not reach their full physical growth until they are about two years old, but most cats usually are sexually mature by 10 months of age. In some breeds, such as the Maine coon, sexual maturity is delayed for up to two years, and in others, cats are sexually mature as early as 5 months of age.

Q: **What changes occur as kittens mature, and when do they occur?**

A: Kittens can orient to their mother by smell at birth. They can hear in the first week, and hearing is fully developed by one month of age. It takes two or three days for the eyes to begin opening, and they are fully open during their second week. Once this happens, kittens are quickly able to locate their mother visually and approach her. In their third week, they take their first wobbly steps and learn to avoid barriers. In their fourth week, their paw placement, guided by their depth perception, is developed to the point that they freeze rather than walk off an elevated shelf. Their eye fluids become

Once a kitten's eyes open during its second week of life, it is immediately able to find its mother by sight.

totally clear by five weeks. If a kitten falls from a height, it can begin to right itself in the air while falling during its fifth week and is fully capable of doing so by about 40 days. A kitten's visual acuity is 16 times better at 10 weeks than it is at 2 weeks, but it continues to improve until it is three or four months old. By week five, kittens try their first clumsy running. They begin to play with their siblings during their sixth week, and predatory behaviors begin to appear in their play during their seventh week. By week five or six, kittens voluntarily defecate and urinate and no longer need their mother to stimulate them to do so by licking their perineums. Their ability to control their body temperatures is fully developed by week seven. They walk and run like adults in their seventh week, but these skills are not perfected until they are three months old. Kittens begin to respond to threatening social stimuli by about week six.

Q: How do mothers wean kittens?

A: Mothers eat more during pregnancy to shore up their energy reserves, mostly stored as fat tissue. Milk takes a lot of energy to produce, and mothers lose several grams of body weight a day while nursing. With an average-size litter, half of a female's energy reserve is depleted in the first three weeks, but larger litters can use three quarters of this reserve in that same time. When the suckling kittens have reached a critical weight, the mother simply cannot produce enough milk to sustain them. Mothers become less tolerant of their kittens at about day 30 and are less apt to initiate suckling; instead, they wait for the kittens to demand a feeding. Weaning begins in week four and is mostly complete by seven weeks, although the kitten may intermittently suckle without any milk transfer for several months after this. During the weaning period, mothers respond aggressively to the kittens' suckling attempts. Kittens seem to lose their nipple preferences as there is less milk and they are searching for more. During weaning the kittens begin to eat solid food. In wild cats this new food is provided by the mother's hunting prowess; we provide this first solid food for our growing kittens.

A mother cat uses a lot of energy to produce milk for her kittens. The gradual process of weaning begins when kittens are about four weeks old and is complete by about seven weeks. As mother provides less milk, kittens replace it with solid foods.

If only cats grew into kittens.
—*R. Stern*

Learning

Q: Are there critical or sensitive periods in the kitten's early development?

A: Normally, kittens mature into competent adult predators with social skills that allow them to meet and mate, and females to rear kittens. Their development, however, can be upset. A cat's brain is more plastic in early life than it is later, and, further, getting the right inputs during early and limited stages of kittenhood is essential for the normal expression of social and other behaviors in adult life. Events that occur or do not occur during these sensitive periods of a kitten's development often have long-term effects. For example, kittens that are handled early tend to develop more rapidly, both behaviorally and physically. Kittens separated from their mother early have emotional and physical problems; they become fearful and aggressive toward other cats and people and do not learn as well. Pioneering studies done in the 1920s demonstrated that kittens raised in the same cage with rats never killed rats of the same strain when they became adults, although some would kill rats of other strains. Cats isolated as kittens from seven weeks on killed the kittens in their own first litters.

Q: Why do kittens play?

A: Many people think that because the motor patterns used in play resemble those used in catching and killing prey, play is practice for adult predatory behavior. Experience is necessary to hone hunting skills, but kittens that have never killed a

rat, for example, can become rat-killers by watching another cat kill a rat. Even kittens reared in social isolation, without opportunities to see another cat kill or even play, showed normal predatory behaviors when presented with a moving mouse model at 11 weeks of age. Also, kittens that had no opportunity to play with objects developed normal predatory behavior later. We simply do not yet know what the role of play is in behavioral development.

Q: How does play develop and recede?

A: Kittens begin to play with siblings by week four, and this social play continues until they are about three months old.

At this point, play bouts can escalate into serious fights. Social play declines after 14 weeks. Kittens begin to play with objects as they develop their eye-paw coordination starting in week seven, and this declines at about three months as well. Beginning at week six, as the end of weaning approaches, some social play shifts to object play. Also, patterns used in aggressive encounters, such as arching, rearing, and chasing, become increasingly associated with predatory motor patterns such as approaching, pawing, and biting. Scientists believe that after weaning there is a divergence in how motor patterns are controlled in the cat's brain, with the centers controlling social and agonistic, or fighting, behaviors becoming different from those controlling predatory behavior.

Kittens continue to play with their littermates until they are about three months old. As they mature into adults, their social play can develop into real fights.

Q: How do kittens learn to be predators?

A: Mothers play a major role in the education of their young to become good hunters, acting as both facilitators and teachers. In domestic cats, a mother begins bringing the prey she kills to her young when they are about four weeks old, so they can watch her eat it and eventually begin eating it themselves. Next, she brings them live prey, either intact or disabled, and vocalizes to call their attention to the animal. The young play with the prey and eventually kill it; the mother helps only if the prey is about to escape, in which case she will retrieve it, or if the kittens lose interest before killing it. Finally, she takes young with her on hunts so that they can practice their skills. Young cats appear to learn a lot about how to be good predators by watching, imitating, and simply being with their mothers. For instance, kittens that learn to hunt with their mothers are much better at biting prey on the nape of the neck, the way domestic cats typically and most efficiently kill.

Q: When are kittens independent of their mothers?

A: Kittens' independence from their mother occurs in stages. After weaning, they go through a period when they are learning to hunt by themselves and spend time alone, but with the mother still nearby. Then, by three to four months of age, they are living independent lives.

CHAPTER 9

A DAY IN THE LIFE

The behavior of cats, whether that of our pets or of their wild relatives, intrigues us because it is at once similar to ours and infinitely different. As do humans, cats sleep, but do so much longer each day, and also indulge in the "cat naps" we so envy. They dream, but we may not ever know what they dream of. We know that our cats are smart, but not what they think about. Cats have athletic abilities that outshine those of our most agile sports heroes. They are even capable swimmers, although they do not like to get wet. Cats can fall great distances and land on their feet often enough to be the stuff of legends, but they do not land safely every time—although they certainly do better than people who fall from similar heights. Yet this ability does not render them fearless: Everyone knows that cats get stuck in trees, afraid to descend. And cats, for all their predatory prowess, have many enemies that kill them. Paradoxically, among their greatest enemies are our proverbial best friends, dogs.

Above: Cats spend most of their days sleeping, and appear to dream as do sleeping humans.

Left: Cats are agile climbers and can survive falls from great heights.

Sleep, Perchance to Dream

Kittens have different sleep patterns than adults, only gradually adding periods of light sleep to periods of deep sleep and wakefulness.

Q: How much do cats sleep?

A: When they are not out and about hunting or patrolling territories, wild cats and free-ranging domestic cats generally hole up in some relatively safe place, such as a thicket of dense vegetation, a burrow, or a crevice among rocks. This is where they rest and sleep. Lions may be seen sleeping with reckless abandon, sprawled out in open shade, and we see our pet cats do this sometimes, too. But generally cats seek secure places to let down their guard.

Most mammals experience two kinds of sleep: light sleep and deep sleep, which are differentiated by the brain-wave patterns seen in an electroencephalogram (EEG). In light sleep, there is very little brain activity, and the animal is in quiet repose. In deep sleep—also called REM sleep, for the rapid eye movements that

occur—intense brain activity is observed. During REM sleep, mammals, including cats and humans, twitch, jerk, change positions, and the like, but are completely relaxed and more difficult to arouse than during light sleep—although once aroused they are more alert than when coming out of light sleep. In adult cats, light sleep, REM sleep, and wakefulness follow a regular cycle, with light sleep as a transition from wakefulness to deep sleep, which is followed by wakefulness. A newborn domestic cat goes directly from being awake to deep sleep, dividing its time about equally between the two for its first few days. Gradually it adds light sleep to the mix until, as an adult, it spends about 35 percent of its time awake, 50 percent in light sleep, and 15 percent in deep sleep.

Mammals that have safe sleeping sites and are predators generally spend more time in REM sleep than mammals that are prey and lack safe beds. As expected, lions, tigers, and domestic cats are known to experience high amounts of REM sleep; they also have relatively large amounts of light and REM sleep combined.

Cats prefer to sleep in places where they feel safe, such as a burrow in the wild or a cozy bed in a home.

Although all mammals sleep at least a little, and long-term sleep deprivation can lead to death, the function of sleep and its two different forms is unknown. Some ideas include tissue repair, energy conservation, recharging the supply of neurotransmitters, and learning and the formation of memories. Support for the learning and memory hypothesis came recently from a study of young domestic cats during the critical period for visual development. Scientists found that kittens that slept for six hours following visual stimulation formed twice the number of brain connections as those that were kept awake and either left in the dark or examined immediately after the visual stimulation. Cats kept awake and exposed to an additional six hours of stimulation also showed fewer changes in the brain than those allowed to sleep. This study also found that light sleep was responsible for the effect.

Q: Do cats dream?

A: People dream only during REM sleep, and dreams may be the result of the intense activity of the brain during this kind of sleep. Cats in REM sleep certainly behave as if they were dreaming: They twitch their paws, whiskers, and tail, and even vocalize. We have no way of knowing, however, whether their dreams are like the often-bizarre filmlike experiences we remember when we wake up. If dreams are merely side effects of the host of physiological events that occur during REM sleep, it seems likely that cats would dream. But, if dreams have functions in humans, such as promoting creative thought through linking ideas in bizarre ways normally suppressed by rational thinking during waking hours, as proposed by one scientist, it is hard to imagine that they serve that same function in cats. Assuming that cats do dream, whether they remember their dreams upon waking, even fleetingly as humans usually do, is unknowable at this stage of our ability to measure and compare how brains work. Even if they do remember their dreams, cats are unlikely to spend any time interpreting them.

Cats in REM sleep behave as if they are dreaming, but we have no idea what their dreams, if they have them, are like.

Clever Cats

Q: **How smart are cats?**

A: The measurement of intelligence is fraught with difficulty, even when dealing only with humans. Many scientists now object to the notion that there is a single IQ ("intelligence quotient") that reflects much more than the ability to take standardized tests. Instead, they recognize multiple intelligences that include linguistic intelligence, logical-mathematical intelligence, spatial intelligence, kinesthetic (physical or bodily) intelligence, interpersonal intelligence, and naturalist (or nature) intelligence. Students of animal behavior confronted a similar issue many years ago, when they tried to compare the intelligence of diverse species using the same tests. Cats, for instance, would quickly learn to escape puzzle boxes for a food reward, but did worse than pigeons when asked to press a lever for a reward. This does not mean that pigeons are smarter than cats, only that cats, given their naturally complex predatory behavior, do not expect to find prey in this predictably easy way.

Another way that scientists have attempted to compare intelligence is by measuring the encephalization quotients of diverse species. The "EQ" is a number reflecting the increase in brain size over and beyond that explainable by an increase in body size. Thus, human beings have a very high EQ, with a far larger brain size relative to body than that of other primates. In turn, primates have higher EQs than carnivores, and carnivores have EQs higher than rabbits. This fits with our intuitive notions about intelligence: Monkeys are smarter than dogs and cats, which are smarter than rabbits. Canids have higher EQs than felids, which may be related to the fact that canids tend to live in groups and thus have more social intelligence than mostly solitary felids. This is one reason why it is easier to train a dog than a cat.

Different parts of the brain may be relatively larger, or smaller, indicating different abilities. The olfactory lobes of primate brains, for instance, are relatively

small, while in carnivores these lobes are relatively large, and those of dogs are larger than those of cats. Thus carnivores have better "smell smarts" than primates, and canids are better smellers than felids. Felids have relatively large cerebellums—the area of the brain that coordinates movement on a minute-to-minute basis—not surprising in light of cats' hunting and killing skills, which depend on stalking and precision attacks. Thus cats have kinesthetic intelligence that may exceed that of the average human. Similarly, cats must have keen spatial intelligence that enables them to find the boundaries of their large home areas, know where prey and water are likely to be found, where others of their species are living, and the best routes to take to find prey and avoid predators.

Asking whether cats think is related to asking how smart cats are. Definitions of thinking include concepts such as intention, planning, foresight, and flexibility in the face of obstacles or change. No domestic cat owner will tell you that his or her cat does not perform intentional behavior, plan, have foresight, or flexibility. And each owner will have one or more favorite examples to show how smart his or her cat is. Wild cats appear to have these same abilities. Servals learn to use car headlights to illuminate prey crossing the road. Lions learn the location of carcasses potentially available to scavenge by noting the circling of vultures. Cats are also capable of learning by observation. Young cats, for instance, learn what is appropriate prey by watching what their mothers eat.

Q: **How does a cat find its way home?**

A: Cats' high degree of spatial intelligence includes excellent visual memory. Cats seem to have mental maps of the areas in which they live. Scents provide further information. Free-ranging cats and domestic cats that spend time outdoors know where they get fed and return to those places regularly. At least some domestic cats also have the remarkable ability to find their way "home" over very long distances of unfamiliar terrain. Some scientific evidence suggests that cats (and other animals that home) are sensitive to Earth's magnetic field and thus have built-in compasses; but much remains to be learned about how this works.

Cats have a remarkable ability to map their home ranges and remember places they have been.

Enemies and Friends

Cats and dogs are natural-born enemies, and a cat running away from its foe actually stimulates a dog to chase it.

Q: What natural enemies do cats have?

A: Humans, parasites, viruses, and bacteria—all may be the enemies of cats. But day to day, the worst enemies of cats are cats and other carnivores, especially members of the dog family.

In general, any larger carnivore will kill a smaller one, including both adults and young of the smaller species, while a smaller one may kill the young of the larger species. Cheetahs are a good example. One study in the Serengeti found that lions, leopards, and spotted hyenas accounted for 68 percent of the deaths of cheetah cubs, and throughout these animals' ranges in sub-Saharan Africa, if lion numbers are high, cheetah numbers are low. Cheetahs may be forced to hunt in the middle of the day to avoid lions, which tend to hunt at night. On the other hand, leopards and hyenas

kill lion cubs that have been left alone, accounting for about 8 percent of lion cub mortality in the Serengeti. Closer to our subject, caracals are known to kill African wildcats, while pumas, Eurasian lynx, and Iberian lynx all kill domestic cats that they encounter.

From a cat's point of view, other nonfelid carnivores are also enemies. In North America, coyotes account for many bobcat deaths, while gray wolves have recently been reported to be killing pumas (these animals are meeting for the first time in a century as a result of the gray wolf's restoration in the Yellowstone area and the puma's expansion in the American West). Coyotes also kill domestic cats, as will domestic dogs. Other potential predators of feral cats, and of pet cats that go outdoors alone, are foxes, raccoons, and large predatory birds such as eagles and owls.

Just as domestic dogs may kill domestic cats, wild canids such as gray wolves kill wild felids such as pumas.

Q: Can cats learn to get along with dogs?

A: As the previous answer suggests, felids and canids—cats and dogs—are natural enemies. Domestic cats generally avoid dogs, but if surprised by one, they run. Because a cat's running triggers a dog's predatory chasing urge, the encounter may end badly for the cat, unless it can escape up a tree or into an area the dog cannot enter. It is not unusual, however, for cats and dogs living in the same home to learn to get along—if not become fast friends—but this requires human intervention. The best way to ensure that your cats and dogs get along is to raise kittens and puppies together from their infancy. If you do this, they will often form close ties and maintain companionable relationships as adults. It is trickier to introduce adult dogs and cats to each other and teach them to get along. The key to success is your ability to control the dog, which must never be allowed to chase the cat, and letting the cat take the lead, at its own pace, in overcoming its fear of approaching and investigating the dog. Depending on the breed and temperament of both dog and cat, it may take many weeks or longer before the cat becomes comfortable with the arrangement, and the dog learns not to chase; however, this may never happen, in which case you will have to keep your pets physically apart, or give one of them up. And even after a cat and dog have lived together peacefully for some time, there is always the chance that tempers will flare and the dog will attack and injure or even kill the cat.

A cat and dog raised together from kittenhood and puppyhood may remain close friends—or at least not mortal enemies—for life.

Fast and Agile

Q: How fast can cats run?

A: Cats are sprinters, not long-distance runners like dogs. This means that cats accelerate to top speeds very quickly, run at that pace for a short distance, in the range of tens or hundreds of yards, and then must rest. In contrast, dogs run at slower speeds but can maintain that speed over many miles. This difference is related to how cats and dogs hunt. A cat slowly stalks its prey and then puts on a sudden burst of speed to capture it and deliver a killing bite. If this rush fails, the cat gives up. In contrast, a dog chases its prey relentlessly until the prey tires and slows down or falls, making it easier for the dog to attack and kill it with multiple bites.

Although it is difficult to measure running speed under natural conditions, domestic cats have been clocked at speeds of up to 30 miles per hour (48 km/h), considerably faster than the 19 to 20 miles per hours (30–32 km/h) measured in sand cats and jungle cats. Among very large cats, lions can reach speeds of 30 to 37 miles per hour (48–59 km/h).

Cheetahs, though, epitomize the running cat. Well known as one of the fastest land mammals, cheetahs reach top speeds estimated at 56 to 65 miles per hour (90–104 km/h)—fast enough to capture speedy gazelles. But key to cheetahs' success is not just speed, but acceleration. From a standstill, cheetahs can reach speeds of 46 miles per hour (75 km/h) in just two seconds—so fast that human eyes just see a blur when a cheetah takes off. This is what gives cheetahs, and most cats, an edge on their slower prey.

Q: How far can cats jump?

A: Running in cats consists of a series of leaps. When a cat is running, there are stages when all feet are off the ground—when it is, however briefly, essentially sailing through the air. Leaping, or jumping, is the most typical movement of cats, and, propelled by relatively long, powerful hind legs and strong thigh muscles, some cats can leap lengths that Olympians would envy. A puma's record long jump, for instance, is nearly 40 feet (12 m), its high jump nearly 20 feet (6 m). Tigers are reported to jump 26–33 feet (8–10 m), aand snow leopards at least 20 feet (6 m).

Although not as astonishing as pumas and some other cats, domestic cats are

The world's fastest cats, cheetahs reach top speed in the blink of an eye, but cannot maintain that pace for long.

All cats are great long jumpers. A tiger can jump up to 33 feet, about three times its body length.

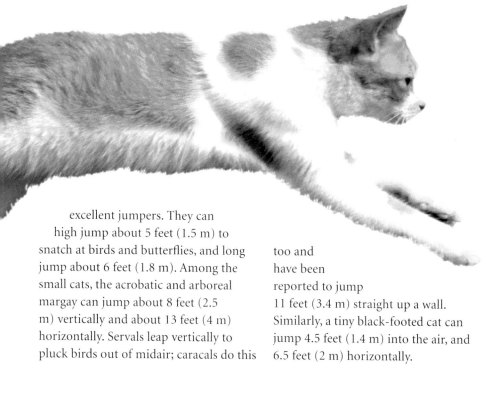

With each of the leaps that make up a run, a cat is briefly flying through the air.

excellent jumpers. They can high jump about 5 feet (1.5 m) to snatch at birds and butterflies, and long jump about 6 feet (1.8 m). Among the small cats, the acrobatic and arboreal margay can jump about 8 feet (2.5 m) vertically and about 13 feet (4 m) horizontally. Servals leap vertically to pluck birds out of midair; caracals do this too and have been reported to jump 11 feet (3.4 m) straight up a wall. Similarly, a tiny black-footed cat can jump 4.5 feet (1.4 m) into the air, and 6.5 feet (2 m) horizontally.

Careful Climbers

Q: How do cats climb?

Below: Climbing trees is natural for cats, which use their front claws like pitons to help scale vertical trunks.

Below right: Cheetahs' stiff legs make climbing difficult for them, but they can walk up a tree whose trunks and branches are more horizontal than vertical.

A: All cats, wild and domestic, can climb trees; one folktale claims that a cat's only trick is to climb a tree. Most adult tigers and lions are too heavy to climb easily and do so only when absolutely necessary. Cheetahs' tibia and fibula are bound together by fibrous tissue, an adaptation that gives stability to the leg. This means that they have little ability to rotate their legs or feet to grasp a branch, making climbing difficult, as it is for dogs. But other than these exceptions, cats in general are adept climbers. The anatomical features that let cats climb are similar to those used to bring down and hold struggling prey. As described by biologist Alan Turner, "A leopard climbing . . . proceeds with a series of bounds in which both forelimbs and both hind limbs act together. Lateral movements of the forelimbs are important, permitting the trunk to be grasped, while the hind limbs continue to move in line with the body. The muscles controlling flexion and extension of the spine are also very important during climbing." To climb a tree, cats rely on strong back muscles, strong hind feet, and splayed front toes tipped with curved claws that act as pitons (mountain-climbing spikes or pegs).

The hard part is getting back down, as anyone who has seen a domestic cat stuck in a tree knows. Leopards can run down trees, but with the exception of margays and clouded leopards, most other cats, including domestic cats,

cannot climb down headfirst, as tree squirrels do. For one thing, the ankles and toes on the hind limbs are less mobile, so most cats cannot grasp a limb with the hind paws. Neither can the claws help in descending headfirst because they are curved in the wrong direction. Therefore, if the cat cannot leap to the ground, it must descend feetfirst, basically sliding down the branch while it alternates limbs in disengaging the claws from the bark.

Q: **How do you rescue a treed cat?**

A: From time to time a domestic cat climbs a tree, either out of curiosity or fear, and then is afraid to climb back down. If your pet cat does this, the first thing for you to do is try to remove any threat, such as a barking dog, that may have driven the cat into the tree. Next, be patient and remain calm. A visibly upset owner may only add to the cat's fear. Most cats will eventually come down of their own volition, but if the cat remains reluctant, placing a favorite food item on or adjacent to the tree may encourage its descent. If time and hunger fail to lure the cat down, you may have to use a ladder to climb up and retrieve it, or call your local animal control officer for assistance. A cat left treed overnight is in danger of being preyed upon by owls and raccoons.

Above: Although climbing up a tree is easy for cats, the climb down is much more challenging.

Left: To encourage a treed cat to descend, take away the dog or other threat that sent it upwards in the first place.

The reason cats climb is so that they can look down on almost every other animal.

—*K. C. Buffington*

Life Span

Q: How long do cats live?

A: The expected life span of a domestic cat is between 9 and 15 years, but there is a poorly documented record for maximum longevity of 36 years, and a more reliable record of 34 years. Feral domestic cats have a much lower expected life span, as little as only two years. Not enough data exist for any wild cat species to compute average life expectancy, but few wild cats survive to adulthood, far less to old age. For example, tigers can live up to 15 years in the wild, but most do not. Only half of all cubs survive to the age when they become independent of their mothers. Only 40 percent of these survivors live to establish territories and begin to produce young. Among these territorial adults, the risk of death remains high. Among big cats, reported maximum longevities, mostly seen in zoo animals, are in the 20s—for instance, about 26 years for tigers, 22 for jaguars, more than 23 for leopards, and nearly 30 for lions. Records for other cats tend to fall in the high teens.

This cat, at 19 years of age, is very old, but in rare cases cats may live much longer.

Q: Do cats have nine lives?

A: This expression is based on both the domestic cat's amazing ability to escape from peril and the fact that in some religious traditions, a trinity of trinities was considered lucky and thus nine was associated with the lucky cat. Of course, cats' success as escape artists is a result of skill, not luck. Alert senses, speed and agility, quiet movement, and camouflage coats enable cats to disappear in the face of danger, if discretion is the better part of valor. If not, with powerful limbs, long claws, sharp canines, and swift attack capabilities, cats can put up fierce defenses.

Q: Do cats always land on their feet?

A: Domestic cats' reputation for having nine lives stems in part from their ability to survive long falls, and they, in fact, do this remarkably well.

In 1987, veterinarians at the Animal Medical Center in Manhattan tracked the survival rates of 115 domestic cats whose owners brought them in for treatment after the cats fell from high-rise apartment buildings. Of the 115 cats, which had hit the pavement after falling from 2 to 32 floors, an astonishing 90 percent survived. The most intriguing part of the results was that cats that fell from 7 to 32 stories were half as likely to die as cats that fell from 2 to 6 stories. Several factors account for both high survival rates after falls and even higher rates after falling greater distances.

First, cats have an excellent sense of balance and exhibit what is called a righting reflex. Like a gyroscope, a cat's inner ear detects its orientation in space. As a cat falls, this gyroscope tells the cat to straighten up, and it does so by twisting its body in one direction and its tail in another, then stretching its legs and reversing the twist. The stretched-out legs keep it from swinging back to the original rotation before its body and tail can twist in the opposite directions. This is repeated until the cat is right side up, usually within two to three feet (0.6–0.9 m). Thus cats land on their fronts, not their backs.

Second, a cat is relatively small. This means that its bones, relative to its body size, are actually stronger than those of larger animals and are thus less likely to break under stress. Small size and light weight also mean that cats fall more slowly than larger animals, and their maximum falling speed, known as terminal velocity, peaks at a slower speed. A cat's terminal velocity is about 60 miles per hour (96 km/h); a person's is about 120 miles per hour (193 km/h). Cats further reduce the impact by slowing their fall after reaching terminal velocity. To do this, cats relax and spread their legs widely, creating a parachutelike effect comparable to the gliding of flying squirrels; this also spreads the impact of the landing over a larger area. Finally, they land with legs flexed, not straight, which also reduces the force of the impact. This helps explain why longer falls may do less damage than shorter ones. Cats reach terminal velocity after about five floors, so if they land

sooner they do not have time to break their fall by parachuting or spreading the impact throughout their body. By seven floors, they have relaxed, stretched out, and flexed their legs, giving themselves the best physical conformation to reduce the risk of death.

There is, however, at least one flaw in the original Animal Medical Center study. The scientists measured mortality rates by looking at the survival of cats whose owners sought treatment. What of the unknown number of cats that fell from high-rises and died instantly or at least before any veterinary help was obtained? Moreover, many of these cats had serious injuries that may have been fatal without treatment.If these deaths could have been taken into account, the survival rate after falls would have dipped below 90 percent, but how far is unknown. This flaw, however, probably does not change the conclusion that cats can survive longer falls better than shorter ones.

Cats exhibit a "righting reflex" that gives them the ability to twist their bodies as they fall so that they tend to land on their feet.

In the Swim

Q: Can cats swim?

A: An old proverb says, "Never was a cat drowned that could see the shore." Domestic cats, and likely all species of cats, can swim. A few wild cat species live in harsh, dry environments with little free water available, but most live close to water, and water is an important part of their environment. Some seem fully at home in the water, even if they are not regularly observed using it.

Wild cats can be aligned along a continuum from those living with little or no water in their environment to those living with a good deal of water. At the driest end is the sand cat, which can live in true desert without any free water. The black-footed cat, Chinese desert cat, Pallas's cat, and Andean mountain cat live in very harsh, dry environments. Can they swim? Probably, but no one has reported seeing them doing so. Lions, which live in

Pumas live in diverse habitats, often near water, but seem to avoid immersing themselves in it.

As do many wild cats, tigers enjoy spending the hottest part of the day in cooling water.

habitats that range from dry to virtually waterless, are adept swimmers but, like domestic cats, prefer to avoid immersion. Pumas, which live in diverse habitats, are strong swimmers but seem merely to tolerate being in water.

Wildcats fall somewhere near the middle of this continuum, occupying diverse habitats across their ranges. In some areas they are associated with rivers and wetlands, in others they are not. But they do not seem to occupy the driest habitats, those that receive less than six inches (100 mm) of rainfall per year, unless watercourses flow through them. There are also no reported observations of wildcats swimming—although they most likely can—or of their resting or hunting in the water.

At the other end of the spectrum are cats that live in or even prefer wetland and riparian (riverside) habitats. These include fishing cats, flat-headed cats, and perhaps Geoffroy's cats, known in some parts of their South American range as fishing cats. Tigers and fishing cats are completely at home in thick mangrove

" The cat loves to fish, but she's loath to wet her feet. "

—*PROVERB*

forests that nearly flood twice a day from the tides. Tigers and ocelots rest in water to keep cool during the hottest part of the day. Tigers, fishing cats, and flat-headed cats are strong swimmers and even swim submerged, enabling them to grab prey, such as a floating duck, from underneath. Tigers have been found swimming far from shore, crossing tidal rivers more than three miles (5 km) wide. Jungle cats are also strong swimmers, often found in wetland habitats, where they may dive to catch fish in their mouths. The jaguarundi, a strong swimmer, is sometimes called an otter cat, while the leopard cat gets it species name, *bengalensis*, because the first one captured by Westerners was swimming in the Bay of Bengal. Jaguars, closely associated with streams and watercourses, are strong swimmers capable of crossing large rivers, and like tigers and ocelots may rest in streams in the heat of the day. Leopards, even those that live in arid environments, seem at ease in water. They play in water and swim well, even over distances of about 3,000 feet (900 m) or more.

Q: Why do domestic cats avoid immersing themselves in water?

A: Domestic cats are often fascinated by water dripping from a faucet or the sound and sight of a flushing toilet. Domestic cats are also often good fishers, scooping goldfish from small indoor bowls as well as large outdoor ponds. But rare is the domestic cat that dives in (as some of the wild cats mentioned above would do), and cats are

notorious for disliking a bath—although individual cats can get used to it. Their wildcat ancestors are not known to immerse themselves either, so the domestic cat's avoidance of water could have ancient origins. Another idea is that soaked fur has poor insulating ability; but this would only account for a cat's propensity to avoid immersion in cold weather. Cats of the Turkish Van breed are exceptions among domestic cats in their affection for water and are sometimes called "swimming cats." The texture of their fur makes it particularly water-resistant.

Although they do not like to immerse themselves in water, cats are attracted to dripping water.

Most domestic cats look bedraggled after a soaking dunk, and their wet fur may not insulate them against the cold.

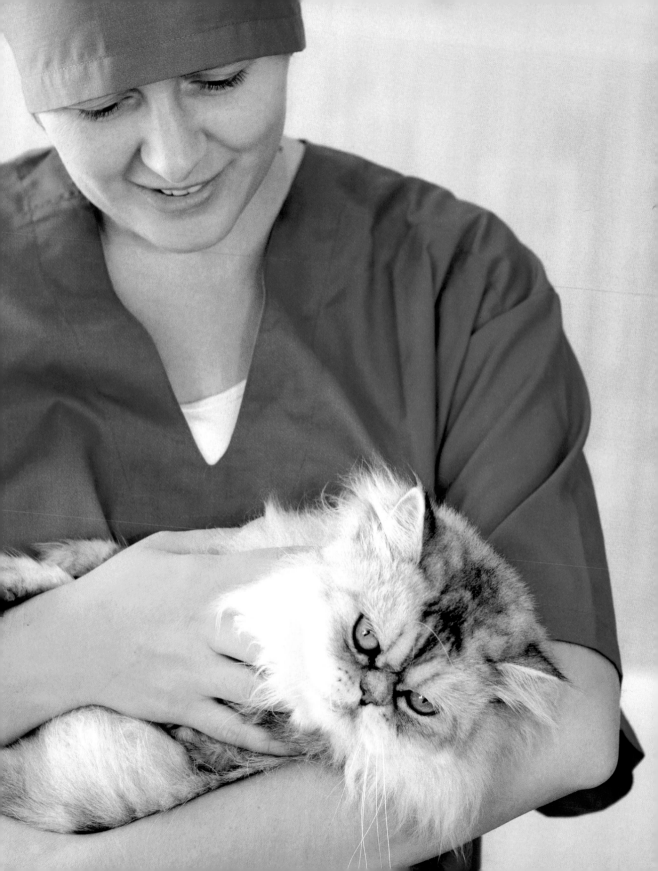

CHAPTER 10

IN SICKNESS AND IN HEALTH

Cats are generally robust and not delicate, as their sleek form might suggest. Yet, cats do get sick from time to time. Cats get internal and external parasites, catch viral and bacterial infectious diseases, and are attacked by various kinds of fungi. They can be ill from too much food and from nutritional deficiencies in their diet. Sometimes they are dealt a bad genetic hand and suffer a genetically based disease. The most important way to ensure your cat's good health is to feed it properly and to vaccinate it on the recommended schedule.

To further protect your cat's health, examine it while petting it each day, gently inspecting its ears and rear for discharges, and for any other general changes in body condition. A key early-warning signal that something is not right is when your cat's fur loses its sheen. If you suspect your cat is sick, consult your veterinarian. Never try to medicate it with over-the-counter human medications, because most, including aspirin and Tylenol, are poisonous to a feline. A trip to the vet once a year is smart maintenance. Your veterinarian may detect symptoms of chronic problems that you do not notice in your daily examination, especially if he or she can refer to your cat's long-term health record.

Above: Early signs of illness or abnormalities may be detected in a daily examination of your cat at home.

Left: An annual veterinary checkup will help ensure your cat's good health.

When Your Cat Gets Sick

There are many obvious signs that your cat may be sick; others, such as dull fur, are harder to spot.

Q: What are some signs of a sick cat?

A: You will know immediately that something is wrong with your cat if it has difficulty breathing, has a distended stomach, diarrhea, constipation, blood in the urine, if it strains to urinate, or is sneezing or coughing.

Yet, as any good predator does, cats tend to hide the symptoms of illness when they sense a decline in their own health. So the first thing your sick cat may do is find a secluded spot. Because each cat is different, owners must be on the alert for what is not normal for their individual cat. When your cat is listless, has obviously been in a fight or is injured, or simply looks bad, see the veterinarian.

As every owner knows, a cat sometimes has an "off day," and yet by the next day everything seems back to normal. We

A sick cat may hide to conceal signs of weakness that, in the wild, might make it a victim of competitors or predators.

may never know what the problem was, or even if there was a problem. When the off day extends to the next day, or beyond, it is time to make an appointment with your veterinarian. Because we live so closely with our pets, we know almost intuitively when ours is not normal. But defining what is "not normal" is a challenge. You may detect small warning signs of a problem before it shows any serious symptoms. For example, your cat may be sleeping in its usual sunny spot, but what catches your eye is its dull fur. You may hear a cough or sneeze in the night, or notice that it has left food in its bowl or not touched its last meal at all. It may be drinking more than usual, or be listless, or have watering, blurry eyes. It may be scratching and grooming itself more than usual, or be less agile. Your cat could have some less obvious problem that develops over time. Your pet's gums may become pale or blue, or either thinner or thicker than usual. If there are no evident reasons for any of these signs, it is time to go to the veterinarian.

Q: What is the normal body temperature of a cat?

A: The cat has a higher temperature than our 98.6°F (37°C). The cat's normal temperature ranges from 100.4°F (38°C) to 102.5°F (39.2°C). A cat's temperature is in the danger zone if it goes up to 105°F (40.6°C) and life threatening when it exceeds 108°F (42.2°C). Your otherwise friendly cat may resist having its temperature taken. You need to use a rectal human thermometer, not an oral one, because those are too thin-walled and likely to break. Coat the thermometer with some K-Y jelly and slowly and gently insert it into the cat's anus. Never try to take a cat's temperature orally; it will simply bite and shatter the thermometer. You can get a less accurate measure under the cat's forelegs or between the hind legs. The temperature of a cat's nose does not reveal anything about its health; that is a myth.

Above: A cat's normal body temperature is some two to three degrees higher than ours.

Below: A veterinarian will examine a cat from head to toe, looking for signs of anything out of the ordinary, just as a doctor would in a medical examination.

Cat Diseases

Q: **What are common diet-induced cat diseases?**

A: Obesity is the most common cat disease in the United States. Obese cats are at a high risk of developing diabetes mellitus and liver disease. Fat cats do not move enough and are likely to develop arthritis at an early age because their excessive weight stresses their joints and tendons. Fat cats may also have trouble reaching to groom themselves, which may lead to skin problems.

Right: Grooming is an important way cats keep their skin clean and healthy. When a cat grows obese, it may become difficult for it to complete this task effectively.

Below: An obese cat is destined to become a sick cat; keeping a cat fit is its owner's responsibility.

Other common diseases may result from poor nutrition. Diets deficient in essential vitamins such as thiamin (B_1) lead to neurological disorders, while those deficient in vitamin D cause rickets and osteomalacia, or bone softening. Too little vitamin E together with too much unsaturated fat in the diet leads to steatitis, or yellow fat disease. Diets deficient in calcium produce hyper-parathyroidism, leading to bone fractures. Taurine deficiency leads to central retinal degeneration. Providing a complete diet in the proper amounts to prevent obesity is the cat owner's primary responsibility.

Q: **Do cats suffer from genetically based diseases?**

A: Scientists have discovered nearly 260 genetic diseases in domestic cats, including diabetes, hemophilia, retinal degeneration, and spina bifida. This compares with about 450 canine genetic diseases. Many of these diseases can be prevented by not inbreeding cats.

Q: **What are some common infectious diseases of cats?**

A: Cat respiratory infections are caused by several different viruses or bacteria. The most common are feline rhinotracheitis virus (FRV), which is a herpesvirus, and feline calicivirus (FCV). Both of these are called "cat flu" because of their symptoms, which include runny nose, sneezing, fever, and loss of appetite;

but they are not usually fatal in domestic cats. There are vaccines available to prevent these diseases. Another cat flu, called feline pneumonitis, is caused by the bacterium *Chlamydia psittaci*. The primary symptom is conjunctivitis, or "pink eye." Humans may also be infected with chlamydia.

Feline infectious peritonitis (FIP) is caused by a coronavirus infection. Many coronaviruses infect cats, but most do not cause serious diseases. The mutant strain that causes FIP invades the white blood cells and spreads the virus through a cat's body. The immune response to the virus results in inflammation, and this interaction causes the disease. The cat's first exposure to FIP may result in mild symptoms or none at all. Weeks, months, or years later the disease flares up in a small percentage of infected animals, and death is inevitable. Young, old, or stressed cats are the most susceptible to the disease. Cats that succumb are often also infected with feline leukemia virus.

Scientists rate feline leukemia virus (FeLV) as the most dangerous fatal disease complex of American cats today. It occurs in three forms. One weakens the immune system, another causes cancerous tumors and abnormal growths, and the third causes severe anemia. FeLV kills more domestic cats each year than any other disease.

Feline panleukopenia virus (FPV), also known as feline infectious enteritis (FIE), or feline distemper, is a highly contagious viral disease usually transmitted through contact with other cats or their excretions. It is primarily a disease of kittens, and its symptoms are a sudden fever, loss of appetite, vomiting, and diarrhea. A vaccine is available to prevent FPV.

Above left: Cats suffer from several different types of respiratory infections or "flus." Recently, domestic cats have been reported for the first time to become infected and die of one strain of avian influenza, or "bird flu."

Above right: Kittens are especially susceptible to feline distemper.

Protecting Your Cat and Yourself

If a human fetus catches toxoplasmosis from its mother's contact with a cat carrying the parasite, miscarriage results.

A cat may bring home a blacklegged tick, which carries Lyme disease, but cats generally do not suffer from this disease.

Q: Can people catch diseases from coming into contact with cats?

A: Some of the viruses and bacteria that cause disease in cats also cause disease in people; however, of the more than 200 animal diseases communicable to people, called zoonoses, people are at risk of catching only a few from their cats. In a worst-case scenario, it is possible for a person to contract bubonic plague, anthrax, tularemia, salmonella, rabies, or tuberculosis from a cat.

Immune-depressed persons and women who are pregnant face the greatest risk of disease from a cat, or its ticks or parasites. Rabies is a risk that can be avoided by vaccinating your pet; an infected cat has to bite for you to contract rabies. Nonetheless, a person should be treated for tetanus after any animal bite. Cat-scratch disease is caused by a bacterium, *Afipia felis.* Sporotrichosis is also transmitted by a bite or scratch. There are certain diseases you could be exposed to when your cat brings home a mouse, such as hantavirus or plague, or from its ticks or fleas, such as Lyme disease or Rocky Mountain spotted fever. Q fever has recently been shown to be transmitted from cats to humans in Japanese urban areas. Cats can pass their ringworms (actually a fungus), tapeworms, and roundworms onto you as well, usually through your contact with soil the cat has infected with these parasites.

Q: What is toxoplasmosis?

A: Probably the most dangerous cat zoonosis is toxoplasmosis, which infects a human fetus through the mother's placenta and results in miscarriage. Cats are the only animal in which the protozoan parasite *Toxoplasma gondii* can complete its life cycle. Cats are infected through eating rodents and uncooked meat, and they shed the parasite in their feces. Infected kittens usually die, but older cats do not, and continue to shed parasites. Rodents infected with this parasite suffer from brain lesions and develop odd behaviors. Toxoplasmosis recently made it into the Pacific Ocean, where it killed hundreds of sea otters. Scientists suspect the source was flushable cat litter or runoff from feral cats. Some scientists believe that the brain lesions

Although flushable cat litter is convenient for owners to use, it may spread toxoplasmosis to coastal-living animals, such as sea otters, through discharge of wastewater into the ocean.

in humans caused by *Toxoplasma gondii* may cause schizophrenia and bipolar disorder. This has not been definitively established, but if initial findings are correct, then scientists may be able to develop a cure for a disease that affects 1 percent of the human population.

Vaccination prevents many common and dangerous diseases of cats, including rabies.

Q: What is a vaccination and for what diseases do you vaccinate a cat?

A: Protecting your cat through vaccination is essential. When you vaccinate your cat, its immune system is stimulated to recognize and respond to an infectious agent, thus dampening or eliminating its harmful effects. This internal body process is called immunization. The duration of immune responsiveness varies with the infectious agent and the vaccine used.

Vaccines are created in different ways. If the infectious agent has been treated so it can no longer infect or replicate in your cat's body, it is called an inactivated vaccine. These are safe but take longer to immunize your cat, and the immunization usually is effective for shorter periods. Attenuated or modified live vaccines are composed of viruses that have been treated to prevent them from producing clinical disease. The viruses do reproduce, however, and there is a rapid immune response developed in the cat's body, but the vaccinated cat can shed the virus and, in some cases, infect other cats. This vaccine should not be administered to a pregnant cat. Subunit vaccines have some of the infectious agent in them but not the whole virus; they are regarded as safe. A new class of vaccines is being genetically engineered, and we will see increased use of them in the future.

Your veterinarian will provide you with the recommended schedule for the various vaccines necessary to protect your cat from certain diseases. For each disease agent there may be several different vaccines. You should wait until a kitten is two months old to vaccinate it. Before that age, it has acquired an immune response through its mother's colostrum and milk, and this will render a vaccination ineffective. The typical list of feline vaccinations includes those for feline panleukopenia (FP), feline viral rhinotracheitis (FVR), feline calicivirus (FCV), chlamydiosis, rabies, feline leukemia virus (FeLV), and feline infectious peritonitis (FIP).

Cat AIDS and Allergies

Scientists recently found that cats get a disease very similar to human HIV/AIDS.

Some people are allergic to a certain protein in cat saliva, and many people become allergic with long exposure to cats.

Q: Do cats get AIDS?

A: Cats do not get human HIV/AIDS, but they have their own closely related form of the disease, feline immuno-deficiency virus (FIV). FIV follows a very similar course in its felid victims to that of HIV/AIDS in humans, but affects only cats. Because it is similar to FeLV, this virus went undetected as a unique disease agent for some time until it was discovered in domestic cats in California during the late 1980s. It is now thought that up to 3 percent of the domestic cats in the United States are infected with this fatal domestic cat disease. Interestingly, many wild cat strains of FIV do not appear to cause immunodeficiency, suggesting a natural selection for genetic resistance to the fatal virus.

Q: What causes some people to be allergic to cats?

A: Many people are said to be allergic to cats. They are not allergic to the whole cat but to a protein called Fel d 1 found in a cat's saliva and sebaceous glands, the simple saclike structures attached to the hair follicles. This protein is actually part of the cat's secretory immune system, but when it affects a person it is called an allergen. When a cat grooms itself, its hair and skin become coated with this protein, which is subsequently shed as dander and inhaled by anyone in the environment. Human allergic reactions range from itchy eyes, runny noses, and sneezing to life-threatening asthma attacks. Cat allergies are common around the world. An estimated 5 to 10 percent of people in the United States suffer from cat allergies, and nearly a third of people who work with cats in laboratories develop allergies.

Not all cats are equal when it comes to triggering allergic reactions. In one study, scientists rated a person's response to cat dander as severe symptoms, moderate symptoms, mild symptoms, or no symptoms. Human subjects with dark-colored cats were two to four times

more likely to report severe or moderate symptoms than those with light-colored cats or no cats. There was no difference in the symptoms for subjects who had light-colored cats and those with no cats. The conclusion was that dark cats produce greater amounts of Fel d 1.

may include diarrhea and vomiting. Hypersensitivity rashes, caused by rubbing against certain plants and sometimes against rubber and plastic dishes, occur in cats. An extreme response to an allergen is sometimes seen in cats, during which the cat's airways and the blood vessels in the lungs constrict. The treatment is an injection of epinephrine, but anaphylaxis, a severe systemic reaction, happens within minutes of contact with the allergen, and the cat may not survive long enough to get to veterinary care. People allergic to bee stings suffer anaphylaxis, too.

Black and dark-furred cats cause stronger allergic symptoms in human than lighter-colored ones.

Q: Do cats have allergies?

A: Allergies are a disorder of the immune system, and the antigen, or substance that causes an allergic reaction, can be ingested (food allergies), inhaled, touched, or obtained from fleas. In many instances, exposure to an antigen results in a skin allergy, and the cat scratches itself desperately to relieve the irritation. Some cats are genetically disposed to a condition called atopy, in which a cat becomes increasingly sensitive to inhaled substances such as house dust, pollen, and molds. This results in thinning fur and excessive licking and chewing.

Some cats have a hypersensitivity to certain foods such as fish, liver, or dairy products. Sometimes the reaction is similar to that caused by atopy, but it

Cats, just as humans, can develop allergies to certain foods, inhaled substances, plants, or other things in their environments.

Cat Parasites and Other Surprises

Cats may be infected by a flea unique to cats as well as by dog and human fleas.

Q: Do cats have external parasites?

A: Ticks, fleas, lice, mites, and other external parasites, called ectoparasites, plague cats as well as all other mammals. Ectoparasites cause tissue damage and inflammation of the cat's skin. The cat responds with excessive scratching. Mites, which are related to spiders, are microscopic in size, and different mite species produce several different skin symptoms, all of which are commonly referred to as mange. Treatment is frequently a parasiticidal dip or washing with special shampoos.

Ticks are not as troublesome for cats as they are for dogs and humans, but outdoor cats are likely to acquire them. Care should be taken when you remove a tick to be sure that all of the buried head is extracted. Cats have their own louse species, *Felicola subrostratus*, which feeds on exfoliated skin. A cat has to get its lice from another cat, directly, or indirectly by lying on the other's bed, for example.

Fleas are by far the most common external parasite that cats endure, especially in warm climates. Cats have their own flea,

Cats and dogs that live together may share parasites, such as fleas.

Ctenocephalides felis, but fleas are not host specific, and cats can be infected by dog fleas and by human fleas. Some cats are hypersensitive to the flea salivary antigens. You should consult your veterinarian for tick and flea treatment, because new products to manage them continue to be developed.

Occasionally, a cat will become infected with fly larvae, or maggots, a condition called myiasis. Watch for this in an outdoor cat that has a cut or bite wound. Fungal diseases (including yeasts and molds) are of concern for the cat, and ringworm (caused by dermatophytes) is the most common fungal disease of cats. It is highly contagious and must be treated. Toxoplasmosis and leishmaniasis are two internal protozoan infections that can also cause skin lesions in cats.

Q: Do cats have internal parasites?

A: Cat owners are generally shocked to discover a long segment of a tapeworm (cestode) or a roundworm (nematode) in their cat's feces. These internal parasites affect all mammals, including humans. Single-celled protozoa, including *Giardia* and *Trichomonas*, are transmitted from one cat to another and live in the cat's intestinal tract. *Trypanosoma* and *Leishmania* are protozoa that are transmitted by infected insects and live in various cells within the cat's body. Both are potential contributors to diseases in humans. The protozoan *Cryptosporidium parvum* lives in the small intestine of its host but is spread by passing oocysts (encapsulated eggs) in the feces and is transmitted to other hosts through contaminated water. The very dangerous protozoan *Toxoplasma gondii* is discussed earlier in this chapter.

The cat's roundworms include its own named species (*Toxocara catii*) and hookworms (*Ancylostoma*). The lungworm (*Aelurostrongylus abstrusus*) threads itself through lung tissue. Cats can also become infected by the heartworm *Dirofilaria immitis*. Tapeworms are long and segmented. They do not have their own gut and instead absorb their nutrients directly through the surfaces of their bodies. Their front section is called a scolex, or holdfast, by which they

anchor themselves to a host's gut mucosa, the moist tissue that lines particular organs and body cavities. The most common tapeworm infecting cats is *Dipylidium caninum,* which can grow to two feet in length inside a cat's intestine. Gastrointestinal parasites deprive the cat of its nutrition and its good health by causing diarrhea, dehydration, vomiting, and anemia. They weaken its immune system, making it more susceptible to viral and bacterial infections.

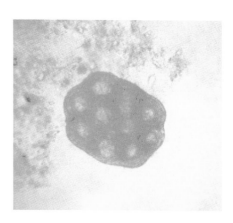

A cat ingests the eggs of tapeworms found in soil, which then develop in the cat's gut and rob the cat of nutrition.

Termatodes, or flukes, that infect cats and humans in the Far East include some schistosome species that enter the body by directly penetrating the skin. In the United States, cats become infected with the liver fluke *Platynosomum concinnum*, which lives in the cat's bile ducts, by eating infected lizards. A high proportion of cats living in southern climates are infected with this fluke.

All of these internal parasites need to be treated, but it is a constant effort because your cat will usually continue to come into contact with a parasite's source populations. Although there are over-the-counter medications for some, you should consult your veterinarian for the most parasite-specific advice available.

> Which came first the intestine or the tapeworm?
>
> —WILLIAM S. BURROUGHS

CATS AND PEOPLE

No group of animals compels more interest and fascination from people than do cats. Our relationship with them, whether predatory tigers or purring house cats, is ancient and universal. According to Greek legend, the Sun god Apollo created the lion and his twin sister, Diana, who was identified with the Moon, fashioned a miniature copy of it—the cat—to ridicule him. This legend shows that people have long recognized the similarity of lions and small cats, despite their enormous size disparity, and it suggests that part of the appeal of domestic cats is that they symbolize mastering the awesome big cats. The legend also encapsulates cats as symbols of Sun and Moon, good and evil, life giver and life taker. Cats have long appeared in the art and literature, myths, and religious beliefs of people around the globe. They have been worshipped as gods, vilified as the agents of evil, envied as symbols of freedom from the constraints of society. In the modern world, they are used in advertising to market diverse products and are popular characters in films, books, and cartoons. And, for better or for worse, people use cats as pest controllers, sources of food and fur, and as subjects in scientific studies to better understand human biology.

Above: At various points in history, cats have been vilified as agents of evil and worshipped as gods.

Left: Humans have a history of developing long-standing, powerful, and sometimes mysterious relationships with cats.

Cats in Culture

Q: What roles did cats play in different early cultures throughout the world?

A: Everywhere that wild cats are found, people have incorporated them symbolically into their culture, as creatures to worship, as symbols of gods and rulers, and as totems or protectors. But most often, the cats so featured were the big cats—lions, tigers, or jaguars, depending on geography. In Europe, Africa, and parts of Asia, lions represent power and strength and serve as protectors of sacred buildings, while tigers and jaguars play similar roles in much of Asia and South America, respectively. Leopards and pumas were also important in some places, while the Eurasian lynx was associated with Freya, the goddess of love and beauty in Norse mythology. Only in the culture and religion of ancient Egypt did domestic cats achieve significant ascendancy over their bigger relatives. The religious practices and beliefs of ancient Egypt were complex and changed

The Eurasian lynx was associated with Freya, the goddess of love and beauty in Norse mythology.

The Norse goddess Freya in a chariot pulled by cats; cats of various species are often depicted as magical transporters of gods and goddesses.

over the thousands of years spanning the reign of the pharaohs. As early as 2300 BCE, people wore charms in the shape of cats to deflect evil. Later, cats, particularly male cats, were associated with or represented the Sun god, Ra. In one rendering, Ra had to fight a battle with the power of darkness every day. Darkness was embodied in a serpent, so Ra daily turned himself into a tomcat—an animal well known as a snake killer. A destructive lion-headed goddess, Sekhmet, and a benevolent cat-headed goddess, Bastet, are sometimes named as daughters of Ra, although other accounts depict Bastet as being lion-headed before her transformation into a cat.

The cult of Bastet is most famously associated with the worship of cats in Egypt. It began

many were sacrificed as offerings. Cats are almost always present in artistic representations of everyday life in Egypt.

This granite statue depicts Sekhmet, the destructive lion-headed goddess of ancient Egypt.

Q: What are cat mummies?

A: Just as Egyptians mummified the bodies of loved ones before burying them for their entry into the afterlife, so did they mummify their cats. At first, this was relatively uncommon, the prerogative of the wealthy, who often had their cats buried with them. Later, millions of cats were killed and mummified as votive offerings to Bastet. Votive offerings were essentially bribes—a way to get Bastet to look favorably on one's prayers by using a dead, or ghost, cat as an intermediary. As this practice grew in popularity, temple priests turned creating cat mummies for people to purchase as votive offerings into big business, with mummies created on a near-industrial scale, filling vast cat cemeteries. Some of these mummies show evidence of shoddy workmanship, or even fraud—some "cat" mummies contain the bones of frogs and other animals. In many other cases, cats were mummified with every bit as much care as people were—evidence of Egyptians' respect and affection for cats.

Bastet, Egypt's benevolent cat goddess, represented much that is good in life, including motherhood and home.

about 950 BCE, when she was made the chief goddess, and lasted at least until the fifth century BCE. Bastet reigned over motherhood, fertility, female sexuality, and the home, so cats represented much that was pleasant in life. (Later, among Europeans, some of these same qualities contributed to cats' reputation as evil.) Cats were kept in sacred temples with worshipful attendants, but also in the homes of ordinary people who cherished them as pets. It was a capital crime to take a cat out of Egypt, or kill one, although

Cats as Evil

Q: Why are some cats, especially black cats, associated with witches?

A: Although we think of black cats and witches as natural companions, this was not always so. Witches were believed to turn themselves into a variety of animals when conducting evil deeds, or to have an animal companion—a familiar—that carried out their mischief. In England, for instance, the original witch's

Black cats have been associated with Satan and with witches, which led to their being persecuted in Europe.

familiar was a hare, associated with Eostre, a pagan fertility goddess, according to medieval chronicles. Like cats, hares are nocturnal, elusive creatures; like hares, cats were pagan symbols of female fertility and sexuality. This last may help account for singling out cats for opprobrium. The early Catholic Church sought to eliminate all vestiges of pagan belief; the Church also condemned the female sexuality that cats symbolize. Affection for a cat was in itself suspect. Cats' aloof indifference to people, their refusal to recognize people as masters, violated the natural order— God gave people dominion over animals, and thus cats, with their secretive ways, must be on the side of Satan.

From the twelfth century through the fourteenth, the Church accused heretics of worshipping Satan in the guise of a large black cat, and, later, witches were accused of flying to their nocturnal meetings on the backs of large black cats.

But during the heyday of European witch persecution, in the 1500s and 1600s, legal records show that association with cats of any color, as well as with dogs, mice, toads, lambs, rabbits, and polecats, might cause a woman to be accused as a witch. Cats were typecast in the role of witch's companion only when witchcraft became the stuff of literature, and writers found cats more attractive as familiars than other small animals. And, by the 1800s, when belief in witchcraft was largely a thing of the past, witches and their cats began to acquire an exotic allure.

Q: Why were cats sometimes persecuted?

A: Apart from their association with witches and Satanic forces, for centuries cats were the pets of the poor: Compared to dogs, they required no extra feeding, demanded no special care, and performed a useful service. Moreover, while dogs were admired for their subservience to people, cats were disliked for their lack of it. Depicted in paintings, a cat represented greed and a threat to domesticity. Cats were casually persecuted and tortured with shocking indifference, both officially—they were burned alive inside an effigy of the pope during Elizabeth I's coronation—and at the hands of small

Popular culture images often depict witches flying at night in the company of cats. In fact, a witch's "familiar" may also be a hare or any number of other small animals.

For centuries, cats were the pets of the poor because these independent animals demanded no special care and required no additional feeding.

boys who might fling them from windows or tie two together by the tails in order to watch them fight. Even influential naturalists reviled cats. In 1607, Edward Topsell, in *The History of Four-footed Beasts and Serpents and Insects,* portrayed cats as dangerous beasts with venomous teeth and poisonous flesh that cause illness, and joined in branding them as familiars of witches.

The Romantic movement, which began in the late 1700s, changed all that. Romantics glorified wild, untamed nature, and suddenly the cat became the dog's superior. Dogs were denigrated for their servility; cats were celebrated for their insistence on freedom. A greater appreciation for cats finally led to the creation of breeding societies in the late 1800s, when, for the first time, cats were valued enough to be shown by the wealthy and bred for desirable and attractive traits.

In ancient times cats were worshipped as gods; they have not forgotten this.

—*Terry Pratchett*

The Uses of Cats

This dozing cat is "guarding" a library. Some librarians welcome cats, which kill mice that munch on books.

Q: What practical uses do people have for domestic cats?

A: The domestic cat is well known and much admired as a rodent killer around farms and even in urban and suburban environments. But cats have also performed this function is some less well-known places. "Refrigerator cats," also called Eskimo cats, were a breed developed in the nineteenth century to thrive in the icy temperatures of commercial refrigeration plants and combat the rats that had already adapted to the frigid temperatures. Cats are still welcomed in some libraries, where mice are apt to nibble on books. An organization called the Library Cat Society keeps track of library cats around the world. As of 2005, the society reported 170 resident library cats; although many of these are actually statues or stuffed animals, some are living, working cats, often strays adopted by a librarian.

Although the trading of domestic cat fur has been banned in many places, a large market still exists for cat fur, which can be fashioned into coats, hats, and gloves and is often labeled as rabbit fur.

Q: Do people wear domestic cat fur?

A: Although the thought is abhorrent to those who love cats, there is a very large market for domestic cat fur, although it is often labeled as rabbit fur. The fur is fashioned into coats, hats, and gloves and used as trim for various garments. Cat skin is also used to make drums. China and a few other Asian countries are the source of a significant proportion of the cat fur that is in trade. Many cats are raised on "farms" in northern China, where the cold climate results in lush fur; others are raised by individuals who then sell the fur and skin in the market. During the annual cat slaughter season, an estimated half million cats are killed each year in China alone, while the Humane Society of the United States estimated the total international trade at about two million cats annually. In the United States, the Dog and Cat Protection Act of 2000 banned the import, export, or sale of products containing cat or dog fur, and many European nations as well

as Australia and a few Asian countries now have similar laws pertaining to trade in domestic cat fur. Deceptive labeling, however, and dying the fur, which makes it hard to tell cat fur from other legally traded fur, make enforcement of these laws spotty. Banning the trade in domestic cat fur was done on humane grounds; these cats are often maintained under terrible conditions before being cruelly slaughtered or even skinned alive. Illegal trade in the skins of wild cats, however, threatens to push some species, such as tigers, to extinction.

Q: Do people ever eat cats?

A: Cats, wild or domestic, do not form a significant part of the human diet anywhere, but some people do eat cats at times. In China, domestic and wild cats form part of the cuisine of the southeastern Guangdong province. One famous dish called "dragon and tiger head" is actually a stew of snake and domestic cat. Some Australian Aboriginals are reported to eat feral cats as a source of meat. People who would otherwise shun dining on cats have resorted to eating them in desperate times, when other food was unavailable. Like their fur, the meat of domestic cats is sometimes advertised as rabbit or hare. This must not have been an uncommon practice among unscrupulous people in at least some parts of the world. The Spanish idiomatic expression *"Pasar gato por liebre"* means "to pass a cat off as a hare" and is equivalent in meaning to the English expression "to pull the wool over his eyes." Parts of domestic cats, such as bones, are also ingredients in Asian folk medicine, often as substitutes for more difficult to procure tiger bones. Prescriptions involving cat parts were also part of European folk medicine.

Bones and other parts of tigers are in demand for use in traditional Asian medicine. Although this trade is illegal, there is a large black market in these products that threatens to doom tigers to extinction.

Inspiration and Superstition

Superstitions about black cats abound, but they are considered bad luck in some cultures and good luck in others.

Q: **What are some cat proverbs, expressions, and metaphors?**

A: Feline references abound in proverbs, as well as in literary metaphors and poetry. So familiar and apt are the proverbs that we do not even stop to think about what they really mean. "A cat among the pigeons," "a cat-and-mouse game," "enough to make a cat laugh," and "when the cat's away, the mice will play" do not need explanation to anyone who knows anything about cats. The meaning of calling the overcomfortable wealthy "fat cats" or a person "catty" is unmistakable, and it would take a dozen or more words to express either idea in any other way. Other proverbs are more obscure. "To let the cat out of the bag" comes from the eighteenth century, when shady dealers would put a cat in a bag and try to sell it as a piglet. Letting the cat out of the bag exposed the scam.

In the Tennessee Williams play *Cat on a Hot Tin Roof*, the sly female protagonist Maggie compares herself to a cat, priding herself on her ability to get out of difficult situations unharmed.

Sounding envious, Scottish poet Alistair Reed likens human freedom and curiosity to that of cats:

Imagination prowls at night,
cat-like, among odd possibilities.
Only our dog-sense brings us
faithfully home,

But every night, outside, cat voices call
us out to take a chance, to leave
the safety of our baskets and to let
what happens happen.

Q: **What are some superstitions about cats?**

A: Superstitions arise when some event is coincidentally associated with another several times and people mistake that for cause and effect. Given the abundance of cats, it is not surprising that both good and misfortune might often befall people in the presence of cats. Black cats have signified bad luck for centuries, and even today superstitious Americans consider a black cat crossing their path bad luck. In Britain, however, this is a sign of good luck, based on the idea that evil has passed you by; and in many other contexts, such as on ships and backstage at a theater, cats are good luck. A cat on stage, however, is bad luck.

A cat washing its face is sometimes believed to predict either fair weather or an impending storm.

to allergies, black cats may indeed be unlucky. Finally, many superstitions about cats relate to the idea that cats can predict the weather. For instance, a cat washing its face predicts good weather, or is a sign of rain, as is a cat sneezing or scratching a table leg. A behavior a cat performs all the time and that predicts both good and bad weather (or good and back luck) is correct half the time, a good basis for the development of superstitions. Some speculate, however, that cats' sensitivity to vibrations and to sounds beyond our hearing may enable them to detect coming storms or earthquakes. This hypothesis is attractive until you consider the number of other animals believed to be able to predict the weather. For instance, a whistling parrot, a hooting owl, a quacking duck, a sitting cow, and a noisy sparrow all are said to predict rain.

Other superstitions about cats relate to their effect on human health. Cats were once believed to cause rheumatism and tuberculosis. People still keep cats away from babies, believing that cats suffocate them or suck their breath out. These beliefs may have some basis in the fact that many people are allergic to cats, or, more specifically, to a protein called Fel d 1 found in saliva and sebaceous glands. Dark and black cats may produce more of the Fel d 1 allergen than cats with paler fur, so for people susceptible

Below left: The superstition that cats can kill human infants by sucking their breath away means many cat owners keep their cats and their babies apart.

Below right: Owls, parrots, ducks, and cows are among the other animals believed to be able to predict the weather.

What's in a Name?

Q: What does the cat's scientific name, *Felis catus*, mean?

A: The genus name *Felis* comes from the Latin word *feles*, which means "cat," "wild cat," or "marten." *Catus* is a Latin form of very many similar words for cat in European languages. Carolus Linnaeus, who invented modern scientific nomenclature that gives each species a unique two-word name that includes the genus and species, essentially called this common animal "cat cat." The wildcat relative of *Felis catus* is *Felis silvestris. Silvestris* means "of the forest," which describes the habitat of the European wildcat.

Q: What are "ailurophobia" and "ailurophilia"?

Above right: The scientific name of the giant panda, *Ailuropoda melanoleuca,* means "black-and-white cat-foot," although pandas are actually bears.

Below: An ailurophile is one who loves cats.

A: The word *ailouros* is of unknown origin, but it may be from the Greek for "tail waver"—referring to cats as well as other small predators such as ferrets. Combined with the Greek word for fear, *phobia,* it means a morbid fear of cats. An ailurophobe is a person who loathes cats. Combining *ailouros* with a form of the Greek word *philos,* or loving, ailurophilia means being fond of cats; an ailurophile is one who loves cats. The word also appears in scientific names. *Proailurus* is the genus name for the dawn cat, the oldest fossil cat

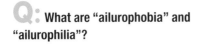

known; another early cat is *Pseudoailuria.* Among modern mammals, the scientific names of both giant pandas, *Ailuropoda melanoleuca,* which means "black-and-white cat-foot," and red pandas, *Ailurus fulgens,* or "shining red" cat, retain forms of *ailouros,* although neither animal is a member of the family Felidae.

Q: What are cats called in languages other than English?

A: According to the *Oxford English Dictionary,* the word "cat" is of unknown origin. It may be from similar Arabic words for this animal, such as *quttah* and *qutt,* or from a north African language, such as Nubian, where the word is *kadis.* "Cat" and variants of this word are found in modern European languages as far back as records go. It appears in Greek as *gata* and in Latin as *catus* or *cattus* between the first and fourth century, although Latin also had another word for cats, *feles,* as described above. Egyptian also has two

Q: Where do the words "kitten" and "pussycat" come from?

A: "Kitten" is a modern English spelling of a French word for a young cat, *chaton*, a diminutive form of the French word for cat, *chat*. "Puss" or "pussycat" comes from Teutonic languages, such as Dutch, in which the word for cat is *poes*. But according to the *Oxford English Dictionary*, "puss" along with its variants was not originally synonymous with cat, but rather was a sound used to call a cat. From this, puss became a pet name for a cat, later replaced with the more affectionate-sounding "pussy."

Ailurus fulgens, the scientific name of the red panda, means "shining red cat," but red pandas are not closely related to cats.

words for cat, *kut* and *mau*. *Mau* may be imitative of a cat's meow call, and similar words for cat appear in other languages, such as *meo* in Thai.

WORDS FOR CAT SIMILAR IN SOME OTHER LANGUAGES

Armenian: *gatz/ gadoo*

Basque: *catua/ catus*

Bulgarian: *kotka*

Finnish: *katti*

French: *chat*

Nubian: *kadis*

Polish: *kot*

Spanish: *gato*

Turkish: *keti*

Yiddish: *kats*

WORDS FOR CAT DIFFERENT IN SOME OTHER LANGUAGES

Arabic: *biss*

Chinese: *miu/ mio/mao*

Dutch: *poes*

Hindi: *billy*

Indochinese: *puss*

Japanese: *neko*

Rumanian: *pisica*

Swahili: *paka*

Thai: *meo*

Vietnamese: *meo*

Although the word *ailouros* is of unknown origin, it may be from the Greek for "tail waver."

Cats and Science

Q: **What have scientists learned by studying cats?**

A: Although using live animals such as cats in research is controversial, scientific studies using feline subjects

have considerably advanced our understanding of diverse aspects of human biology.

For example, in 1981, Neuro-biologists David H. Hubel and Torsten N. Wiesel won the Nobel Prize in Physiology and Medicine for work that elucidated the structure of the primary visual cortex of the brain. They discovered, among

Above: Although animal research remains controversial, scientific studies using cats as subjects have helped advance our understanding of human biology.

Right: Cats have binocular vision and are good models for understanding the human visual system.

other findings, that there is a critical period in early life for the development of visual pathways from retina to cortex; if stimuli are blocked during this period, permanent visual impairment will result. Hubel and Wiesel undertook much of their ground-breaking work in this field using domestic cats as subjects. Cats are good models for understanding the human visual system because, like us, cats have binocular vision. Hubel and Wiesel shared the Nobel Prize that year with Roger W. Sperry, who also used cats in his studies of the relation-ship between the two hemispheres of the brain. And six other Nobel Prizes have been awarded to scientists who studied cats to gain a better understanding of the nervous system.

The knowledge that calico cats, with their black and orange splotches of fur, are almost always female, and

that coat color in cats resides on the X chromosome, inspired British geneticist Mary Lyon's discovery that one of the X chromosomes in each cell of a female mammal is turned off, but not every cell turns off the same one. In the calico cat, this leads to a mosaic of cells, some with genes that code for black fur and others that code for orange.

Domestic cats suffer and die of a virus, feline immunodeficiency virus (FIV), very similar to the HIV virus that causes AIDS in humans, providing the only natural model in which to study this disease. Using insights gained from studies of cats with FIV, scientists are looking for ways to prevent AIDS.

Scientists at the National Cancer Institute, led by Stephen O'Brien, are in the process of mapping the entire genome (genetic code) of the domestic cat, which will provide a powerful model for the study of human hereditary and infectious diseases.

Studies of domestic cats are also helping scientists to better understand the physiology and behavior of wild cats, critical information they can use to help conserve the many threatened and endangered wild felid species. For example, scientists learned to successfully artificially inseminate domestic cats before applying the same technique to augment zoo populations of cheetahs. Controversially, domestic cats have now been successfully cloned, and the techniques have been used to clone African wildcats and caracals.

Above: Scientists learned to artificially inseminate domestic cats before applying the technique to cheetahs.

Left: The splotches of different-colored fur seen in calico cats, which are almost always female, result from certain genes on the X chromosome in each cell of a female cat coding for black fur and others coding for orange.

CHAPTER 12

WILD CATS

Wild cats can be found virtually the world over. Only Australia, Antarctica, and a few isolated islands lack native wild cats. Because humans have left domestic cats nearly everywhere they have traveled, feral domestic now inhabit nearly everywhere as well. The center of felid diversity and abundance is Asia, home to 22 species. Africa claims 9 species and South America 12. Europe has only 3 species, while North America north of Mexico now has 4 (puma, bobcat, Canada lynx, and a small population of ocelots

in Texas). For all their fundamental similarities to domestic cats, wild cats are marvelously diverse. Some are fishers while others specialize in eating hares and rabbits. Most hunt on the ground, but two are true acrobats comfortable hunting in trees. Their habitats range from hot, humid tropical rain forests to deserts to cold northern forests and windswept high mountains. Unfortunately, all wild cats are in more or less danger of extinction, largely because of human activities. The legions of people who love their domestic cats can help change that grim outlook for their pets' wild relatives.

Above: The small ocelot of Mexico and Central and South America is just one of the 40 diverse species of wild cats.

Left: The Eurasian lynx is one of the world's many geographically wide-ranging medium-sized cats.

Small Wild Cats of Asia

True to their name, adaptable, sturdy fishing cats catch and dine on fish and other animals that live in water.

Q: **What are some small Asian wild cats?**

A: The nearest wild relatives of domestic cats are six species that live in Africa and parts of Eurasia (see "What species are the closest relatives of domestic cats?"). Asia is also home to another six species of small cats in the leopard cat lineage, which is a near relative to the domestic cat, or felis, lineage. All of these cats are spotted.

Both the rusty-spotted cat and the flat-headed cat are tiny. Adult rusty-spotted cats may weigh only a little more than two pounds (1 kg), while flat-headed cats range from about three to five pounds (1.4–2.2 kg). Little is known about either of them. Rusty-spotted cats live on the island of Sri Lanka (at the southern tip of the Indian subcontinent) and in parts of India, while the flat-headed cat is confined to southern Thailand, Malaysia, Borneo, and Sumatra. Both eat the usual small-cat fare of small mammals, birds, reptiles, and amphibians. Rusty-spotted

cats include large insects in their diets, and flat-headed cats eat fish and are closely associated with water.

Leopard cats and Iriomote cats are reported to eat both fish and insects along with the usual feline fare. Leopard cats have a very large Asian distribution and range in size from less than 7 pounds (3 kg) on the island of Borneo to as large as 22 pounds (10 kg) in the Russian Far East. The very closely related Iriomote cat (some scientists consider them to be the same species) lives only on a single Japanese island near Taiwan; fewer than 100 of these cats exist.

Fishing cats, as their name implies, include fish and other aquatic vertebrates in their diets and even dive into the water to catch their prey. These are robust cats, with the largest males reaching 33 pounds (15 kg), and seem fairly adaptable. They live in Southeast and South Asia, including on the island of Sri Lanka, where they even live in wet habitats within big cities.

Found only on a single Japanese island, the Iriomote cat is rare and endangered while its closest relative, the leopard cat, is widespread and fairly common.

Pallas's cat, named after German naturalist Peter Pallas, is the most unusual cat in this group, with its short legs and long, thick, pale gray fur. Also called the manul or rock wildcat, it lives in harsh semideserts and rocky steppes of central Asia. Its squat body is adapted to climbing on rocks. This cat tolerates both hot and very cold weather but does not live where snow accumulates deeply because deep snow hinders its movements. Pallas's cat feeds on rodents, pikas, partridges, and hares.

Three other small cats of Asia form yet another lineage, called the bay cat lineage. The bay cat, which weighs less than about 22 pounds (10 kg), is probably the rarest cat in the world. It lives only on the island of Borneo, where it is apparently restricted to rain forest. The bay cat is know from only a few museum specimens and very few others that have been captured and photographed, or caught in a camera trap. There are none living in zoos. Biologists believe that it has always been very rare. Just across the way, on the island of Sumatra, biologists regularly see and camera trap its slightly larger close relative, the Asian golden cat, which may also be found in various kinds of forest in other parts of South and Southeast Asia. Little is know about these cats, but they are likely terrestrial hunters. The marbled cat is the third member of this lineage and equally mysterious. A very small cat at 4.5 to 11 pounds (2–5 kg), it lives only in Southeast Asian rain forests and is thought to be arboreal. Its tail is very long, and it has large feet for its size.

Like its relatives, the bay cat and marbled cat, the Asian golden cat is little known but it is seen much more often than these other rarer, more secretive cats.

More Small Wild Cats

Q: What are some small wild cats of South America?

A: Nine species of small, spotted cats, all closely related, live in various parts of South America, with a few ranging through Central America and into northern Mexico. Ocelots are the best known of the cats in this group, so scientists call this the ocelot lineage. All the cats in this lineage are small, weighing less than 44 pounds (20 kg), and the oncilla, kodkod, and some Geoffroy's cats are extremely small, at less than about 7 pounds (3 kg).

Scientists have very few details about the lives of most of these cats, but all are believed to be solitary, with diets of small rodents supplemented with birds, snakes, lizards, and other small animals. They hunt primarily at night but sometimes during the day. The margay and oncilla are primarily arboreal hunters but also hunt on the ground, while the others are primarily terrestrial hunters. Geoffroy's cats also fish in some parts of their range. The margay is the most acrobatic of all cats and is unusual in its ability to race down trees as well as up them. Margays have flexible hind limbs, especially the grasping toes, and ankles that can rotate 180 degrees.

Although their geographic ranges may overlap, these cats generally occupy different habitats. The Andean mountain cat, for instance, is confined to open landscapes at high elevations in the central Andes, while the kodkod lives in evergreen and deciduous forests of Chile and Argentina. Margays inhabit only moist tropical forests. Ocelots, which are the largest cats in this group, are also the most adaptable, living in diverse habitats from rain forest to dry scrub, and can survive in areas disturbed by human activities. Ocelots also range farther north than the others; a small population still hangs on in the Rio Grande Valley of Texas.

The cats in this lineage have a different number of chromosomes from all other cats (36 instead of the usual 38), and they

Below left: The margay is one of nine species of closely related spotted cats, all of which live in South America.

Below right: The serval, native to sub-Saharan Africa, specializes in catching rodents as they emerge from underground burrows.

Once believed to be related to lynxes, the caracal boasts similar tufted ears and eats a similar diet.

cat has a small distribution in west and central African forests, and the serval is largely confined to moist grasslands in sub-Saharan Africa. The little-known African golden cat is robust, weighing 17 to 35 pounds (8–16 kg), with a short tail. Its diet is composed of the usual small mammals and birds, but it is big and strong enough to take on larger prey, such as duikers (smallish forest-living antelope) and monkeys.

Servals, which are slim and tall with very large ears, are fairly specialized cats, with bodies designed to catch small rodents in tall grass. The serval's large ears and excellent hearing enable it to detect the ultrasonic calls of rodents in their underground burrows. Servals often sit and wait for a mouse to emerge from a burrow, then pounce on it, in what is called a "capriole jump." Similar to a fox, the serval jumps into the air and then, coming down, hits and stuns the prey with its powerful feet. A single pounce may cover nearly 12 feet (3.6 m) horizontally and from 6.5 to nearly 10 feet (2–3 m) vertically. Servals also leap vertically to pluck birds from midair.

Caracals are also prodigious leapers, reported to jump more than 11 feet (3.4 m) straight up to snatch birds. These beautiful cats, with black-tufted ears and plain coats, are slender and long-legged, but less so than servals. Though weighing from 17 to 44 pounds (8–20 kg), caracals are capable of killing large prey, including livestock such as goats and sheep; most of a caracal's diet, though, consists of hares and other mammals and birds under about 11 pounds (5 kg).

also tend to have smaller litters—one is typical—after relatively longer gestation periods than other cats.

Q: What are some small wild cats of Africa?

A: Apart from the cats in the domestic cat lineage, three other small cat species, in the caracal lineage, live in Africa, although the caracal itself also ranges through Arabia and the Middle East and central Asia as far as central India. In contrast, the African golden

Wide-ranging Medium-sized Cats

The jaguarundi is related to pumas and, more surprisingly, to cheetahs. Although pumas and jaguarundi today are found in the Americas, and the cheetah in Africa, this lineage probably first arose in Eurasia.

Q: What are lynx?

A: All cats of the lynx lineage are spotted and have soft hair, face ruffs, and black-tasseled ears. The Iberian lynx, the Canada lynx, and the bobcat are relatively small, weighing 11 to 44 pounds (5–20 kg), while the Eurasian lynx can weigh up to nearly 90 pounds (40 kg). All four species are the foremost predators of hares and rabbits, although the Eurasian lynx also hunts large roe deer and red deer. Eurasian lynx live in the northern forests of Europe and Asia. Canada lynx occupy the cold northern forests of North America, mostly in Canada but dipping into the United States in Maine and in the Rocky Mountains in the West. Bobcats replace lynx in most of the United States and into northern Mexico.

The Canada lynx's distribution matches that of its primary prey, snowshoe hares, while bobcats live where cottontail rabbits are plentiful. The Iberian lynx, which is the world's most endangered cat species (with a remaining population of about two hundred), lives in only a few tiny populations in Spain and Portugal. Its diet consists almost exclusively of European rabbits, which are abundant everywhere they have been introduced by people, such as in Australia and parts of Europe, but becoming rarer every day in their native Iberia.

The bobcat, named for the short tail that all lynxes have, is the only wild-cat species that is almost exclusively a resident of the United States.

Q: What is the connection between pumas and cheetahs?

A: People are often surprised to learn that the puma and the cheetah are fairly close relatives that, with the jaguarundi, form the puma lineage. The origin of the lineage is probably Eurasia, with a subsequent dispersal of the puma and jaguarundi ancestor into North America, where they diverged and expanded their ranges into South America about four million years ago. The cheetah's ancestor dispersed into Africa and North America, where the speedy pronghorn antelope probably evolved in response to predation from the cheetah in western North America. The cheetah and the puma disappeared from North America at the end of the Pleistocene, about 10,000 years ago, along with many other cat species. Based on genetic evidence, the puma re-colonized North America from South America sometime later. The cheetah and puma are medium-size cats, weighing less than about 175 pounds (80 kg), and the jaguarundi is a small cat of about 11 pounds (5 kg).

The solitary jaguarundi, whose plain fur may be either reddish or grayish, lives from northern Mexico to northern Argentina in a great diversity of habitats, ranging from thorn forest to wetlands to tropical forest. It hunts on the ground and also apparently in trees, and eats small mammals, supplementing its diet with birds, amphibians and reptiles, and fish. It is sometimes called the otter cat because of its resemblance to an otter.

The tawny-coated puma lives in a wide range of American habitats from Patagonia in South America to the Yukon in North America. The solitary, terrestrial puma kills ungulates (hoofed mammals), including white-tailed and mule deer, elk, and bighorn sheep, in the northern reaches of its range and the llama-like guanacos in the southern reaches. Pumas supplement their diets seasonally with larger rodents, such as squirrels, and other mammals, including rabbits and hares.

The cheetah is widely known as the world's fastest land mammal. Once widely distributed in Africa and in Asia into India, it now lives only in sub-Saharan Africa and in small relict populations in Iran and the central Sahara. Among cats, cheetahs are unique in that the females live alone but males live in small groups called coalitions. They are primarily predators of gazelles, but they also take hares and larger ungulates from time to time. They live in grasslands and in dry savannas and woodlands. They do not eat carrion, and they lose many of their kills to larger predators, including lions and spotted hyenas.

The Thomson's gazelle is the primary prey of sub-Saharan cheetahs.

Pumas are all-American cats that once ranged throughout North America as far north as the frigid Yukon and from the east to the west coast, as well as through Central and South America as far south as Patagonia.

Big Cats

Tigers are the largest of the big cats and equally at home in cold and hot climates.

Q: What are the big cats?

A: The largest of the living cats are lions and tigers, weighing up to 440 pounds (200 kg) for the largest lions today, and 550 pounds (250 kg) or more for the largest tigers. But four other species join lions and tigers in the big-cat group known as the Panthera lineage: jaguars, leopards, snow leopards, and clouded leopards. Leopards, snow leopards, and most jaguars are medium-sized cats, between 45 and 175 pounds (20–80 kg), although a few of the very largest jaguars weigh as much as 220 pounds (100 kg). The largest snow leopards are 110 pounds (50 kg). Clouded leopards are far smaller, weighing 25 to 50 pounds (11–23 kg).

Lions live only in sub-Saharan Africa and in one small population in a single area of western India called the Gir Forest, although they once had a huge distribution that included most of Eurasia and North America. Both male and female lions live in social groups composed of

Left: Among the cats, only male lions grow long flowing manes that advertise their fitness.

Right: Leopards are versatile cats, able to survive in a wide variety of Asian and African habitats and hunt prey both large and small.

close relatives, an adaptation for living in open country where other lions are abundant and dangerous competitors. The other members of this lineage live in solitary social systems. Lions, usually hunting in groups, kill medium and large open-country ungulates, such as wildebeest and zebras. The male lion's conspicuous mane signals his age, health, and social status; female lions prefer to mate with males with the showiest manes, while lesser males avoid fighting with them.

Tigers today are confined to select parts of Asia, where they live in habitats ranging from mangrove forests and rain forests to tropical wet savannas and cold temperate forests. Tigers are specialized predators of large deer and pigs and also prey on livestock, bringing them into conflict with people.

The jaguar lives in moist savannas and rain forests from northern Mexico through Central and South America. A particularly robust, stocky cat, it kills deer, peccaries, and also caiman and large terrestrial and aquatic turtles.

Leopards live in habitat as diverse as the Kalahari Desert, dry and wet forests, savannas, and woodlands, and have the largest distribution of the big cats, ranging throughout the African continent and most of Asia. Highly adaptable, they kill medium-sized ungulates and primates, supplemented with smaller mammals and birds, but are capable of killing animals many times larger than themselves.

In contrast, the snow leopard is a specialized predator of alpine goats and sheep that share its high-elevation habitat in the rugged mountain ranges of central Asia. Snow leopards have huge paws to grip rocks in their mountain homes and can walk easily through deep snow.

Although all the large cats are primarily terrestrial hunters, clouded leopards are also adapted for hunting in trees. They kill terrestrial species such as muntjac, a small deer, and tree-living monkeys and apes. Biologists say that the clouded leopard has a large-cat head, with the longest canines relative to body size of any cat, on a small-cat body. The clouded leopard lives in forested habitats in South and Southeast Asia.

Smallest of the big cats, the clouded leopard is a secretive forest-living animal that hunts both on the ground and in trees.

Oh, the tiger will love you. There is no sincerer love than the love of food.
—GEORGE BERNARD SHAW

Saving Wild Cats

Above: An illegal trade in the beautiful fur of cats threatens the survival of many species of cats.

Right: A small number of surviving Florida panthers are the last remnants of a once large population of pumas that roamed the southeastern United States.

Q: Why are wild cats threatened?

A: One or more populations of every cat species except the domestic cat are threatened or endangered for one or more of four reasons: habitat fragmentation and destruction; overkill; effects of introduced species; and secondary extinctions (which occur as a result of the extinction of another species or the disruption of an ecological process). Pulitzer Prize–winning biologist E. O. Wilson refers to these as "the mindless horsemen of the evolutionary apocalypse."

Extinction and human presence go hand in hand. Wild cats are in decline because they are being killed accidentally—by vehicles, for example—or deliberately, because of their predation or to supply illegal markets for fur and other parts. The habitat they require is disappearing. The prey they need to survive is overexploited by people or is dying from introduced diseases. In many parts of the world, effective protective programs for wildlife and their habitats in general, or for cats specifically, do not exist. Confrontations continue between people and cats that threaten people and their livestock, resulting in dead cats.

Q: Have any cat species gone extinct in recent years?

A: No cat species that we know of has gone extinct within historical time, but many populations or subspecies have been wiped out. The tiger subspecies that lived on the Indonesian islands of Bali

and Java, those that lived around the Caspian Sea, and the wild tiger of central China all disappeared in the twentieth century and of the remaining five subspecies of tiger, only the Bengal tiger of the Indian subcontinent exists in numbers greater than 750. In the past 10 years alone, the tiger habitat in Asia has declined by nearly 40 percent, to less than one-tenth of its historic range.

The pumas that once lived in the eastern part of North America are now gone, except for a remnant population in Florida, called the Florida panther. Fortunately, protection in the U.S. West has led to an upsurge in puma numbers there. The South African Cape lion is gone, as are the lions, leopards, cheetahs, and servals that lived north of the Sahara. Snow leopards, despite the remoteness of their harsh mountain habitats, are also in decline. The Iberian lynx is so critically endangered that it may not survive for many more years.

Q: How can cat lovers help wild cats?

A: First, learn as much as you can about the conservation challenges facing the wild cat species in which you are particularly interested. Visit your local zoo and closely observe the cats that live there. Compare them to one another. Ask zookeepers about the different species and about particular individuals and their temperaments and about other species until you have a greater number of questions than they can answer. Seek answers to these questions from other authorities and through reading. Get to know the many nongovernmental conservation organizations (NGOs) that use cats as flagship species. Find out just how each organization is addressing the conservation issues for the wild cat species that has caught your attention. Use your knowledge of wild cat biology and conservation issues to increase awareness among your family and friends. NGOs are always looking for monetary and human resources. Contribute where you can, both in dollars and by volunteering. Wild-cat biologists are always looking for volunteers—to help to maintain paper filing systems, for example, or to update electronic databases.

Go see a cat in the wild. Be an ecotourist or join a study tour in which volunteers help a wild-cat biologist in the field. Ecotourism and study tours add value to living wild cats because they bring attention and money to local economies. You may never actually see a wild cat, because that is the nature of wild cats, but your interest makes the lives of wild cats matter, and that is an enormous contribution. The inspiration for many wild-cat biologists and conservation-minded NGOs is the anthropologist Margaret Mead's declaration: "Never doubt that a small group of thoughtful, committed citizens can change the world. Indeed, it is the only thing that ever has."

With a visit to your local zoo, you can learn about tigers and other cat species and what it will take to ensure a future for them in the wild.

Taking an ecotour to see cats in their natural habitats, such as cheetahs in Kenya, is one way you can contribute to the conservation of cats.

Glossary

ADAPTATIONS. A set of features—anatomical structures as well as behaviors—enabling animals to survive and reproduce successfully in the habitats in which they live.

ALTRICIAL YOUNG. Young born helpless, naked, blind, and incapable of survival independent of their mother for some relatively long time after their birth. Altricial and its opposite (precocial) are actually the ends of a continuum that describes the relative maturity of animals at the time of their birth.

ALLELE. A form of a gene.

ARBOREAL. Living in trees; adapted to life in trees.

BINOCULAR VISION. The ability to focus both eyes at once on an object. This ability enables cats to accurately pounce on prey.

BIRDS OF PREY. Flesh-eating birds, such as hawks, eagles, and owls.

BREED. A subdivision of a species, created by artificial selection, whose members have distinctive genetic features that are consistently reproducible.

CAMOUFLAGE. The way an animal blends into its environment in order to sneak up on prey and hide from predators. The coats of most cats help them blend into the habitat in which they live and hunt.

CANID. A member of the family Canidae, which includes dogs, wolves, and foxes.

CANINE TEETH. The teeth between the front incisor teeth and the side molars. Long, sharp canine teeth are a feature of all cats, which use them to kill prey.

CARNASSIALS. Scissorlike molar teeth that tear chunks of meat from a carcass.

CARNIVORA. An order of mammals most of which are meat-eaters, including cats, dogs, bears, and others.

CARNIVORE. An animal that eats meat or flesh.

CLADE. A group of animals whose members all derived from a common ancestor; also called a lineage. The family Felidae (cats) is a clade, and each lineage within the cats is also a clade.

COLOSTRUM. Milk mothers produce in the first day or two after birth; it contains antibodies to boost newborns' immune systems.

COMPETITORS. Two or more animals that may fight for the same food, territory, habitat, or mating partners.

CONSERVATION. The effort to maintain the earth's natural resources, including wildlife, for future generations.

CONVERGENT EVOLUTION. Similar features or behaviors evolved independently by distantly related animals. The saber teeth of saber-toothed cats and saber-toothed marsupials is an example of convergent evolution.

DESERT. Dry region receiving less than 250 millimeters of rain annually. Desert-living cats include sand cats and black-footed cats.

DIGITIGRADE STANCE. Walking on the toes, so that the heels do not touch the ground. The foot bones of cats are modified so that only their toes touch the ground. Human stance, walking with the entire foot on the ground, is called plantigrade.

DIURNAL. Active during the day.

DISPERSAL. The process of an animal leaving the place of its birth to find a home range elsewhere.

DOMESTICATION. The process of changing, through artificial selection, the genetic makeup of a species in order to increase the species' usefulness to humans.

ENDANGERED SPECIES. Species that are likely to die out (become extinct) unless people take action to prevent this. In casual usage, many species are called endangered, but the word has a legal and scientific definition under the U.S. Endangered Species Act and a strict scientific definition on the *IUCN Red List of Threatened Species*.

ESTROUS CYCLE. The reproductive cycle of an adult female mammal.

ESTRUS. The period when a female mammal is ready to copulate with a male. Estrus usually occurs around the time a female ovulates, or produces an egg or eggs that can be fertilized by male sperm. Also called "in heat" or "in season".

EXTINCT. No longer living. When the last living member of a species dies, the species is extinct.

FELID. A member of the family Felidae, or cats.

FERAL CAT. A free-living domestic cat that lives without direct human care or influence.

FLEHMEN. A behavior in which cats curl their lip into a grimace after sniffing another cat or its scent mark. Flehmen may serve to draw chemicals into the vomeronasal organ.

GENE. The basic unit of heredity; a gene may come in more than one form, each of which is called an allele.

GENOME. An animal's genetic material.

GESTATION. The period during which a fertilized egg develops into a fetus ready to be born.

HABITAT. The place where an animal lives in the wild, such as a forest or grassland. An animal's habitat provides food, water, shelter, potential mates, and the right environment for the animal's survival.

HERBIVORE. An animal that eats primarily plant material. Many of the species that cats prey on, such as deer, antelope, and rabbits, are herbivores.

HYBRIDIZATION. Crossbreeding of individuals from genetically different breeds, populations, or species.

HOME RANGE. The area that an animal travels over during the course of a year to find food and shelter, to find mates, and to rear young.

HYPERCARNIVORES. Animals that eat only meat. Cats are hypercarnivores.

IMMUNIZATION. The process in which an animal's immune system comes to recognize foreign proteins or antigens and produce antibodies against them.

INCISOR TEETH. The front teeth. Cats use their incisor teeth for fine work such as plucking feathers from a bird carcass.

INFANTICIDE. Killing newborn animals. In biology, this usually refers to an animal killing young of its same species (killing the young of another species is called predation).

LACTATION. Producing milk from mammary glands to feed young.

LAGOMORPH. A member of the order Lagomorpha, which includes rabbits, hares, and pikas.

LEUCISM. Light or white coloration of skin, hair, fur, and feathers, such as the white fur of white tigers and the light fur of domestic Siamese cats.

LINEAGE. A group of animals whose members all derived from a common ancestor; also called a clade.

LORDOSIS. A crouching posture adopted by female cats to facilitate copulation.

MAMMAE. Glands that produce milk, ending in a nipple from which babies suck milk.

MAMMAL. A class of animals in which individuals have hair and babies are fed on milk from their mothers' mammary glands.

MELANISM. Dark or black coloration of skin, hair, fur, and feathers. Melanistic cats, such as black leopards, have dark or black fur.

METABOLISM. The life-sustaining chemical processes in the body; conversion of nutrients into energy.

MORPHOLOGY. The form and structure of a body.

MUTATION. A genetic change that may arise spontaneously or as a result of an external influence.

NEUTER. To sterilize an animal by surgical removal of the testicles of a male or ovaries of a female.

NOCTURNAL. Active at night.

OLFACTION. The sense of smell.

OPEN HABITATS. Areas with relatively little plant cover, such as savannas and deserts.

OVULATE. The release of an egg from an ovary.

PARTURITION. The act of giving birth; labor.

PATHOGEN. An organism, such as a virus or bacterium, capable of producing disease in another organism.

PERINEUM. Area between the anus and genitalia.

PHEROMONE. A chemical that conveys information related to reproduction.

PINNAE. The external portions of the ears.

POACHING. Hunting animals illegally.

POLYDACTYLY. Having more than the usual number of fingers or toes.

PREDATOR. An animal that hunts, kills, and eats other animals to survive. All cats are predators.

PREY. Animals that are hunted, killed, and eaten by other animals called predators.

PRIDE. A group of female lions and their young. The females in a pride are usually related. Males attach themselves to prides of females.

PRIMATE. A member of the Primate order, which includes monkeys, apes, and humans.

PSEUDOPREGNANCY. Also called false pregnancy, when a queen displays signs of pregnancy after a nonfertile mating.

QUEEN. An unaltered adult female domestic cat.

RAIN FOREST. A forest that receives at least 2.5 meters of rainfall annually. Most rain forests are in tropical regions of the world. Some tigers and leopards live in rain forests.

RIPARIAN. Relating to the banks of a watercourse such as a river or stream. Fishing cats occupy riparian habitats.

RODENT. A member of the Rodentia order, which includes rats and mice. Rodents are the primary prey of most small cats.

SCAVENGER. An animal that eats meat killed by other predators.

SELECTION. The process whereby biological populations change over time, as a result of the propagation of heritable traits that affect the ability of individual organisms to survive and reproduce. In natural selection, the environment determines whether individuals with particular heritable traits survive and reproduce to pass these traits to their offspring. In artificial selection, human preferences determine this.

SPAY. To sterilize a female cat by removing her ovaries.

SPECIES. A group of animals with very similar features. Individual members of a species are able to breed and produce live young that are fertile (able to breed when they too become adults). Under usual, natural conditions, individuals of different species do not interbreed, but some exceptions occur. The species is the basic unit in scientific classification of animals and plants.

SUBSPECIES. Populations of a species in which individuals consistently differ in certain features from individuals in other populations of the species, but not enough so that the individuals can no longer breed and produce live, fertile young. Subspecies are usually separated from each other by barriers such as seas or high mountains. If subspecies remain isolated from each other for a very long time, they may become different species.

TAPETUM LUCIDUM. Structure in a cat's eye that reflects light back through the eye so that the cells responding to light get a second chance to respond. Many nocturnal mammals and most carnivorans have this structure. This is what causes the "eyeshine" of cats when they look into a light at night.

TAURINE. An amino acid essential to cats, especially for proper functioning of the retina and the heart.

TERRESTRIAL. Living on land; adapted to living on land.

TERRITORY. A home range that an animal or group of animals of the same species lives in and defends from other members of its species, especially those of the same sex.

VACCINATION. Giving a vaccine to create immunity or resistance to certain diseases.

VERTEBRATE. An animal with a backbone.

VIBRISSAE. Long, stiff hairs, or whiskers, that project from the face and other parts of a cat's body. They are sensitive to the lightest touch.

VOMERONASAL ORGAN. Two tiny openings on the roof of the mouth through which chemicals send messages to parts of brain concerned with sexual behavior; also known as Jacobsen's organ.

Further Reading

Beadle, Muriel. *The Cat: History, Biology, and Behavior*. New York: Simon & Schuster, 1977.

Budiansky, Stephen. *The Character of Cats*. New York: Viking, 2002.

Clutton-Brock, Juliet. *Cats: Ancient and Modern*. Cambridge, MA: Harvard University Press, 1993.

Coleman, John S., and others. "Cats and Wildlife: A Conservation Dilemma." http://www.wisc.edu/extension/catfly3.html.

Johnson, Warren E., and others. "The late Miocene radiation of modern Felidae: a genetic assessment." *Science* (2006) 331, 73–77.

Kitchener, Andrew. *The Natural History of the Wild Cats*. Ithaca, NY: Cornell University Press, 1991.

Leyhausen, Paul. *Cat Behavior: The Predatory and Social Behavior of Domestic and Wild Cats*. New York: Garland STPM Press, 1979.

Lumpkin, Susan. *Big Cats: Great Creatures of the World*. New York: Facts on File, 1993.

———. *Small Cats: Great Creatures of the World*. New York: Facts on File, 1993.

Macdonald, David. *The Velvet Claw: A Natural History of the Carnivores*. London: BBC Books, 1992.

Morris, Desmond. *Illustrated Catwatching*. New York: Crescent Books, 1994.

———. *Cat World: A Feline Encyclopedia*. New York: Penguin Reference, 1997.

Nowak, Ronald M. *Walker's Carnivores of the World*. Baltimore: Johns Hopkins University Press, 1999.

O'Brien, S. J., and others. "The Feline Genome Project." *Annual Review of Genetics.* (2002) 36, 657–686.

Rogers, Katharine M. *The Cat and the Human Imagination: Feline Images from Bast to Garfield.* Ann Arbor: University of Michigan Press, 1998.

Schneirla, T. C., and others. "Maternal behavior in the cat." *Maternal Behavior in Mammals.* H. C. Rhingold, ed. New York: John Wiley, (1963), 122–168.

Seidensticker, John, and Susan Lumpkin, eds. *Great Cats: Majestic Creatures of the Wild.* Emmaus, PA: Rodale Press, 1991.

———. *My First Pocket Guide: Cats and Wild Cats.* Washington, D.C.: National Geographic Society, 1996.

———. *Smithsonian Answer Book: Cats.* Washington, D.C.: Smithsonian Books, 2004.

Siegal, Mordecai. *The Cornell Book of Cats*, 2nd ed. New York: Villard, 1997.

Sunquist, Mel, and Fiona Sunquist. *Wild Cats of the World.* Chicago: University of Chicago Press, 2002.

The Cat Fancier' Association (CFA). "World's Largest Register of Pedigreed Cats." http://cfa.org.

Turner, Dennis C., and Patrick Batson, eds. *The Domestic Cat: The Biology of its Behaviour*, 2nd ed. Cambridge: Cambridge University Press, 2000.

Van Vechten, Carl. *The Tiger in the House*, 3rd ed. New York: Bonanza Books, 1936.

At the Smithsonian

Below left: The National Museum of Natural History is home to one of the most important collections of mammals in the world, with exhibits that feature ice-age saber-toothed cats and Imax films that let you get up close to African lions.

Below right: *Cat with Lantern,* a woodblock print by Kobayashi Kiyochika, is one of the many feline-themed pieces of artwork housed in the Freer and Sackler Galleries.

The Smithsonian Institution is home to the largest group of biodiversity and conservation scientists in the world. Many of these scientists focus on cats in their work through the study of their systematics (phylogenetic relationships), paleontology (fossils), ecology, behavior, veterinary medicine, reproduction, genetics, epidemiology, and other exciting areas. For example, Smithsonian scientists were the first ever to radio track wild tigers in Nepal and the first to discover that wild South African cheetahs have very low genetic diversity.

The Smithsonian's Web portal (www.si.edu) is a window into the world of cats as they are found at various Smithsonian museums, research sites, and the National Zoological Park. These Web sites provide up-to-date stories on Smithsonian scientists as they go about their work of learning about the conservation needs of various cats species or tracking wild cats in the wild places they still inhabit or using its advanced laboratories to expose further secrets about cat biology ranging from reproduction to nutrition to the genetic makeup of wild and zoo populations. Go to the Web site and search for cats in general or for any species you may be interested in obtaining additional information about.

Explore the homes of wild cats at the National Zoological Park or marvel at the wild cats on display in the Museum of Natural History's Hall of Mammals. See the cat-related objects and art on display in the Museum of the American Indian and in the Freer and Sackler Galleries. Through the Web, you can explore the cat-related images housed in Smithsonian libraries and in the stunning photo gallery at the National Zoo.

If you like your cats up close and personal, there is no better way to see them than to visit the National Zoo's Great Cats exhibit. This exhibit features lions, tigers, caracals, and servals, and the Cheetah Conservation Station where the first cheetahs ever born at the National Zoo were born in 2004. Other wild cat species can also be found in the Small Mammal House (leopard cats), Beaver Valley (bobcats), and Forest Carnivores (fishing cats). The Zoo's new Asia Trail features fishing cats and clouded leopards. You can also visit the National Zoo's live animal cams (http://nationalzoo.si.edu/Animals/WebCams/) to share the daily lives of individual tigers and cheetahs.

For more information, search the Web site of *Smithsonian* magazine (www.smithsonianmag.com) and *ZooGoer* (http://nationalzoo.si.edu/Publications/ZooGoer) for in-depth articles on nearly every species and topic about cats from fossil saber-toothed cats to the recent sightings of jaguars in Arizona to the natural history of individual wild cat species to the recent discovery of FIV in domestic and wild cats.

The National Zoological Park's Great Cats exhibit on Lion/Tiger Hill features Sumatran tigers and an African lion—living, breathing, roaring great cats. Sumatran tiger Soyono gave birth to three male cubs on May 2, 2004. Their older brother, Berani, was born at the zoo in September 2001.

Index

A

Abyssinian, *2*, 34, 102, 106
African golden cat, 196
African lion, 11
African wild cats, 14, *18*, 196
aggression, 124–125
agouti, 18, 25
AIDS, 174, 191
ailurophilia, 188
ailurophobia, 188
albino, *24*, 25
alleles, 23–24
allergy, 174–175, 187
allogrooming, 50
American bobtail, *102*, 106
American Cat Fanciers Association, 22
American curl, 29, 106
American lion, 11
American Pet Products Manufacturers
Association, 34
American shorthair, 102, 107
ammonia toxicity, 81
amphibians, 85
anaphylaxis, 175
anatomy, 8–9, 40–47, 102
Andean mountain cat, 196
anestrus, 120, 132
Angora, 30, 40
Animal Locomotion, *45*
Animal Medical Center, 162–163
animal research, 190–191
antifreeze, 83
arginine, 81
artificial insemination, 191
Asian golden cat, 195
Asian wild cats, 194–195
aspirin, 167
atopy, 175
Australian Aboriginals, 185
autogrooming, 50–51
awn hairs, 48

B

babies, cats suffocating, 187
bad luck, 186
Bastet, 3, 180–181
bay cat lineage, 12, 195
bells, 85
Bengal, *31*, 102
big cats, 200

binocular vision, 56, 58
bird flu, 171
Birman, 28, 107
birth, 133, 138–139
biting, 42–43, 130
black cats, 33, 52–53, 182, 186
black-footed cat, *16*, 17
bobcats, 198
body language, 92–95
body morphology, 101
Bombay, 107
bones, 40
Borneo, 195
brain, 154–155
breeding. *See* sexual behavior
breeds, 22–26, 28, 30–34, 101–117
British shorthair, 102, 108
British type, 31
brushing, 51
Buffington, K. C., 161
Burmese, 102, 108
Burroughs, William S., 177

C

calico, 53, 105, 190
camouflage, 52
Canada lynx, 49, 198
Canadian Cat Association, 22, 47
canines, 42–43, 73
caracal, 12, 15, 197
carbohydrates, 81
carnassials, 8
Carnivora, 8
castration, 134
Cat Fanciers Association (CFA), 22, 34, 47, 106
cat flu, 170
Cat on a Hot Tin Roof, 186
cat shows, *22*
Catholic Church, 182
catnip, 67
Cats Protection League, 34
cat-scratch disease, 172
Chartreux, 109
chattering, 79
cheek rubbing, 98
cheetah, *15*, *41*, 46, 79, 88–89, 156, *158*, *160*, 191, 198–199
chevrons, 40
China, 184–185
Chinese mountain cat, 17

chirp, 90
chlorine, 83
chromosomes, 9, 53, 191, 196
Church, Joseph Wood, 65
clavicle, 40
claws, 46–47
climbing trees, 160–161
cloning, 191
clouded leopards, 200–201
coalitions, 89
coat color gene chart, 25
cobby morphology, 102
colonies, 89
color vision, 59
color, 18, 23–25, 52, 104–105
colostrum, 133, 173
communication between cats, 87
conjunctivitis, 171
conservation, 203
Cornish rex, 29, 48–49, 109
corpora luteum, 131–132
courtship, 126–129
coyotes, 156
Crete, 26
Cryptosporidium parvum, 177

D

dark, seeing in the, 57–58
dawn cat, 10
declawing, 47
development of kittens, 146–149
Devon rex, 102, 109
dewclaw, 46
diabetes, 170
dichromatic vision, 59
diet, 70–71, 80
digestive system, 9
digitigrade stance, 40, 45
dimorphism, 39
diseases, 170–172
diversity, 21
Dog and Cat Protection Act, 184
dog food, 80
dogs, 29, 34–35, 43, 67, 154–157
domestication, 15
dominance, 124–125
dopamine, 33
down hairs, 48
"dragon and tiger head," 185
dreaming, 151–153
drums, 184
dwarf cats, 38

E

ears, 60–61, 93, 103
earthquakes, cats predicting, 61, 187
eating, 70–75
ecotourism, 203
ectoparasites, 50, 176
Egypt, 3, 14–15, 26, 180–181
Egyptian mau, 110
electroencephalogram (EEG), 152
Elizabeth I, 182
Elizabethan collar, *134*
encephalization quotients (EQ), 154
endangered species, 202–203
enemies, 156
estrus, 120, 126
Eurasian lynx, 180, *192*, 198
European wildcat, *14*, 18, 135
evil, 182
evolution, 7, 10–12, 14
expression, facial, 91–92
extinct cats, 10–11
extinction, 84, 202
eyes, 56–59, 92–93, 102
eyeshine, 58

F

falling from heights, 151, 162–163
fear of cats, 188
feces, burying, 97
feeling, 62–63
Felidae, 2, 6–7, 12
Feliformia, 7
feline calicivirus (FCV), 170
feline distemper, 171
feline immunodeficiency virus (FIV), 174, 191
feline infectious peritonitis (FIP), 171
feline leukemia virus (FeLV), 171
feline panleukopenia virus (FPV), 171
feline pneumonitis, 171
Felis catus, 188
Felis lineage, 13
Felis silvestris, 188
females vs. males, 39, 89, 123
feral cats, 2, 16, 87, 89, 135
fighting, 124–125, 134, 149
fisher, *7*
Fisher, M. F. K., 37
fishing cats, 194
flat-headed cat, 194
fleas, 176
flehmen, 66
flirting chase, 127
Florida panthers, 202

folic acid, 81
food, 70–71, 74–75
foreign morphology, 31, 102
fossils, 10
founder effect, 30
Freya, 180
fungal diseases, 176
fur trade, 184, 202
fur, 48–49, 103–105, 167–168

G

Gallico, Paul, 135
genes, 9, 23–25
genetic diseases, 170
genetic mutation, 31, 32, 44
genome mapping, 191
Geoffrey's cat, 196
George, W. L., 71, 141
Gesner, Konrad, *27*
gestation period, 132
Giardia, 177
Global Invasive Species Specialist Group of the
World Conservation Union (IUCN), 84
gonadotropin-releasing hormone (GnRH),
121, 131
grass, 81
gray wolf, *156*
Greek legend, 179
grooming, 50–51
groups, 88–89
Guangdong province, 185
guard hairs, 48

H

hair. *See* fur
hairball, 51
Harrappa culture, 26
Havana brown, 102, 110
haw, 59
head rubbing, 99, 127
health of cats, 167–177
health, human, 187
hearing, 60–61
Hemingway cats, 44
hemophilia, 170
Himalayan cat, 30
Historia animalium, 27
*History of Four-footed Beasts and Serpents and
Insects*, 183
HIV virus, 191
Hubel, David H., 190
Humane Society of the United States, 184
hunting, 1, *5*, 7–9, 69–70, 72–78, 84–85
hybrid breeds, 102

hybridization, 18, 135
hypercarnivore, 8–9

I

Iberian lynx, 2, *3*, 198, 202
inbreeding, 170
induced ovulation, 130–131
infanticide, 122, 138
intelligence, 154
intention movement, 99
interestrus, 132
intermediate morphology, 102
International Progressive Cat Breeders'
Alliance, 22
invasive species, 84
IQ, 154
Iriomote cat, 12, 194

J

Jacobsen's organ, 66
jaguar, *36*, 53, 200–201
jaguarundi, 53, 198–199
Japanese bobtail, 28, 40, 111
jaws, 42–43
jumping, 158–159
jungle cat, 17

K

kangaroo, 6
Kashmir cat, 31
Key West, Florida, 44
killing bite, 42–43, 62, 73
kinesthetic intelligence, 155
Kipling, Rudyard, 44
kittens, 87, 137–149
kodkod, 196
Korat, 111

L

La Brea tar pits, 10–11
lactation, 145–146
languages, 188–189
LaPerm, 31, 111
leishmania, 176–177
leopard cat, 194
leopard, 9, 160, 200–201
leopard, black, 52
leopard, snow, *12*, 200–202
leopardus lineage, 13
Leyhausen, Paul, 124
Library Cat Society, 184
lice, 176
licking, 63, 142

Life and Adventures of a Cat, The, 121
life span, 134–135, 162
Lincoln, Abraham, 121
Linnaeus, Carolus, 188
lion, *6*, 11, 88–89, *119*, 200–201
lion, mountain. *See* puma
litter size, 138
liver fluke, 177
lordosis, 128–129, 139
Lorenz, Conrad, 26
luteinizing hormone (LH), 131
Lyall, David, 84
Lyme disease, 172
lynx lineage, 12
lynx, *12*, 198
lynx, Canada, 49
lynx, Eurasian, 180, *192*
lynx, Iberian, 2, *3*
Lyon, Mary, 191

M

maggots, 176
Maine coon, 112, 28, 34, 41, 45
males vs. females, 39, 89, 123
Mammal Species of the World, 12
mammals, 6–8
mange, 176
manul, 195
Manx, 28, 40–41, 112
marbled cat, 195
margay, *9*, 196
Martelli's cat, 18
mating, 128–130. *See also* sexual behavior
McMillan, Stuart, 91, 101
Mead, Margaret, 203
meat, cats as, 185
medicine, traditional, 15, 185
melanism, 52–53
meow, 91
metabolic water, 82–83
milk, 144–145
miniature cats, 38
mobile strategy, 73
molecular genetic phylogenetic reconstruction, 10
Morris, Desmond, 18, 22, 30
mountain lion. *See* puma
mummification of cats, 181
Munchkin, 32
muscles, 41
Muybridge, Eadweard, *45*
myiasis, 176

N

National Cancer Institute, 191
natural breeds, 102
natural selection, 30
neophilia, 83
neophobia, 83
nepetalactone, 67
neurobiology, 190
neurological disorders, 170
neutering, 38, 134–135
New York City cats, 27
nictitating membrane, 59
night blindness, 81
Nimravidae, 11
nine lives, 162
nipples, 144
Nobel Prize, 190
nongovernmental organizations (NGOs), 203
Norse mythology, 180
Norwegian forest, 28, 41, 49, 113
Nubian language, 188
nursing, 139, 142, 144–146

O

O'Brien, Stephen, 191
obesity, 170
ocelot, *193*, 196
Ocicat, 102, 113
olfaction, 66
oncilla, 196
orange cats, personality of, 33
organs, 41
Oriental, 113
origins of breeds, 101
ovulation, 130–131
owl, *187*
Oxford English Dictionary, 188–189

P

pads, 45
paleofelids, 11
Palestine, 26
Pallas, Peter, 195
Pallas's cat, *13*, 195
pandas, *188–189*
Panthera atrox, 11
panthera lineage, 12–13
papillae, 64
parasites, 176–177
parenting, 132
parturition. *See* birth
paws, 45
pedigreed cats. *See* breeds

persecution of cats, 182–183
Persian, 28, 30, 33–34, 40–41, 102, 114
personality, 32–33
petting, 63
piebald, 25
pilo-erection, 95
pink eye, 171
pinnae, 61
placental mammals, 6
play, 77, 148–149
pointed pattern, 24, 104
polydactyly, 44–45
polyestrous, 120
polygynous breeders, 122
population, 34–35
Pratchett, Terry, 183
predation. *See* hunting
predatory behavior, 148–149
pregnancy, 132–133
preparturition behavior, 138
prey, 70, 72–78
prides, 89
Proailurus, 10, 188
proestrus, 126
protein, 80–81
proverbs, 186
Pseudoailuria, 10–11, 188
pseudopregnancy, 132
puma lineage, 13
puma, *13*, *88*, *164*, 198–199, 202
pupils, 57
purring, 90

Q
Quammen, David, 3
queen, 121

R
Ra, 180
rabbits, 85
rabies, 172
Ragdoll, 28, 114
rat, *26*
Reed, Alistair, 186
Refrigerator cats, 184
rejection of food, 71
religion, 3, 179
REM sleep, 152–153
repellent odors, 67
reproduction. *See* sexual behavior
research, 190
respiratory infections, 170
retinal degeneration, 170
retractable claws, 46

rhinotracheitis virus (FRV), 170
righting reflex, 163
ringworm, 176
rock wildcat, 195
Romantic movement, 183
Rome, 26
Russian blue, 30, 49, 114
rusty-spotted cat, *38*, 133, 194

S
saber-toothed cats, 10
salt, 64–65
sand cats, *16*, 17
Satan, 182
Savannah, 31
scent marking, 67, 87, 96–98, 126
Scottish fold, *29*, 115
Scottish wildcat, *18*
Sekhmet, 180, *181*
Selkirk rex, 29, 115
semi-altricial young, 140
senses, 55–67
Serpell, James, 15
serval, *13*, *60*, 61, 196–197
sex of kittens, determining, 140–141
sexual behavior, 91, 120–122, 126–128
sexual maturity, 121
sexual selection hypothesis, 39
Shaw, George Bernard, 201
shedding, 49
ships, cats on, 26–27
Siamese, *24*, 30, 33, 34, 40–41, 102, *103*, 115
Siberian forest, 28, *30*, 116
sickness, 167
sight, 56–58
silver vine, 67
Singapura, 28, 39, 116
size of breeds, 28, 38–39, 140
skeleton, 40
skull, *8*
sleep, 151–153
smell, 66–67
Smilodon fatalis, *10*
snow leopard, *12*, 200–202
solitary living, 88
songbirds, 84–85
South African Cape lion, 202
South American wild cats, 196
spatial intelligence, 155
spaying, 134
speciation, 12
speed, 158
Sperry, Roger W., 190
Sphynx, 31, 32, 48, 116

spina bifida, 170
spontaneous mutation, 102
sporotrichosis, 172
spraying, 96–97
Sri Lanka, 194
stationary strategy, 73
Stephens Island, 84
Stern, R., 146
submissive behavior, 97–99
suckling. *See* nursing
Sumatra, 195
superstitions, 186–187
surplus killing, 76
sweet, 64–65
swimming, 164–165
symbolism, 179
symptoms, 168, 171

T
tabby, 23, 104–105
tail, 40, 94–95, 103
tapetum lucidum, 58
tapeworm, *177*
taste, 64–65
taurine, 81
taxonomy, 6–8, 12–14
teeth, 42–43, 73, 145
temperature, body, 24, 169
terminal velocity, 163
territories, 123–124
testosterone, 124
tetanus, 172
Thailand, 30
thermometer, 169
thermoregulation, 52
third eyelid, 59
Thomson's gazelle, 199
ticks, 172, 176
tiger farms, 15
tiger parts in medicine, *185*
tiger, 2, *43*, *52*, *159*, *164*, 200–202
tiger, white, *24*
toes, 44–45
tom, 121, 124
tongue, 64
Tonkinese, 117
Topsell, Edward, 183
torbie, 105
tortoiseshell pattern, *53*, *105*
touch, sense of, 62–63
toxic substances, 83
toxoplasmosis, 172–173, 176–177
treed cat, 161
trill, 91

Turkish Angora, 117
Turkish Van, 41, 102, 117, 165
Turner, Alan, 160
Tylenol, 167
tympanic bulla, 8

U
umami, 64
uses of cats, 184–185

V
vaccination, 173
vegetarians, 80–81
vibration, 61
vibrissae, 62
Vikings, 27
vision, 56–58, 146
visual streak, 57
vitamin deficiency, 170
vocalizations, 90–91
vomeronasal organ, 50, 66

W
water, 82, 164–165
weaning, 147, 149
weather, cats predicting, 187
weight, 38
whiskers, 48, 62
white tiger, *24*
Wiesel, Torsten N., 190
wild cats, 2, 12, 15–18, 35, 78–79, 88
wild hybrids, 102
wildlife, 84
Williams, Tennessee, 186
Wilson, E. O., 202
witches, 3, 182–183
worms, 172, 177

Y
yowl, 91

Acknowledgments & Picture Credits

Our positions at the Smithsonian's National Zoological Park and Friends of the National Zoo have allowed us a matchless opportunity to watch wild cats and to travel frequently to see and study cats in the wild. Friends of the National Zoo has provided much financial support to John over the years. We watch the daily coming and going of cats in our alley and garden in upper northwest Washington D.C., and with "camera traps" we have extended our observations through the night. We thank Ellen Nanney, Senior Brand Manager, Smithsonian Business Ventures, Katie Mann, and Lisa Purcell, Hylas Publishing, for guiding this book into print. We dedicate this book to the late John F. Eisenberg, our mentor who taught us a new approach to understanding the behavior of mammals, and the late Paul Leyhausen, legendary cat biologist who inspired us to begin watching cats.

The author and publisher also offer thanks to those closely involved in the creation of this volume: Collins Reference executive editor Donna Sanzone, editor Lisa Hacken, and editorial assistant Stephanie Meyers; Hydra Publishing president Sean Moore, publishing director Karen Prince, senior editor Lisa Purcell, art director Edwin Kuo, designers Rachel Maloney, Greg Lum, Gus Yoo, Mariel Morris, La Tricia Watford, Brian MacMullen, Ken Crossland, editorial director Aaron Murray, editors Marcel Brousseau, Myrsini Stephanides, Suzanne Lander, Ward Calhoun, Lori Baird, Franchesca Ho Sang, Emily Beekman, Mary Kate Aveni, Kristin Maffei, copyeditor Glenn Novak, picture researcher Ben DeWalt, production manager Sarah Reilly, production director Wayne Ellis, and indexer Jessie Shiers.

PICTURE CREDITS

The following abbreviations are used: IO Index Open; JI © 2006 Jupiterimages Corporation; iSP iStockphoto.com; SS—ShutterStock; PR—Photo Researchers, Inc.; SPL—Science Photo Library; LoC—Library of Congress; SI—Smithsonian Institute; BS—Big Stock Photo

(t=top; b=bottom; l=left; r=right; c=center)

The Nature and Wonder of Cats
IIII IO/Bruce Ando **IIIr** IO/LLC, Fog Stock **IVt** JI **IVb** SS/Dimitri Sherman **IV-V**background JI **Vt** ©2006 Brand X Pictures **Vb** ©2006 Getty Images **VI** IO/photos.com Select **1** SS/Dean Evangelista **2**tl iSP/Catherine Scott **2**br SS/Dragan Trifunovic **3**tr PR/Tom McHugh **3**bc JI

Chapter 1: What is a Domestic Cat?
4 SS **5**background iSP/Bryce Kroll **5**cr IO/photolibrary.com pty ltd. **6**bl SS **6**tr SS/Kris Mercer **7**bl JI **8**bl Illustration by Hylas Publishing/Data Source: Biological Sciences, University of Alberta **9**cl JI **9**bl SS/Keith Levit **10**tr JI **10**bc SS/Michael Ledray **11**bl The Page Museum of the La Brea Tarpits **12**tr JI **12**bl SS/Vladimir Pomortzeff **13**tl SPL/Chris Martin-Bahr **13**tr SS/Ecliptic Blue **13**bl JI **14**bl SS/Vladimir Pomortzeff **14**br Wikimedia **15**br SS/Bryan Brazil **16**tr SPL/Tony Camacho **16**bc PR/Art Wolfe **17**br Alamy/wildphotos.com **18**bl SPL/Tony Camacho **19**tl SPL/Duncan Shaw **19**br SS/Paige Falk

Chapter 2: Domestic Cat Details
20 SS/Dwight Smith **21** SS/Mircea Maiero **22**bl LoC **23**tl SS/Alvaro Pantoja **23**bl SS/Geoff Pelderfield **24**tr ©2006 Brand X Pictures **24**br SS/Marc Goldman **26**bl iSP/Ben Scholy **26**cr SS/Adrian Hughes **27**tc SI **27**br SS/J. Gracey Stinson **28**bl SS/Neil Webster **29**tl PR/Yves Lanceau **29**br SS/Verena Matthew **30**bl Alamy/Juniors Bildarchiv **30**tr SS/Tatiana

31bl SS/Marilyn Barbone **32**bl SS/Anne Gro Bergersen **33**bl IO/LLC, Fog Stock **33**br Alamy/Purestock **34**cl iSP/Anne Gro Bergersen **34**bl iSP/George Cairns **35**tl Sarah Reilly **35**br SS/Joel Banchat Grant

Chapter 3: The Cat's Body
36 JI **37**cr SS/Valeriy Poltorak **38**bl ©2006 BrandX Pictures **38**tr Alamy/Terry Wittaker **39**bl SS/Sarah Gates **40**bl Illustration by Hylas Publishing/Data Source: www.moggies.co.uk **41**tr Alamy/Junior Bildarchiv **41**bl JI **42**tr Illustration by Hylas Publishing/Data Source: Washington State University, Department of Veterinary Medicine **42**bl ©2006 BrandX Pictures **43**br JI **44**br Tracy Boggler **45**tr SS/Nana Lao **45**bl LoC **46**bc Illustration by Hylas Publishing/Data Source: www.moggies.co.uk **47**br SS/Neven Jurkovic **47**tl PR/Nigel J. Dennis **48**bl SS/Jennifer Leigh Selig **49**tl JI **49**br SS/Anne Gro Bergersen **50**bl ©2006 Brand X Pictures **50**br SS/Daniel Gale **51**tl SS/Johanna Goodyear **52**tl SS/Teynold Sumayku **52**br SS/Casey K. Bishop **53**tr SS/Irene Teesalu **53**br ©2006 Getty Images/G.K. and Vikki Hart

Chapter 4: How Cats Sense the World
54 ©2006 Brand X Pictures **55**cr SS/Norman Chan **56**br iS/David Edwards **57**tr SS/Brian Morrison **57**tl SS/Joel Bauchat Grant **58**bl PR/Art Wolfe **58**br iSP/Barbara Henry **59**tl Jonathan Conklin **60**bl SS/Arnold John Labrentz **60**br SS/ijansempoi **61**tl SS/La Tricia Watford **61**tl SS/Cate Frost **62**tc SS/Davier Yoon **62**br Alamy/Juniors Bildarchiv **63**bc Alamy/Gregor Hohenberg **63**tc iSP/Carmen Martinez **64**tr iSP/Sharon Dominick **64**bl PR/SPL **65**bl iSP/John Richbourg **65**cr ©2006 Brand X Pictures **66**tt SS/Evon Lim Seo Ling **66**bl Illustration by Hylas Publishing/Data Source: www.maxshouse.com **67**tr PR/Alan and Sandy Carey

Chapter 5: Domestic Cats as Predators
68 SS/Mrs. Gill Martin **69**cr SS/Lenice Harms **70**tc PhotoObjects.net **70**br SS/Pete Oliveira **71**tll SS/Paige Falk **71**br iSP/dcmainz **72**tr JI **72**cr SS/Aleksandra Duda **73**tl SS **73**tc iSP/Tiniiiii **74**bl SS/Jakob Metzger **75**tll BS/phototrekker **75**br Alamy/ CatsEye Photography **76**cr JI **76**br SS/Jan Stadelmyer **77**tc SS/OxaDesign **77**bl Alamy/Roger Tamblyn **78**bc Alamy/Robert Baronet **79**tl JI **79**br iSP/Graefen **80**bl SS/Kenneth Sponsler **80**br PhotoObjects.com **81**tl IO **82**bl SS/J. Helgason **82**br iSP/hurricanegrady **83**iSP/nrtn **84**bl Alamy/Juniors Bildarchiv **85**tr iSP/snelsonc **85**bl SS/pixelman

Chapter 6: Social Life
86 SS/Ingrid Oliphant **87**tr Joan Johnson **88**cr JI **88**br IO/Keith Levit Photography **89**bc SS/Mircea Maieru **90**bl BS/Adriantj **91**tl SS/Mircea Maieru **91**tr SS/Patricia Freitas **92**bl SS/Aleksander Bocheknek **92**br SS/Mircea Maieru **93**tc SS/Norman Chan **93**cr Jonathan Conklin **94**tr SS/Tiburon Studios **94**br SS/Slobodan Vasic **95**tc SS/RJ Lerich **95**bc SS/Suponev Vladimir Mihailovich **96**cr SS/Ross Dailey **96**bl SS/Dimitrii N. Birykov **97**tl SS/Andre Klopper **97**br Joan Johnson **98**cr iSP/Blair_witch **98**bc iSP/Debibisshop **99**tr BS/Eleonora **99**br **100**bl Bret Reilly **100**br SS/ijansempoi **101**tl iSP/kreicher

Ready Reference
Background Joan Johnson **102**tr SS/Marilyn Barbone **103**bl BS/Charmina **103**tr SS/Robert Redelowski **104**tl SS/Yank Chauvin **104**br SS/Evgeny Itsikson **105**cr SS/Jeff Oien **106**bl SS/Anne Gro Bergersen **107**tr iSP/Anne Gro Bergersen **108**tl BS/Charmina **108**br iSP/Tiburon Studios **109**cr ©2006 Brand X Pictures **110**bl SS/Anne Gro Bergersen **111**tl Alamy/Juniors Bildarchiv **112**tl iSP/Anne Gro Bergersen **112**br SS/Cheryl Kunde **113**tr BS/Charmina **114**tc BS/Laura Pervis **115**br SS/Anne Gro Bergersen **116**tc Sarah Reilly **117**tr iSP/Shaun Lowe

Chapter 7: Males and Females
118 SS/Tiburon Studios **119**cr JI **120**br BS/Kian Khoon **121**tl

JI **122**bc SS/Gaston M. Charles **122**br SS/Jean Schweitzer **123**tl SS/Norman Chan **124**bl BS/Macdeedle **124**tr iSP **125**bl SS/Yvonne McCarthy **126**br SS/Heidi Tuller **127**bl SS/Norman Chan **127**br IO **128**bl SS/James Nickel **128**tr Alamy/Arco Images **129**bl SS/Dan Briski **130**tr Alamy/Arco Images **130**br BS/Sylwia **131**bl SS/Vixique **132**bl SS/Thomas Nord **133**tl Alamy/Terry Whittaker **133**br SS/Sherry Yates **134**bl BS/Maarigard **135**tl SS/Vishal Shah **135**br iSP/Jeremy Voisey

Chapter 8: Bringing Up Babies
136 SS/Jeff Oien **137**cr iSP/Thomas Pullicino **138**tr SS/Jean Schweitzer **138**bl SS/Tony Campbel **139**tr BS/Gitana **140**cl SS/Jean Schweitzer **140**bl SS/Clint Scholz **141**tl SS/Cindy Lyn Dockrill **141**tr SS/Odelia Choen **142**bl SS/Geary LaBell **142**br SS/Jean Schweitzer **143**tr SS/Clint Scholz **144**tr SS/Odelia Cohen **145**bl IO/Bill Romerhaus **146**tr iSP/cronopios **146**bc SS/Cindy Lynn Dockrill **147**br SS/Mike Tolstov/photobank.kiev.ua **148**tl SS/Eline Spek **148**cr IO/FogStock, LLC **149**tr SS/Clara Natoli

Chapter 9: A Day in the Life
150 SS/Davidenko Volodymyr **151**cr Jonathan Conklin **152**bl Joan Johnson **152**tr SS/Sally Cheng **153**br SS/Carole Gomez **154**tr iSP/Roger Branch **154**br Jonathan Conklin **155**br SS/Donald Joski **156**tr SS/David Virtser **156**bl Nicolas Delafraye **157**bc ©2006 Brand X Pictures **158**bl iSP/Mark Wilson **159**cf iSP/Norman Chan **159**tl iSP/eROMAzE **160**bl SS/Marsha Hunter **160**br iSP/Highlander Images **161**tl SS/N. Joy Neish **161**bc iSP/Vaide Dambrauskaite **162**bl iSP/KHR128 **163**cr PR/Agence Nature **164**bl SS/Tan Kian Khoon **164**tr JI **165**tr SS/Trevor Allen **165**br iSP/Kristen Eckstein

Chapter 10: In Sickness and in Health
166 iSP/Andrei Tchernov **167**cr IO/LLC, FogStock **168**bl iSP/Luke Daniek **168**tr SS/Ivan **169**bc SS/Alfred Wekelo **169**cr iSP/Jaimie D. Travis **170**c SS/Allyson Ricketts **170**bl iSP/Heizfrosch **171**bl iSP/Charlotte Erpenbeck **171**tr SS/Jean Schweitzer **172**tl iSP/Jamsi **172**bl Centers for Disease Control and Prevention/Jim Gathany **172**br Joan Johnson **173**tc Alamy/Paul Wayne Wilson/PhotoStockFile **174**tr iSP/Nancy Louie **174**br SS/Galina Barskaya **175**tc SS/Robert W. Ahrens **175**br SS/C.A. Carrigan **176**bl SS/Anne Gro Bergersen **176**tr SS/Carolina K. Smith, M.D. **177**tr Centers for Disease Control and Prevention

Chapter 11: Cats and People
178 SS/ijansempoi **179**cr BS/Dr. Bouz **180**bl JI **180**tr SS/Patrick Hermans **181**tl iSP/Miguel Comas **181**br JI **182**tc SS/Z. Adam **183**tl iSP/Rob Leach **183**cr SS/Andrey Grinyov **184**tr Rachel Maloney **184**br SS/Mikhail **185**bc JI **186**tr SS/Anneke Schram **187**tl SS/Martin Smith **187**bl SS/Francois Etienne du Plessis **187**br SS/Stephen McSweeny **188**bl SS/Peter Hansen **188**tr SS/Wang Sanjun **189**tl SS/Julie Simpson **189**bc SS/Paul Cowan **190**lc BS/Victor PR **190**br SS/Daniel Thomson **191**tr SS/Andreas Gehret **191**br Jonathan Conklin

Chapter 12: Wild Cats
192 SS/Razvan Stroie **193**cr SS/Graham Bloomfield **194**bl Alamy/JTB Photo **194**tr PR/Terry Whittaker **195**rc Alamy/Purestock **196**bl SS/Alvaro Pantoja **196**br SS/Patrick Hermans **197**tl SS/Koval **198**bl iSP/Janine White **198**tr SPL/William Ervin **199**bl IO/Photos.com Select **199**tr iSP/Ogen Perry **200**bc SS/Marina Cano Trueba **200**tr IO/Ralph Reinhold **200**br JI **201**tr iSP/Michael Lynch **202**tl BS/Pomortzeff **202**tr U.S. Fish and Wildlife Service **203**tl iSP/Ira Struebel **203**cl JI

At the Smithsonian
210l Smithsonian Photographic Services/James DiLoreto [2003-8959] **210**r Freer Gallery of Art and Arthur M. Sackler Gallery/SI **211** SI/National Zoological Park/Jessie Cohen